VMware vSphere Security Cookbook

Over 75 practical recipes to help you successfully secure your vSphere environment

Mike Greer

[PACKT] enterprise 88
PUBLISHING
professional expertise distilled

BIRMINGHAM - MUMBAI

VMware vSphere Security Cookbook

First published: November 2014

Production reference: 1181114

Published by Packt Publishing Ltd.
Livery Place
35 Livery Street
Birmingham B3 2PB, UK.

ISBN 978-1-78217-034-1

www.packtpub.com

Credits

Author

Mike Greer

Reviewers

Mike Armstrong

Alexandre Borges

Mario Russo

Aravind Sivaraman

Acquisition Editor

Nikhil Karkal

Content Development Editor

Poonam Jain

Technical Editor

Faisal Siddiqui

Copy Editors

Relin Hedly

Dipti Kapadia

Project Coordinator

Mary Alex

Proofreaders

Simran Bhogal

Stephen Copestake

Maria Gould

Ameesha Green

Paul Hindle

Indexer

Rekha Nair

Graphics

Ronak Dhruv

Production Coordinators

Kyle Albuquerque

Conidon Miranda

Cover Work

Conidon Miranda

About the Author

Mike Greer is an accomplished IT Security Practitioner and Enterprise architect with a proven track record of successful, highly-complex projects over the past 20 years. Infusing security into the core infrastructure is one of his greatest concerns while enabling customers to achieve and preserve a secure business posture. As a consultant or instructor in his professional career, he continues to provide consultancy services on a number of subject matters that include strategy, virtualization, messaging, database, and infrastructure optimization. He is the founder of Evolution Security Solutions, a start-up company focusing on strategy, virtualization, and security. His industry certifications include CCSK, CISM, CISSP, ITIL, VCP, MCSE, and MCITP.

Evolution Security Solutions provides vCIO services in addition to strategy, security, cloud, and virtualization consulting.

I'd like to thank Gloria, Declan, and Colin for their support and understanding during the course of this project.

About the Reviewers

Mike Armstrong is a Sr. Site Reliability Engineer at VMware that supports OneCloud, VMware's private cloud environment. He is also a VMware vExpert and has been working with virtualization technologies since 2005. He has been in the IT industry for 30 years and has worked with various technologies. Mike's certifications include VCAP5-DCA, VCP4 & 5, MCITP, MCSE, and ITILv3.

Alexandre Borges is an Oracle ACE in Solaris and has been teaching courses on Oracle Solaris since 2001. He worked as an employee and a contracted instructor at Sun Microsystems, Inc. until 2010, teaching hundreds of courses on Oracle Solaris (such as Administration, Networking, DTrace, and ZFS), Oracle Solaris Performance Analysis, Oracle Solaris Security, Oracle Cluster Server, Oracle/Sun hardware, Java Enterprise System, MySQL Administration, MySQL Developer, MySQL Cluster, and MySQL tuning. He was awarded the title of Instructor of the Year twice for teaching Sun Microsystems courses.

Since 2009, he has been imparting training at Symantec Corporation (NetBackup, Symantec Cluster Server, Storage Foundation, and Backup Exec) and EC-Council (Certified Ethical Hacking (CEH)). In addition, he has been working as a freelance instructor for Oracle education partners since 2010.

In 2014, he became an instructor for Hitachi Data Systems (HDS) and Brocade. Currently, he also teaches courses on Reverse Engineering, Windows Debugging, Memory Forensic Analysis, Assembly, Digital Forensic Analysis, and Malware Analysis. Alexandre is also an (ISC)2 CISSP instructor and has been writing articles on the Oracle Technical Network (OTN) on a regular basis since 2013. He has also authored *Oracle Solaris 11 Advanced Administration Cookbook* by Packt Publishing.

Dedicated to my wife, Fernanda.

Mario Russo has worked as an IT architect, a senior technical VMware trainer, and in the presales department. He has also been working on VMware technology since 2004. In 2005, he worked for IBM on the first large project Consolidation for Telecom Italia on the Virtual VMware ESX 2.5.1 platform in Italy with the Physical to Virtual (P2V) tool. In 2007, he conducted a drafting course and training for BancoPosta, Italy, and project disaster and recovery (DR Open) for IBM and EMC. In 2008, he worked for the project Speed Up Consolidation BNP and the migration P2V on VI3 infrastructure at BNP Cardif Insurance.

He is a VMware Certified Instructor (VCI Level 2) and has a certificate in VCAP5-DCA. He is the owner of Business to Virtual, which specializes in offering virtualization solutions. He was also the technical reviewer of *Implementing VMware Horizon View 5.2*, *Implementing VMware vCenter Server*, *Troubleshooting vSphere Storage*, and *VMware Horizon View 5.3 Design Patterns and Best Practices*.

I would like to thank my wife, Lina, and my daughter, Gaia. They're my strength.

Aravind Sivaraman is a virtualization consultant with more than 8 years of experience in the IT industry. For the past 5 years, he has been focusing on virtualization solutions, especially VMware products. He holds different certifications from VMware, Microsoft, and Cisco and has been awarded with the VMware vExpert title for 2013 and 2014. He is a VMware Technology Network (VMTN) and Experts Exchange contributor. He maintains his personal blog at `http://aravindsivaraman.com/` and can be followed on Twitter `@ss_aravind`.

He has also technically reviewed *Troubleshooting vSphere Storage* and is the co-author of *VMware ESXi 5.1 Cookbook*, both by Packt Publishing.

I would like to thank and dedicate this book to my wife Madhu, my parents, and my family members, who are always there for me no matter what, for all their unconditional support and for teaching me to never give up.

www.PacktPub.com

Support files, eBooks, discount offers, and more

For support files and downloads related to your book, please visit www.PacktPub.com.

Did you know that Packt offers eBook versions of every book published, with PDF and ePub files available? You can upgrade to the eBook version at www.PacktPub.com and as a print book customer, you are entitled to a discount on the eBook copy. Get in touch with us at service@packtpub.com for more details.

At www.PacktPub.com, you can also read a collection of free technical articles, sign up for a range of free newsletters and receive exclusive discounts and offers on Packt books and eBooks.

PACKTLIB™

https://www2.packtpub.com/books/subscription/packtlib

Do you need instant solutions to your IT questions? PacktLib is Packt's online digital book library. Here, you can search, access, and read Packt's entire library of books.

Why subscribe?

- ► Fully searchable across every book published by Packt
- ► Copy and paste, print, and bookmark content
- ► On demand and accessible via a web browser

Free access for Packt account holders

If you have an account with Packt at www.PacktPub.com, you can use this to access PacktLib today and view 9 entirely free books. Simply use your login credentials for immediate access.

Instant updates on new Packt books

Get notified! Find out when new books are published by following @PacktEnterprise on Twitter or the *Packt Enterprise* Facebook page.

Table of Contents

Preface

This book features two topics that I have a keen interest in: security and virtualization. The virtualization space can be complex in its own right, and like other technological areas, adding sufficient security can prove to be quite labor intensive and often frustrating. As technology evolves, the idea of building an infrastructure or project in a secure manner from the beginning is still somewhat novel in its approach. While more security controls are available in products, I find that such controls and features continue to be underutilized or not implemented at all.

Consider the following: on receiving a plate of pasta at your local restaurant, you are generally asked, "Would you like cheese with that?" This simple scenario and the relationship between pasta and cheese is an apt metaphor for the way security is applied to the Information Technology (IT) infrastructure in many businesses today.

My core philosophy is to help those in need. By and large, given my profession, ensuring privacy and providing some form of data security seems the logical approach. I hope this cookbook that deals with security tasks specific to the VMware vSphere 5.5 product set will enable you to get a better understanding of the virtualization environment with step-by-step instructions.

This book covers implementing specific security features of the vSphere 5.5 virtualization platform in a step-by-step format. Each topic contains a high-level overview to give context to the cookbook recipes. This book is not intended to provide reference architectures or theories behind specific security topics implemented by vSphere.

What this book covers

Chapter 1, Threat and Vulnerability Overview, provides you with an overview of threats and vulnerabilities specific to the virtualization infrastructure. This chapter covers a high-level review of hypervisor, virtual machine, network, storage, and physical threats and vulnerabilities.

Chapter 2, ESXi Host Security, introduces you to hardening the ESXi host from both the console and the vSphere client. This chapter covers the host firewall and configuration of services.

Chapter 3, Configuring Virtual Machine Security, focuses on security of the guest virtual machine, covering both management of the virtual machine and configuration of the virtual machine. Configuration of guest operating system security and virtual machine isolation controls are covered in this chapter.

Chapter 4, Configuring User Management, guides you through the secure user administration of a virtualization environment using vCenter. Topics include configuring Active Directory integration, configuring Single Sign-On, assigning permissions, and administrative roles.

Chapter 5, Configuring Network Security, introduces you to security options in the configuration of virtual network switches and port groups.

Chapter 6, Configuring Storage Security, introduces you to the configuration of storage security from a vSphere perspective. The majority of this chapter covers iSCSI authentication between source and target systems. On completion of this chapter, you will be able to configure iSCSI authentication on a vSphere 5.5 host.

Chapter 7, Configuring vShield Manager, introduces you to the installation and configuration of vShield Manager, from downloading and installing the virtual appliance to configuration of user and group access—including SSL certificate configuration.

Chapter 8, Configuring vShield App, introduces you to vShield App configuration and setup on the ESXi host. The common application firewall settings are also covered.

Chapter 9, Configuring vShield Edge, introduces you to the setup and configuration of vShield Edge. In addition, adding and managing appliances and interfaces is covered, along with VPN, firewall, and gateway configurations.

Chapter 10, Configuring vShield Endpoint, introduces you to vShield Endpoint protection, installation, and configuration, and the importance of endpoint protection in securing the virtual infrastructure.

Chapter 11, Configuring vShield Data Security, introduces you to the configuration of vShield Data Security options and policies. Customizing data polices and reports are also covered.

Chapter 12, Configuring vSphere Certificates, guides you through the tasks involved in assigning issued X.509 certificates to vSphere component services. The SSL tool is used to assign certificates to vCenter, Update Manager, Web Client, Log Manager, Inventory Manager, and Single Sign-On services.

Chapter 13, Configuring vShield VXLAN Virtual Wires, introduces the prerequisites for implementing VXLAN virtual wires, configuring virtual wires and configuring firewall rules for virtual wires.

What you need for this book

You should have knowledge of basic VMware virtualization concepts such as datacenters, clusters, hosts, datastores, networks, and virtual machines.

A background of governance and security is helpful when evaluating how the security procedures covered in this book can provide additional controls in a virtualized environment.

You need to install VMware vSphere Client 5.5 or VMware vSphere Web Client. The web client is heavily referenced in the text and is the preferred VMware management tool going forward.

Who this book is for

This book is intended for the virtualization professional who is experienced with VMware vSphere setup and configuration, but who hasn't had the opportunity to investigate securing the environment properly.

This book covers all the major security options for vSphere 5.5 deployment in a modular fashion where only the recipe pertaining to the task is required. In other words, the book is not meant to be read from cover to cover, but rather used as a toolkit for specific tasks and scenarios in the virtualization infrastructure environment.

Conventions

In this book, you will find a number of styles of text that distinguish between different kinds of information. Here are some examples of these styles, and an explanation of their meaning.

Code words in text, database table names, folder names, filenames, file extensions, pathnames, dummy URLs, user input, and Twitter handles are shown as follows: "The Windows Firewall can also be enabled and disabled by using the `netsh.exe` command via the command line."

New terms and **important words** are shown in bold. Words that you see on the screen, in menus or dialog boxes, for example, appear in the text like this: "Click on **OK** to initiate the snapshot."

> Warnings or important notes appear in a box like this.

> Tips and tricks appear like this.

Reader feedback

Feedback from our readers is always welcome. Let us know what you think about this book—what you liked or disliked. Reader feedback is important for us because it will help us develop titles that you really get the most out of.

To send us general feedback, simply send an e-mail to feedback@packtpub.com, and mention the book title in the subject of your message.

If there is a topic that you have expertise in and you are interested in either writing or contributing to a book, see our author guide on www.packtpub.com/authors.

Customer support

Now that you are the proud owner of a Packt book, we have a number of things to help you to get the most from your purchase.

Errata

Although we have taken every care to ensure the accuracy of our content, mistakes do happen. If you find a mistake in one of our books—maybe a mistake in the text or the code—we would be grateful if you would report this to us. By doing so, you can save other readers from frustration and help us improve subsequent versions of this book. If you find any errata, please report them by visiting http://www.packtpub.com/submit-errata, selecting your book, clicking on the **errata submission form** link, and entering the details of your errata. Once your errata are verified, your submission will be accepted and the errata will be uploaded on our website, or added to any list of existing errata, under the Errata section of that title. Any existing errata can be viewed by selecting your title from http://www.packtpub.com/support.

Piracy

Piracy of copyright material on the Internet is an ongoing problem across all media. At Packt, we take the protection of our copyright and licenses very seriously. If you come across any illegal copies of our works, in any form, on the Internet, please provide us with the location address or website name immediately so that we can pursue a remedy.

Please contact us at copyright@packtpub.com with a link to the suspected pirated material.

We appreciate your help in protecting our authors, and our ability to bring you valuable content.

Questions

You can contact us at questions@packtpub.com if you are having a problem with any aspect of the book, and we will do our best to address it.

1
Threat and Vulnerability Overview

In this chapter, we will cover the following topics:

- ► Risk overview
- ► Hypervisor threats
- ► Hypervisor vulnerabilities
- ► Guest virtual machine threats
- ► Guest virtual machine vulnerabilities
- ► Network threats
- ► Network vulnerabilities
- ► Storage threats
- ► Storage vulnerabilities
- ► Physical threats
- ► Physical vulnerabilities
- ► Security Concepts

Introduction

Risk management, while outside the scope of this book, is a key foundation in the creation of a secure system. Proper risk assessment will not only identify what is being protected, the cost, and the criticality of those assets, but also identify the likelihood of the system or systems being breached. With the state of governance, compliance, and the growing requirement to notify customers of the security breach, it's more important than ever to create an auditable system based on well-defined security policies.

Not long ago, type I hypervisor systems, such as VMware ESX and Microsoft Hyper-V, were considered inferior for the task of running highly secure environments. The virtualization market has made substantial progress in the security space in a short span of time.

This chapter provides a brief overview and review of the risk and the associated components of risk pertaining to the virtualization environment. The ultimate goal is to determine the **acceptable risk**, which is the level of risk that a company is willing to take in order to conduct business.

Risk overview

The risk equation is composed of three components: threat, vulnerability, and cost.

Risk = Threat x Vulnerability x Cost

In brief, **Cost** is the damage measured in currency, as experienced in the loss of hardware or software. The cost also includes consulting hours or quantifiable staff time spent in remediating the damages caused. While cost is a key factor in the risk formula, it falls outside the scope of this book. Please refer to sites such as http://www.isaca.org for further information on risk and risk management.

The **Threat** component of the risk equation is measured in frequency or rate. For example, the threat of a user deleting a file will be greatly reduced if a user only has read permission on the file. By the same token, an organization with 10,000 computers has a much higher potential threat of a virus infection than an organization with 1,000 computers.

While there are threats associated specifically with the virtualization environment, a great deal of risk is caused by the misconfiguration of systems and policies. With the added complexity of virtualization comes additional layers that need to be addressed in order to make the environment secure. Without end-to-end security communication in the **Storage Area Network** (**SAN**), the storage switch, hypervisor host, and virtual machine are at risk. Likewise, communication between virtual networking components and physical networking components presents many opportunities for misconfiguration, thereby leading to the opportunity for a security breach.

The **Vulnerability** component, at a broad level, is measured as a percentage, which is similar to the case of a threat. The term vulnerability is most closely tied to a known deficiency or bug that presents a clear vector for compromise, and as such, caries a likelihood of 100 percent if the system is not patched to protect against said exploit.

Considering the risk equation, vulnerability is the component that has the most control. Vulnerabilities in the hypervisor platform will typically be patched by the vendor, in this case, VMware. By utilizing tools such as Update Manager, system administrators are able to keep the host systems patched in a timely and regular manner.

During the software patching cycle, it's important to do proper testing before applying a patch to a production system. This is even more critical for virtualized systems since a single virtualized host can hold a large number of virtual machines and thus will be affected adversely by a patch crippling a host.

Normal network vulnerabilities are still present in a virtualized environment. The mix between virtual networking and physical networking can present a different set of vulnerabilities based on the environment. It is important for the networking team and the server virtualization team to work together in order to ensure that both the physical and virtual networks are correctly configured and secure.

Understanding defense-in-depth

In addition to risk is the concept of defense-in-depth. The defense-in-depth model uses a layered approach, which not only increases the attacker's risk of detection but also reduces an attacker's chance of success. Defending the organization in depth means the application of a combination of people, processes, and technology to protect against threats at each layer. A good defense-in-depth architecture will build each layer of the security under the assumption that the other layer has been breached. If one layer is missing something, another layer might stop it and thereby stop the attacker.

In brief, the model consists of a series of interconnected components. The fundamental layer of policy and procedure affects every other layer. This layer includes both security policies and security procedures, as shown in the following figure:

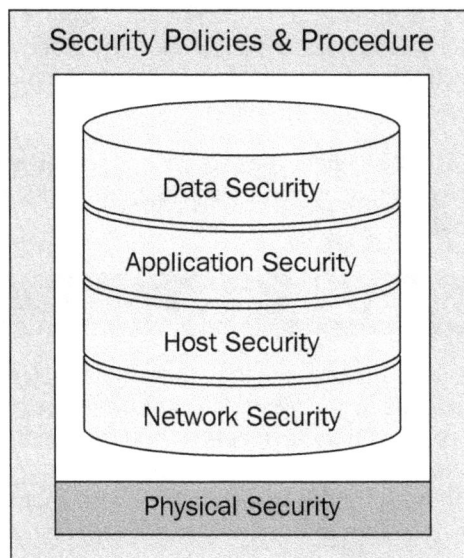

The next layer is the **Physical Security** layer. This layer encompasses the remaining layers and includes secure facilities, mantraps, surveillance, and biometric identification devices.

The traditional host layer is now broken up into the virtual host and the virtual machine. The virtual host, also known as the hypervisor, includes signed drives, a secured kernel layer, and minimal management attack surfaces. The virtual machine layer includes the guest operating system, host hardening, patch management, and strong authentication. The guest operating system might also include a host-based firewall, intrusion detection system, and disk encryption system.

The data layer of the defense-in-depth model includes **Access Control Lists (ACLs)** and encryption.

The application layer includes hardening practices such as mechanisms to prevent SQL injection, as an example.

The network layer consists of an internal network and perimeter layers. These layers are traditionally separated by a security device such as a firewall. In a virtualized environment, both an internal network and a perimeter network can and often do reside within the same set of virtual host machines. In a complex networking scheme, it's even more critical to ensure that trusted network traffic and untrusted network traffic are properly separated in the virtual environment.

In a traditional physical environment, overall security is often more difficult to achieve, simply because there are more components and the risk of misconfiguration is higher. For example, securing a mission-critical application is more efficient when the majority of components are virtual and can be configured together by a team or an individual. In a physical environment, the same tasks could span numerous individuals around the globe. The virtual environment provides the administrator with an encapsulated landscape, which provides a better structure for tracking critical components.

The remainder of this chapter will highlight the threats and vulnerabilities to core services utilized in a virtualization environment, including storage, networks, hypervisors, virtual machines, and physical security.

Hypervisor threats

Hypervisor threats from attackers are growing in popularity. In fact, the vulnerability that allows a virtual machine to escape to the hypervisor has been documented in a certain number of 64-bit operating systems that have been virtualized. In addition, a limited number of Intel CPUs are vulnerable to a local privilege-escalation attack. The attack essentially allows the virtual machine access to a ring of the kernel on the hypervisor host. While this did affect several hypervisor platforms, it did not affect the VMware ESX platform.

VMware continues to innovate in the area of isolating components of the virtual landscape with various products, including **Network Virtualization Platform** (**NSX**). NSX is designed with the **Software Designed Data Center** (**SDDC**) approach in mind. Achieving true isolation in a multitenant cloud model is the goal. Increased isolation and controls will help to minimize hypervisor threats.

The following is an example of a guest VM affecting the host at the workstation level, not at the server level. The vulnerability listed in the National Vulnerability Database (`http://nvd.nist.gov`) is as follows:

National Cyber Awareness System

Vulnerability summary for CVE-2007-4496

Original release date: 09/21/2007

Last revised: 03/08/2011

Source: US-CERT/NIST

Overview

Unspecified vulnerability in EMC VMware workstation before 5.5.5 build 56455 and 6.x before 6.0.1 Build 55017, player before 1.0.5 Build 56455 and Player 2 before 2.0.1 Build 55017, ACE before 1.0.3 Build 54075 and ACE 2 before 2.0.1 Build 55017, and server before 1.0.4 Build 56528 allows authenticated users with administrative privileges on a guest operating system to corrupt memory and possibly, execute arbitrary code on the host operating system via unspecified vectors.

Impact

CVSS severity (Version 2.0)

CVSS v2 base score: 6.5 (medium) (AV:A/AC:H/Au:S/C:C/I:C/A:C) (legend)

Impact subscore: 10.0

Exploitability subscore: 2.5

CVSS Version 2 metrics:

Access vector: Local network exploitable

Access complexity: High

Authentication: Required to exploit

Impact type: This provides administrator access; allows complete confidentiality, integrity, and availability violation; allows unauthorized disclosure of information; and allows disruption of service

In this case, the user with administrative privileges in the guest operating system was able to execute the code against the host. Keep in mind that this was not just any host; this was a VMware workstation, which is a different type of hypervisor.

Hypervisor vulnerabilities

Hypervisor vulnerabilities affect the ability to provide and manage core elements, including CPI, I/O, disk, and memory, to virtual machines hosted on the hypervisor. As with any other software system, vulnerabilities are identified and vendors work toward patching them as quickly as possible before an exploit is found.

Several key vulnerabilities exist at this time, specific to VMware ESXi, including buffer overflow and directory traversal vulnerabilities. The following information is taken from the National Vulnerability Database (http://nvd.nist.gov):

National Cyber Awareness System

Vulnerability summary for CVE-2013-3658

Original release date: 09/10/2013

Last revised: 09/12/2013

Source: US-CERT/NIST

Overview

Directory traversal vulnerability in VMware ESXi 4.0 through 5.0 as well as ESX 4.0 and 4.1 allows remote attackers to delete arbitrary host OS files via unspecified vectors.

Impact

CVSS severity (Version 2.0):

CVSS v2 base score: 9.4 (high) (AV:N/AC:L/Au:N/C:N/I:C/A:C) (legend)

Impact subscore: 9.2

Exploitability subscore: 10.0

CVSS Version 2 metrics:

Access vector: Network exploitable

Access complexity: Low

Authentication: Not required to exploit

Impact type: This allows unauthorized modification and the disruption of service

Note that the access vector for both of these vulnerabilities is termed network exploitable, meaning that the vulnerability is remotely exploitable with only network access. The attacker does not need local access to exploit this type of vulnerability. The vulnerability listed in the National Vulnerability Database (`http://nvd.nist.gov`) is as follows:

National Cyber Awareness System

Vulnerability summary for CVE-2013-3657

Original release date: 09/10/2013

Last revised: 09/13/2013

Source: US-CERT/NIST

Overview

Buffer overflow in VMware ESXi 4.0 through 5.0 as well as ESX 4.0 and 4.1 allows remote attackers to execute the arbitrary code or cause a denial of service via unspecified vectors.

Impact

CVSS severity (Version 2.0):

CVSS v2 base score: 7.5 (HIGH) (AV:N/AC:L/Au:N/C:P/I:P/A:P) (legend)

Impact subscore: 6.4

Exploitability subscore: 10.0

CVSS Version 2 metrics:

Access vector: Network exploitable

Access complexity: Low

Authentication: Not required to exploit

Impact type: This allows unauthorized disclosure of information, unauthorized modification, and the disruption of service

When attackers find a vulnerability such as this and see that no authentication is required to exploit and the access vector is network exploitable, they move this up the list as a potential low-risk, high-value target.

It should be noted that at the time of writing this book, these vulnerabilities were active; however, VMware releases patches on a regular basis and some or all of the example vulnerabilities might have already been remediated.

Guest virtual machine threats

Virtual machine (**VM**) threats vary by the guest **operating system** (**OS**) that is loaded into the VM. Each operating system has its own list of threats, with the Microsoft Windows OS at the top of the list. Given its popularity, the Windows operating system has been a prime target for years as attackers find different ways to compromise the OS itself or the popular Internet Explorer browser within Windows.

Over the past few years, Adobe and its Adobe Reader product have become a target for attackers. Since Adobe Reader is installed on the majority of Windows and Apple operating systems, compromising Adobe can potentially allow an attacker to access a very large number of computers.

Although the guest operating system is contained within each virtual machine, it interacts with the hypervisor by way of the virtual hardware that supports the VM as well as by the specific tools that allow the VM to interact with the hypervisor, through which the hypervisor provides specialized services to the VM.

There is evidence reported by Symantec that certain malware attempts to determine whether the operating system is running in a virtual machine. This detection can be done in a number of ways, including checking whether VMware tools are running. For more details, check the Symantec link in the *References* section.

Guest virtual machine vulnerabilities

The vulnerabilities listed here are likely to be out of date as they have been remediated by the respective vendors. The following are a few guest operating system vulnerabilities at the time of writing this book.

The following vulnerability is one of an ever increasing number of vulnerabilities from Adobe, Adobe Reader, and Acrobat listed in the National Vulnerability Database (`http://nvd.nist.gov`):

National Cyber Awareness System

Vulnerability summary for CVE-2013-5325

Original release date: 10/09/2013

Last revised: 11/03/2013

Source: US-CERT/NIST

Overview

Adobe Reader and Acrobat 11.x before 11.0.05 on Windows allow remote attackers to execute an arbitrary JavaScript code in a JavaScript: URL via a crafted PDF document.

Impact

CVSS severity (Version 2.0):

CVSS v2 base score: 9.3 (high) (AV:N/AC:M/Au:N/C:C/I:C/A:C) (legend)

Impact subscore: 10.0

Exploitability subscore: 8.6

CVSS Version 2 metrics:

Access vector: Network exploitable; Victim must voluntarily interact with the attack mechanism

Access complexity: Medium

Authentication: Not required to exploit

Impact type: This allows the unauthorized disclosure of information, unauthorized modification, and the disruption of service

The following vulnerability is for a kernel-mode driver in Windows 7, listed in the National Vulnerability Database (http://nvd.nist.gov):

National Cyber Awareness System

Vulnerability summary for CVE-2013-3881

Original release date: 10/09/2013

Last revised: 11/03/2013

Source: US-CERT/NIST

Overview

win32k.sys in the kernel-mode drivers in Microsoft Windows 7 SP1 and Windows Server 2008 R2 SP1 allow local users to gain privileges via a crafted application, also known as "Win32k NULL Page Vulnerability."

Impact

CVSS severity (Version 2.0):

CVSS v2 base score: 7.2 (HIGH) (AV:L/AC:L/Au:N/C:C/I:C/A:C) (legend)

Impact subscore: 10.0

Exploitability subscore: 3.9

CVSS Version 2 metrics:

Access vector: Locally exploitable

Access complexity: Low

Authentication: Not required to exploit

Impact type: This allows the unauthorized disclosure of information, unauthorized modification, and the disruption of service

Any vulnerability found in a standalone desktop machine might have applicability in a virtualized environment. In fact, an infected Windows desktop, for example, has the opportunity to do more damage in a virtualized environment than if it were a standalone machine. If a virtualized environment was not configured correctly, a runaway desktop machine could take resources away from other virtual machines on the same host, impacting the performance of many as opposed to a single machine.

Network threats

Network threats are the largest in number due to the nature of the Internet and enterprise data connectivity. Since virtual switches function similar to physical switches, most, if not all, threats that have faced the traditional networking environment continue to face the virtualization environment. Even threats to specific Cisco IOS versions, for example, can affect the virtual network environment since there is a Cisco Nexus 1000 virtual switch available for VMware. There are several types of network attacks that generally fall into the following categories:

- **Denial of service attack**: This attack is usually focused on large commercial websites with the intent of making the website unavailable. A denial of service takes place when the web server or network device is overloaded by legitimate requests. In the case of an e-commerce website, a denial of service attack can cost the company millions of dollars. In another example, a recent attack used **Network Time Protocol** (**NTP**) to take down popular gaming services including League of Legends and www.ea.com.

- **Hijacking or man-in-the-middle attack**: This attack takes advantage of the TCP/IP protocol stack between endpoints. Hijacking is an attack where the attacker takes control over a legitimate user session that has already been connected and authenticated. In a man-in-the-middle attack, the attacker is able to observe, intercept, read, and modify messages between two systems. As an example, an attacker might set up a fake Wi-Fi hotspot at a coffee shop and observe traffic that passes from the users to the Internet.

- **Sniffing**: This is the process of capturing and collecting network packets regardless of their destination. A sniffer is either hardware or software that can listen on a wired or wireless network interface. Common sniffer software includes Wireshark, TCPdump, and Network Monitor. A full view of the data within each collected packet is provided by a sniffer if the packets are not encrypted.

- **Trojans**: This is also known as malware or spyware. Once installed by the unwitting user, the code can collect certain information from the user's system and send it back to the attacker.

- **Spoofing**: IP spoofing is when an attacker sends IP packets from a false source address. This technique is used to trick the destination address into allowing the traffic since the source address is seen as valid. IP spoofing is often used in distributed denial of service attacks. In this example, the attacker sends a flood of packets that appear to have originated from multiple valid source addresses to a specified target address in an attempt to overload the network device.

Other types of network threats do exist, but for the purposes of this overview, the general types explained give you the background required for configurations in the virtual environment.

Network vulnerabilities

Network vulnerabilities are the most exploited type of vulnerability due to the large population of devices connected to the Internet. Network vulnerabilities affect endpoint devices, such as web servers, and core devices, such as routers and switches.

Network vulnerabilities across many vendors currently exist. Here are two example vulnerabilities from Cisco. Both represent bugs in the switch-level OS. This vulnerability is listed in the National Vulnerability Database (`http://nvd.nist.gov`) as follows:

National Cyber Awareness System

Vulnerability summary for CVE-2013-5566

Original release date: 11/08/2013

Last revised: 11/08/2013

Source: US-CERT/NIST

Overview

Cisco NX-OS 5.0 and earlier-on MDS 9000 devices allows remote attackers to cause a denial of service (supervisor CPU consumption) via the **Authentication Header** (**AH**) authentication in a **Virtual Router Redundancy Protocol** (**VRRP**) frame, also know as Bug ID CSCte27874.

Impact

CVSS severity (Version 2.0):

CVSS v2 sase score: 5.0 (MEDIUM) (AV:N/AC:L/Au:N/C:N/I:N/A:P) (legend)

Impact subscore: 2.9

Exploitability subscore: 10.0

CVSS Version 2 metrics:

Access vector: Network exploitable

Access complexity: Low

Authentication: Not required to exploit

Impact type: This allows the disruption of serviceUnknown

The next vulnerability allows an attacker to cause a denial of service using a modified packet sent to the device. This example is listed in the National Vulnerability Database (`http://nvd.nist.gov`) as follows:

National Cyber Awareness System

Vulnerability summary for CVE-2013-5565

Original release date: 11/08/2013

Last revised: 11/08/2013

Source: US-CERT/NIST

Overview

The OSPFv3 functionality in Cisco IOS XR 5.1 allows remote attackers to cause a denial of service (a process crash) via a malformed LSA Type-1 packet, also known as Bug ID CSCuj82176.

Impact

CVSS severity (Version 2.0):

CVSS v2 base score: 4.3 (MEDIUM) (AV:N/AC:M/Au:N/C:N/I:N/A:P) (legend)

Impact subscore: 2.9

Exploitability subscore: 8.6

CVSS Version 2 metrics:

Access vector: Network exploitable

Access complexity: Medium

Authentication: Not required to exploit

Impact type: This allows the disruption of serviceUnknown

The two examples are very specific, but both reinforce the common threat of denial of service and why frameworks such as defense-in-depth are important. If an attacker is able to cause a denial of service in the network device, a sensor somewhere on the network should be in place to send the proper alert.

Storage threats

There are many different types of storage that can be used by VMware vSphere; however, for the purposes of this brief explanation of storage threats, we will focus on **storage area networks (SAN)** and **network-attached storage (NAS)**. From a protocol perspective, Fibre Channel and **Internet Small Computer System Interface (iSCSI)** will be briefly reviewed in the context of which threats and potential vulnerabilities they bring to the risk equation.

In the past, there was a clear delineation between SAN storage and NAS, but in recent years, high-performing devices have become much more popular for small- and medium-sized businesses. Likewise, most enterprises that historically used Fiber Channel exclusively now tend to have some iSCSI in their storage environment. Both protocols are inherently insecure on their own. In the case of Fiber Channel, sending information in clear text would seem to be the major risk; however, this is mitigated largely due to the physical characteristics of the fiber that the data passes over. That's not to say that Fiber Channel can't be exploited, but the nature of its closed-loop system makes it a lower risk.

iSCSI, on the other hand, uses the same RJ-45 network cables and physical switches that the normal IP traffic utilizes within the network. Without a proper process for securing iSCSI, traffic is very vulnerable to attack and exploit. It's crucial to isolate iSCSI traffic in order to separate switches or by VLAN. Additionally, the use of **Challenge Handshake Authentication Protocol (CHAP)** authentication will ensure that only approved iSCSI endpoints can communicate with the storage system.

Storage vulnerabilities

At the time of writing this book, there were no publicized vulnerabilities for any of the major SAN or NAS vendors specific to the access protocols' Fiber Channel or iSCSI. The following two vulnerabilities are for storage vendor management, listed in the National Vulnerability Database (http://nvd.nist.gov).

A number of the vulnerabilities listed specific to storage center around some form of management and authentication information being sent or stored in clear text:

National Cyber Awareness System

Vulnerability summary for CVE-2013-3278

Original release date: 10/01/2013

Last revised: 10/02/2013

Source: US-CERT/NIST

Overview

EMC VPLEX before VPLEX GeoSynchrony 5.2 SP1 uses cleartext for storage of the LDAP/AD bind password, which allows local users to obtain sensitive information by reading the management-server configuration file.

Impact

CVSS severity (Version 2.0):

CVSS v2 base score: 4.9 (MEDIUM) (AV:L/AC:L/Au:N/C:C/I:N/A:N) (legend)

Impact subscore: 6.9

Exploitability subscore: 3.9

CVSS Version 2 metrics:

Access vector: Locally exploitable

Access complexity: Low

Authentication: Not required to exploit

Impact type: This allows the unauthorized disclosure of information

Another example from Hitachi shows vulnerability in the Network Node Manager that allows remote attacks:

National Cyber Awareness System

Vulnerability summary for CVE-2012-5001

Original release date: 09/19/2012

Last revised: 09/20/2012

Source: US-CERT/NIST

Overview

Multiple unspecified vulnerabilities in Hitachi JP1/Cm2/Network Node Manager i before 09-50-03 allow remote attackers to cause a denial of service and possibly execute the arbitrary code via unspecified vectors.

Impact

CVSS severity (Version 2.0):

CVSS v2 base score: 7.5 (HIGH) (AV:N/AC:L/Au:N/C:P/I:P/A:P) (legend)

Impact subscore: 6.4

Exploitability subscore: 10.0

CVSS Version 2 metrics:

Access vector: Network exploitable

Access complexity: Low

**NOTE: Access complexity is scored low due to insufficient information

Authentication: Not required to exploit

Impact type: This allows unauthorized disclosure of information, unauthorized modification, and the disruption of service

Both of these example vulnerabilities are in the management layer of the storage device, not within the data stream specific to the protocol transferring information between the SAN or NAS drivers and the hypervisor.

Physical threats

The topic of physical security might seem out of place in a book on virtual security; however, it plays a key role. As referenced in the defense-in-depth model, the most thorough design and implementation can be breached if physical security fails. For example, if one can physically access a console logged in with administrative credentials, security controls are effectively neutralized.

Physical threats by nature are threats that require physical access to the hardware in order to exploit the systems. In the case of virtualization hardware, the threat vector is somewhat lessened if you assume that the hardware will reside in some form of secure datacenter structure, be it a secure facility or room. In addition, carrying out administrative tasks on management desktops situated in secure locations without access to any public networks will also reduce risk.

Even with equipment residing in a secure facility, there are a number of threats that remain, including nonmalicious factors such as extreme weather and power outages. Other threat vectors include security and authentication mechanisms to the facility and within the facility to the server location. Typically, in a highly secure facility, a cage within the datacenter is used to secure the server hardware. Entry into the cage is limited to certain personnel and controlled by biometric or card reader devices.

Another potential threat is the personnel that staff the facility. A dishonest employee, even one who has been fully vetted and background-checked can gain access to sensitive equipment and potentially the data residing on that equipment. Alternatively, a dishonest employee can grant access to an outsider who is intending to attack a particular company's server or virtualization environment contained in the facility.

Physical vulnerabilities

Physical vulnerabilities include any weak links between the outside and the server equipment within the facility belonging to the customer. Vulnerabilities can mean the existence of the threats mentioned in the previous section, most notably weak authentication and questionable personnel.

Vulnerability such as a poor location or inadequate power grid should be immediately remediated by moving equipment to another facility without said vulnerabilities. Additional vulnerabilities that need to be considered include any aspect of the facility that will lend itself to a single point of failure, including the lack of redundant power or redundant Internet connections. Commercial datacenters are usually happy to showcase their redundancy.

As with all the threats and vulnerabilities mentioned in the previous sections, a detailed plan and checklist should be used when evaluating the design and implementation of each of these parts that make up a secure infrastructure. Adequate disaster recovery planning is also key as well as ensuring data security during a disaster. Confirm that should a disaster occur, the data will be secure at the disaster recovery website or websites.

Security concepts

This book contains a number of security, compliance and encryption topics that might not be second nature to the reader. This section will provide an overview of concepts and methods discussed in the book along with references for further information.

Data classifications

Data classifications are used to assign data at the right level of protection and security based on the content type and sensitivity required. **Personally Identifiable Information (PII)** and **Protected Health Information (PHI)** are two of the classifications referenced.

> ▸ **PII**: Information that can uniquely identify an entity is considered PII. An example includes **Social Security Number (SSN)**, home address, birthdate, e-mail address, and application login information.

> ▸ **PHI**: Information created or derived from a hospital, physician, and healthcare providers specific to an individual's past, present and future medical condition. There is also a growing concern over the activity information recorded by wearable devices by privacy experts.

Cryptography

Symmetric Encryption: This utilizes a shared secret key to encrypt and decrypt messages. Both the sender and recipient utilized the same key to encrypt and decrypt information passed between them. The key can take the form of a complex string, for example. The encryption algorithm along with its key length determine the relative strength of the key. The strongest current block cipher is **Advanced Encryption Standard (AES)**.

Asymmetric Encryption: This utilizes a public key and a private key. A message encrypted by the private key can only be decrypted by the public key and vice versa. The public key is available to anyone, while the private key is kept secret. Public key certificates utilize asymmetric encryption and provide information about the organization to which the certificate was issued.

Certificates

Certificates provide digital identification and a mechanism to establish trust. We can think of a certificate as a driver's license or government issued ID card. The trusted root authority can be thought of as the government in this example. The license or ID can be thought of as the certificate. When someone checks our ID to verify our identity, they trust the authority that issued that ID. Likewise, when a certificate is issued from a trusted authority, we can be assured the identity represented by the certificate is genuine.

Also known as digital certificates or X.509 certificates, these certificates are widely used by websites to prove their identity to the web browser. Certificates can also be used for mutual authentication where not only does the web browser trust the website, but also the web site trusts the web browser.

Public Key Infrastructure (**PKI**) generates certificates in both public and private scenarios. A **Certificate Authority** (**CA**) is the mechanism that responds to proper certificate requests and returns certificates to the requesting party. Verisign, Thawte, and Digicert are examples of public CAs, meaning a certificate issued by them is trusted by the majority of commercial web browsers by default. A private CA is usually set up within a corporate network, and the certificates issued are only trusted by machines on the corporate network.

Virtual Private Networks

Virtual Private Networks (**VPN**) provide a network tunnel between two endpoints through which information is encrypted (protected) from the network traffic outside the VPN tunnel. There are two main types of VPN tunnels in use today: **IPSEC** and **SSL**. IPSEC stands for **Internet Protocol security,** while SSL stands for **Secure Sockets Layer**.

References

The following references give a background on topics covered in this chapter:

- Malware detecting Virtual Machines: `http://www.symantec.com/connect/blogs/does-malware-still-detect-virtual-machines`
- IP Spoofing overview: `http://www.cisco.com/web/about/ac123/ac147/archived_issues/ipj_10-4/104_ip-spoofing.html`
- Man-in-the-middle attack: `https://www.owasp.org/index.php/Man-in-the-middle_attack`
- Known vulnerability database resources include the following:
  - National Vulnerability Database: `http://nvd.nist.gov`
  - Common Vulnerabilities and Exposures: `http://cve.mitre.org/cve`
  - Latest vulnerability exploit tracking at Internet Storm Center: `http://isc.sans.edu`
- PII Reference: `http://csrc.nist.gov/publications/nistpubs/800-122/sp800-122.pdf`
- PHI Reference: `http://www.hipaa.com/2009/09/hipaa-protected-health-information-what-does-phi-include/`
- Encryption Reference: `http://support.microsoft.com/kb/246071`
- Cipher Reference: `http://www.encryptionanddecryption.com/encryption/index.html`
- PKI Reference: `https://developer.mozilla.org/en-US/docs/Introduction_to_Public-Key_Cryptography`

- ▶ IPSEC VPN Reference: `http://csrc.nist.gov/publications/nistpubs/800-77/sp800-77.pdf`

- ▶ SSL VPN Reference: `http://csrc.nist.gov/publications/nistpubs/800-113/SP800-113.pdf`

Summary

The goal of this introductory chapter was to provide an overview of the threats and vulnerabilities that apply to a virtual infrastructure. From a security and compliance standpoint, every system should undergo a proper risk assessment. The risk equation has been presented along with a high-level introduction to the defense-in-depth philosophy.

Example threats and vulnerabilities have been highlighted for the hypervisor, guest virtual machine, network, storage, and physical categories. As threats continue to evolve and vulnerabilities are identified, vendors such as VMware provide patches and updates to keep their products secure and ensure system integrity. It is always a good idea to check new software versions for vulnerabilities before performing an upgrade.

While this chapter provided an overview and baseline information, the remainder of the book will be presented in the typical cookbook format. Each chapter will provide specific recipes for securing your vSphere infrastructure.

2
ESXi Host Security

In this chapter, we will cover the following recipes:

- ► Hardening the host via Console
- ► Hardening the host via vSphere Client
- ► Configuring host services
- ► Configuring the host firewall

Introduction

Securing the hypervisor platform is critical for building a secure virtualization infrastructure. VMware has made substantial progress in reducing the threat surface of the ESX hypervisor. Beginning with Version 4.0, the traditional ESX hypervisor was joined by the ESXi version of the hypervisor. The ESX version of the hypervisor had a larger footprint and a greater threat profile. ESXi versus ESX is similar to Windows Server Core versus the full version of Windows Server.

Starting with vSphere 5.0, the ESXi hypervisor replaced the ESX hypervisor; as a result, the console's interface was changed to a more streamlined and simple **Graphical User Interface (GUI)**. In fact, the ESXi hypervisor is often run from a memory card instead of a dedicated hard drive due to its size.

Hardening the host via Console

The ESXi console is very straightforward and provides easy keyboard navigation to access basic options. The most common use of the console is to configure the management network so that the host can be accessed from the network by vCenter and directly by the vSphere client management tool.

There are two primary areas to be highlighted with regard to security:

► Troubleshooting mode
► Lockdown mode

Getting ready

ESXi 5.5 must be installed on the physical host, and we must have direct access available to the keyboard and monitor in order to proceed with the local console steps. ESXi is part of the vSphere 5.5 download file and can be found at `https://my.vmware.com/web/vmware/evalcenter?p=vsphere-55`.

How to do it...

Perform the following steps:

1. Press any key to wake the server and change the black and gray screen to yellow. Once the system is awake, we need to log in.

2. Press *F2* to enter configuration mode. We'll need to enter the *root* password by default.

3. Once the password is accepted, we move our cursor down to the **Troubleshooting Mode Options** menu item.

4. Selecting **Troubleshooting Mode Options** gives us the following configuration options, shown in the following screenshot:

   ❑ **Enable ESXi Shell**
   ❑ **Enable SSH**
   ❑ **Modify ESXi Shell and SSH timeouts**
   ❑ **Restart Management Agents**

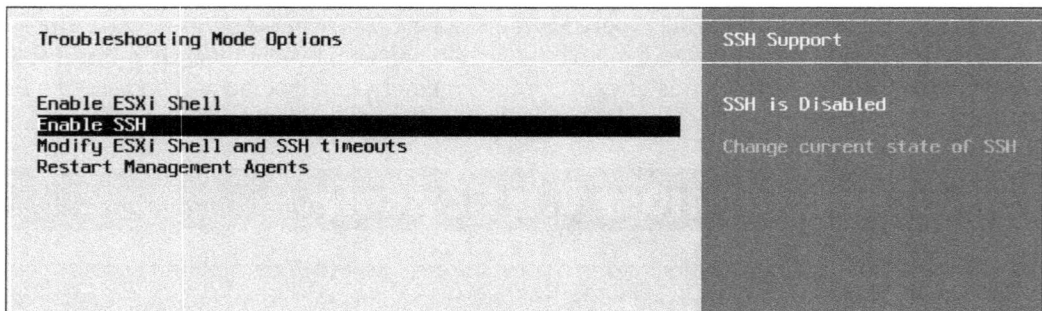

```
Troubleshooting Mode Options                      SSH Support

Enable ESXi Shell                                 SSH is Disabled
Enable SSH
Modify ESXi Shell and SSH timeouts                Change current state of SSH
Restart Management Agents
```

Specifically, we want to ensure that both the ESXi Shell and SSH are disabled.

5. Toggling between **enabled** and **disabled** can be done by using the Space bar to make the proper selection.

6. The second area to be noted is **Configuration Lockdown Mode**.

> You cannot set the lockdown if the host is not yet added to a vCenter. The option is disabled as shown in the following screenshot.

7. **Configure Lockdown Mode** is an option to lock down the host to the point where you cannot log in locally and only through vCenter. This option is enabled or disabled by selecting the option from the main **System Customization** menu (shown in the following screenshot):

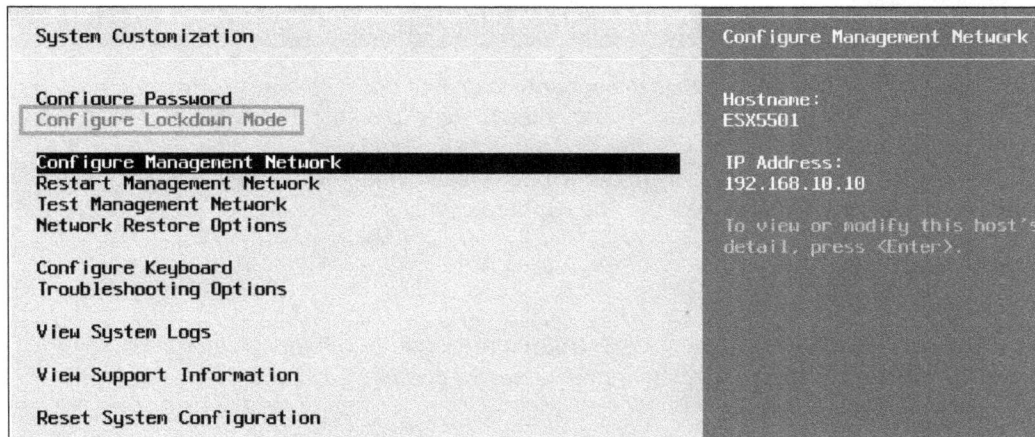

How it works...

The console is used to configure remote access to the ESXi host that is not under the control of a vCenter server. In such cases, remote access can be provided by allowing SSH and remote shell connections to the host. The steps mentioned in the preceding section provide an example for enabling SSH.

Lockdown mode is recommend when the physical host is remote or in a location with questionable security. Ensure that a highly available vCenter configuration exists prior to enabling lockdown mode. If a single virtual vCenter server is used and this server becomes unresponsive, it is not possible to connect to the ESXi server by any remote means to restart the vCenter VM.

There's more

Configuring ESXi at the console is usually only done in smaller environments and special circumstances. More complex scenarios take advantage of deployment tools and host profiles to simplify the configuration.

ESXi Shell is a method used to script and speak to the host via command-line tools such as **PowerCLI**. In general, these options should remain disabled unless there is a specific need to manage the host outside vCenter. SSH is a key that service attackers use to infiltrate systems that are returned from a port scan run by the attacker. While SSH can be very helpful for troubleshooting or even for transferring files with programs such as FileZilla, it should be kept disabled until needed.

Hardening the host via vSphere Client

The most common way to configure the security stance of our ESXi hosts is through the vSphere Client. vSphere Client can be connected directly to a host that is not managed by vCenter or can be connected to vCenter and manage the host centrally. While vSphere 5.5 has features that are only available in the vSphere Web Client, for the purposes of configuring the ESXi host security profile, we'll use the vSphere client.

Getting ready

In order to proceed, we require access to a vSphere Client. The client can be run on any modern Windows desktop operating system or server operating system.

> The vSphere 5.5 Client will not run from a Windows Domain Controller.

The vSphere Client can be downloaded from the link provided on the ESXi host web page, in our example http://192.168.10.10, or from www.vmware.com as a component of the vCenter server: https://my.vmware.com/web/vmware/evalcenter?p=vsphere-55.

How to do it...

Perform the following steps:

1. Open the vSphere Client and enter the IP address of the host that we'll connect. In this example, the host IP is 192.168.10.10.

2. Enter the username and password with access to the host; the default username is root.

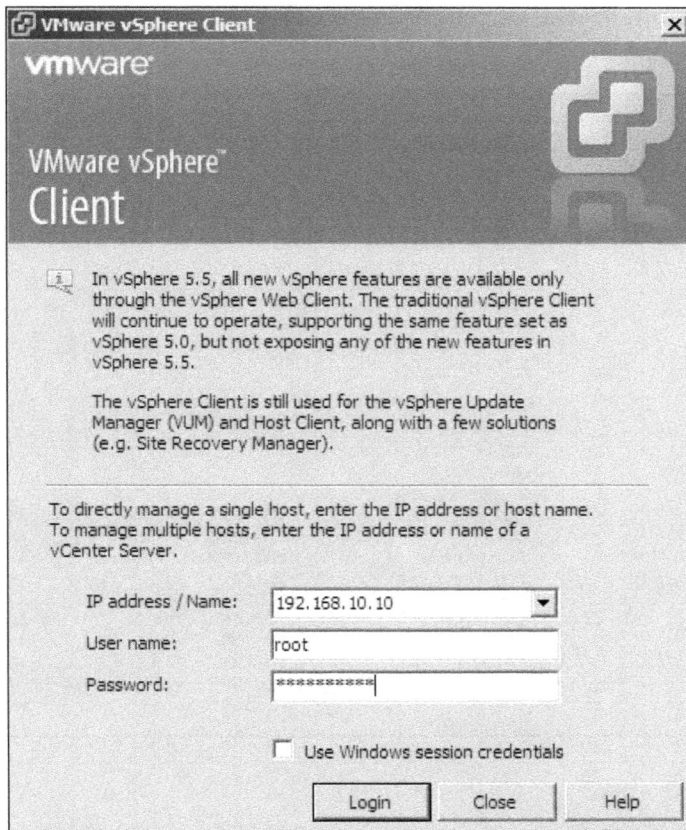

3. Once the client is open, we'll navigate to the inventory section.

> In most cases, a dialog box will present a warning due to an untrusted certificate. Ignore this warning as we will assign proper certificates later in *Chapter 12, Configuring vSphere Certificates*.

4. After selecting the inventory, click on the **Configuration** tab.

5. Once on the **Configuration** tab, locate the **Security Profile** section in the left-hand side pane under the **Software** heading, as shown in the following screenshot:

6. From **Security Profile**, we can observe our firewall ports and services running on the host:

| Getting Started | Summary | Virtual Machines | Resource Allocation | Performance | Configuration | Local Users & Groups | Events | Permissions |

Security Profile

Services — Refresh

I/O Redirector (Active Directory Service)
snmpd
Network Login Server (Active Directory Service)
lbtd
vpxa
ESXi Shell
xorg
Local Security Authentication Server (Active Directory Service)
NTP Daemon
vprobed
SSH
Direct Console UI
CIM Server

Firewall — Refresh

Incoming Connections

vsanvp	8080 (TCP)	All
ipfam	6999 (UDP)	All
Fault Tolerance	8100,8200,8300 (TCP,UDP)	All
DNS Client	53 (UDP)	All
SSH Server	22 (TCP)	All
SNMP Server	161 (UDP)	All
NFC	902 (TCP)	All
CIM Server	5988 (TCP)	All
rdt	2233 (TCP)	All
CIM SLP	427 (UDP,TCP)	All
vSphere Client	902,443 (TCP)	All

Hardware:
Health Status
Processors
Memory
Storage
Networking
Storage Adapters
Network Adapters
Advanced Settings
Power Management

Software:
Licensed Features
Time Configuration
DNS and Routing
Authentication Services
Virtual Machine Startup/Shutdown
Virtual Machine Swapfile Location
▶ Security Profile
Host Cache Configuration
System Resource Allocation
Agent VM Settings
Advanced Settings

How it works...

The security profile options are the same regardless of whether the vSphere client is connected directly to the host or vCenter is managing the host.

> The important thing to note in **Security Profile** is that once a configuration is updated, the change takes place immediately.

In complex designs, administrators might open ports or start services that are not needed in order to eliminate any potential security problems that might impede the proper configuration of the environment.

Care should be taken in verifying the security services and firewall settings, particularly after any changes to the systems or the environment, including upgrades or patches to the ESXi hosts themselves. This also includes changes or an upgrade to vCenter after any remote troubleshooting has been completed by a third party.

Details on making changes to the firewall and the services are discussed in the following sections; however, it should be noted that a service has the potential of automatically starting or stopping depending on how firewall ports are configured.

Configuring host services

The host services work in concert with the firewall rules to enable or disable a functionality on the ESXi host. Services provided by the vCenter agent allow communication and management of the host by a vCenter server, for example.

The way host services are configured can cause trouble sometimes since we expect to communicate with the host because the port is open, but that is only half of the equation most times. Unlike a Windows server that has services running irrespective of whether they are being used or not, an ESXi host does not have services running that are not called or configured to do so.

Getting ready

In order to proceed, we require access to the vSphere Client. The client can be run on any modern Windows desktop operating system or server operating system.

> vSphere Client will not run from a Windows Domain Controller.

vSphere Client can be downloaded by the link provided on the ESXi host web page or from www.vmware.com.

How to do it...

Perform the following steps:

1. From the **Configuration** tab, select the security profile.
2. Then, select a particular service from the list; in this example, we've selected SSH (highlighted in the following screenshot), which is a common service used for troubleshooting. The status of the service is shown in the dialog box.

3. In order to make changes to the service, select the **Options...** button, as shown in the following screenshot:

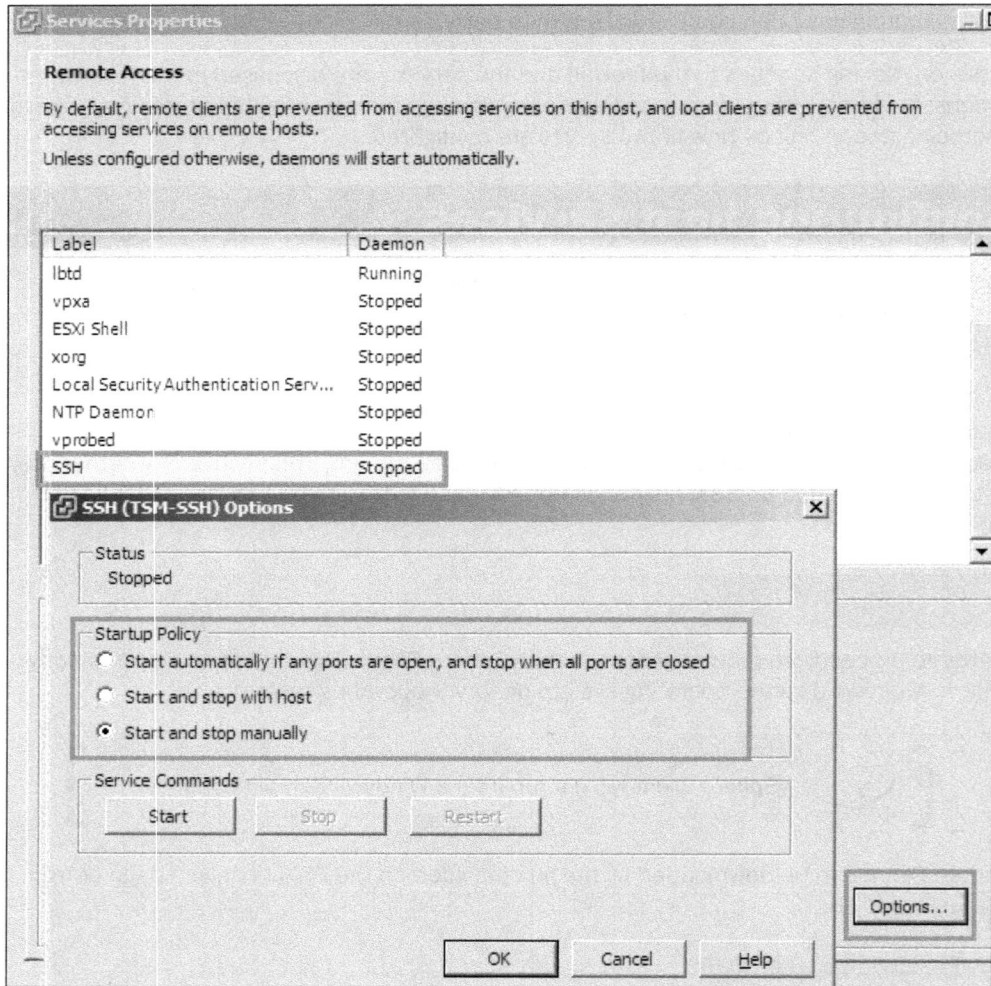

4. This presents us with three options for the service:

   ❏ **Start automatically if any ports are open, and stop when all ports are closed**

   ❏ **Start and stop with host**

   ❏ **Start and stop manually**

5. Select the **Start and stop manually** option since we are only enabling the service for the purpose of remote troubleshooting by a third-party vendor.

6. Click on **OK** to complete the configuration change.

How it works...

The services allow the host to receive processes and respond to commands and data sent by the remote machine. These services work in conjunction with the firewall ports. For example, if we set the SSH server service to start manually but did not open port 22 for inbound traffic, no SSH commands will be processed.

Third-party services also appear in this list when loaded. Hardware-specific services, such as HP Smart Start, will also appear in the list and their corresponding ports will appear in the firewall's list of ports.

Configuring the host firewall

The ESXi firewall configuration is very similar to many firewalls that we are already familiar with from our day-to-day work duties. It is important to note that even though a port might be configured as open in the firewall configuration, should the corresponding service or daemon be stopped, an unexpected connection error might result. For example, the SSH server port is open by default on a new ESXi build. An SSH connection will fail, however, because the SSH service is not running to respond to the request.

Getting ready

In order to proceed, we require access to vSphere Client. The client can be run on any modern Windows desktop operating system or server operating system.

> vSphere Client will not run from a Windows Domain Controller.

The vSphere Client can be downloaded from the link provided on the ESXi host web page or from www.vmware.com.

How to do it...

Perform the following steps:

1. Navigate to the **Configuration** tab and select **Security Profile**.

2. Click on **Properties...** in the **Firewall** section, as shown in the following screenshot:

3. In our example, we're selecting the **SSH Client** rule.

4. After you select the rule, you will be presented with a dialog box, as shown in the following screenshot.

5. We have the option to allow traffic from all networks or to restrict the allowed traffic from specific hosts or known subnets.

> It is always a good idea to restrict inbound traffic if the network where the host resides is well-defined. This takes extra work and the configuration should be documented thoroughly.

6. After you make changes to your IP address range, save the changes; in our example, we'll select the **Allow connections from any IP address** option.

7. Then, you can enable your firewall rule for the SSH client by clicking on **OK** to close the dialog box, as shown in the following screenshot:

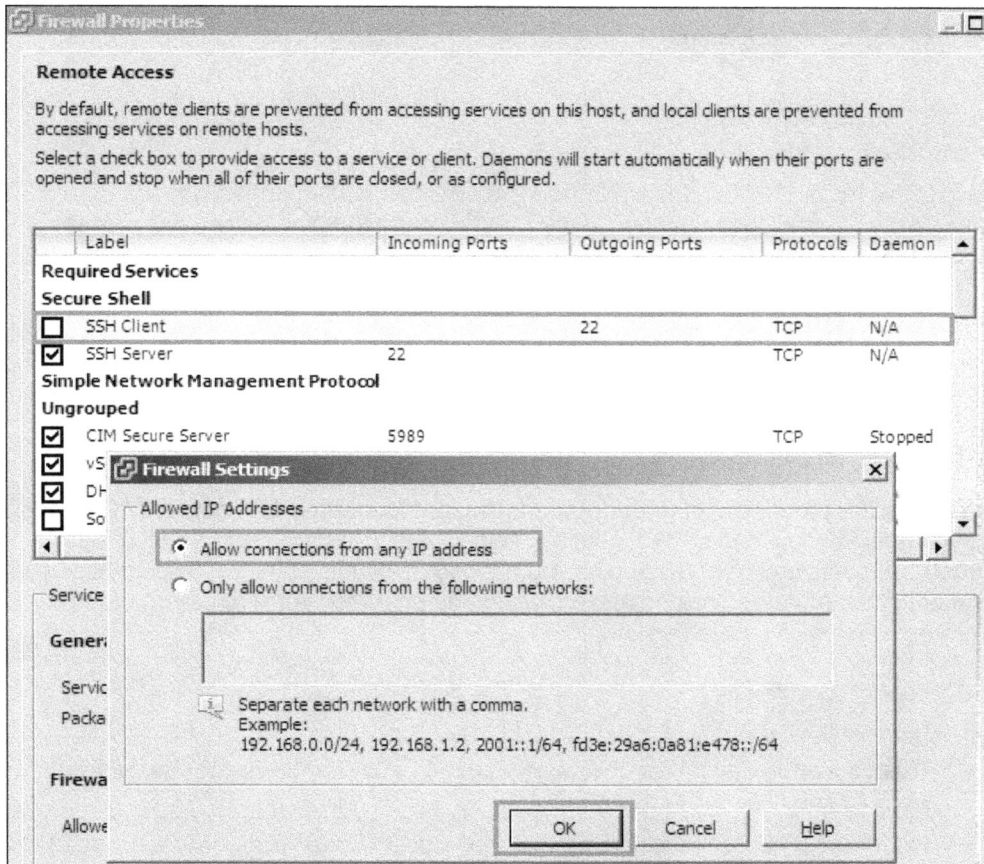

Firewall Properties ⌐ ☐

Remote Access

By default, remote clients are prevented from accessing services on this host, and local clients are prevented from accessing services on remote hosts.

Select a check box to provide access to a service or client. Daemons will start automatically when their ports are opened and stop when all of their ports are closed, or as configured.

Label	Incoming Ports	Outgoing Ports	Protocols	Daemon
Required Services				
Secure Shell				
☐ SSH Client		22	TCP	N/A
☑ SSH Server	22		TCP	N/A
Simple Network Management Protocol				
Ungrouped				
☑ CIM Secure Server	5989		TCP	Stopped
☑ vS				
☑ DH				
☐ So				

Firewall Settings ✕

Allowed IP Addresses

◉ Allow connections from any IP address

○ Only allow connections from the following networks:

ⓘ Separate each network with a comma.
  Example:
  192.168.0.0/24, 192.168.1.2, 2001::1/64, fd3e:29a6:0a81:e478::/64

Service

Gener:

Servic

Packa

Firewa

Allowe

[OK]   Cancel   Help

How it works...

The firewall rules allow and disallow inbound and outbound ports to send or receive traffic from the ESXi host. It is critical that the ports be configured appropriately since unauthorized access to the host could potentially affect a large number of guest machines being hosted on the hypervisor.

The firewall rules are updated once the **OK** button is clicked.

[If a service is in an autostart configuration, it will start if a port is opened.]

There's more

An exhaustive list of ESXi hardening controls are available in the hardening guide from VMware, including the command line and PowerCLI commands for the settings presented in this chapter.

TPM encryption

Trusted Platform Module (**TPM**) is offered on Intel-based systems. Systems with a TPM chip provide protection of the hypervisor, including third-party drivers. TPM provides cryptographic processing on the motherboard that operating systems and applications, such as disk encryption, can take advantage of.

In order to utilize protection, both the TPM and **Trusted Execution Technology** (**TXT**) settings must be enabled in the server BIOS settings. Once the settings are enabled, ESXi will automatically configure TPM/TXT at boot. During boot, TPM measures the VMkernel and a subset of loaded modules, looking for corruption and unauthorized changes or updates. The current version of TPM is Version 2.0.

See also

> ▶ Trusted platform guide: `http://www.intel.com/support/motherboards/server/sb/CS-032413.htm`

> ▶ vSphere 5.5 hardening guide: `http://blogs.vmware.com/vsphere/2013/10/vsphere-5-5-hardening-guide-released.html`

3
Configuring Virtual Machine Security

In this chapter, we will cover the following recipes:

- ▶ Configuring administrative access options
- ▶ Securing the guest OS
- ▶ Configuring virtual machine hardening
- ▶ Configuring virtual machine resource isolation
- ▶ Configuring the standard image templates
- ▶ Managing snapshots

Introduction

The proliferation of **Virtual Machines** (**VM**) has promoted a lack of security in many instances as well as oversight, especially in cases of development or test lab scenarios. Much of the blame can be placed on the ease with which a VM can be brought online and made functional with a variety of capabilities. The term *sprawl* has been used to describe the state of many virtualization projects; that extends to private cloud scenarios as well.

The ease with which a VM can be provisioned is the heart of the problem when we consider the security surrounding the guest operating system. Each guest VM and its encapsulated operating system is analogous to a physical workstation or server being set up and deployed in a production, business, or test lab environment. Due to the perception of users and some administrators that these VMs are free when it comes to physical resources and even software licenses, in some cases, attention is not given to the proper security of the VM as it relates to other assets on the virtual and physical networks.

For many customers, a test or development machine will be created and not necessarily segmented from the rest of the virtual or physical environment in terms of network segmentation or host resource usage. In some cases, the development VM is not loaded with proper anti-malware and antivirus software or a host-based firewall is not configured. In addition, these development or test machines are left running frequently until such time that the host runs low on resources, and an administrator reviews and shuts down unnecessary VMs.

This chapter outlines the steps to be taken to ensure that the VMs and their guest operating systems are secure as a baseline to reduce the attack surface and lower the likelihood of a VM adversely affecting the environment, either by the consumption of resources or compromise by an attacker.

Configuring administrative access options

The nature of the VM is such that no local access exists in the same way a physical machine has a keyboard, mouse, and monitor. Therefore, access methods must be thought of in the same context as access to a physical machine. From a VMware perspective, the console is the classic **Keyboard, Video, Mouse** (**KVM**) interface.

The primary options to access a VM are either through the vCenter console or through a remote connection method directly to the VM. The remote connections for Windows-based machines are primarily achieved through **Remote Desktop Protocol** (**RDP**). For Linux and UNIX machines, **Virtual Network Computing** (**VNC**) is a popular tool along with PuTTY for terminal sessions.

In this recipe, we'll focus on controlling administrative access through vSphere only since this is the platform we are focusing on for controls.

Getting ready

In order to proceed with this set of steps, we must be logged into vSphere Client with a user account in the administrators group.

How to do it...

For pure administration from the virtualization administrator perspective, the vCenter console is the preferred method since no specific rights need to be given to the VM in order to allow remote access. For example, the console bypasses any RDP permissions needed for remote access to the VM since the console equates to the KVM and is seen as local access by the VM.

In this example, we'll open a console session though vSphere Web Client.

Perform the following steps:

1. Navigate to the vSphere Web Client web address (in our example, `https://vcenter55.traing.lag:9443/vsphere-client`).

2. Log in with administrative privileges and navigate to **Home | vCenter | VMs and Templates**.

3. Expand **Datacenter** and select the appropriate server (in our example, **File Server**).

4. Click on **Launch Console** in the **Summary** tab.

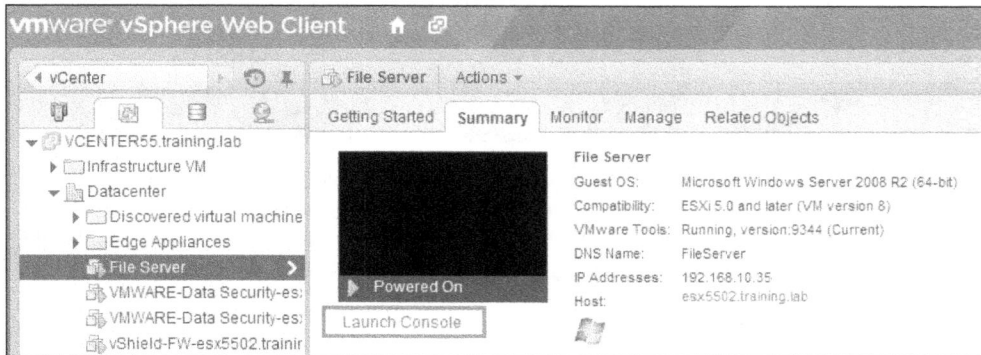

5. The console will launch in another tab of the browser. Click on the **Send Ctrl-Alt-Delete** link to log in.

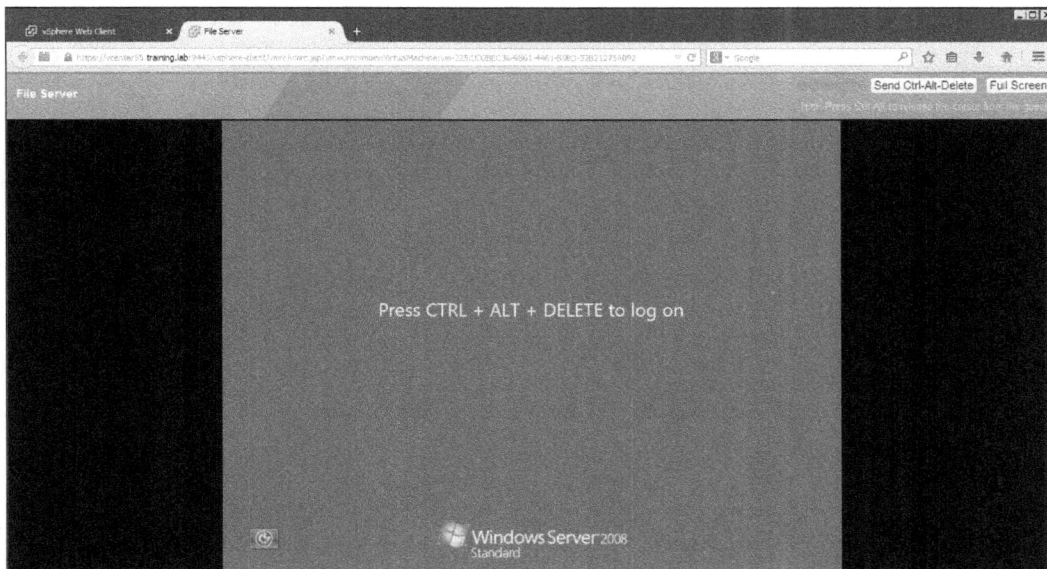

How it works...

The vCenter console sessions are initiated from vSphere Client only. Controlling access to vSphere Client is critical to secure the VMware virtualization platform as a whole, and more detail will be covered in *Chapter 4, Configuring User Management*. Console access can also be gained through vSphere Web Client.

When utilizing a native remote connection to the guest operating system, the access and method of connection should be secure and should follow the best practices associated with the given product. It is always a good idea to restrict the accounts that are able to remotely administer the OS irrespective of whether it is physical or virtual in nature.

Securing the guest OS

A VM and its associated guest operating system should be treated the same as a physical machine with regard to a proper security stance given the location and the function of the machine. Standard practices including up-to-date antivirus, anti-malware, and firewall rules should all be implemented. The lack of standard security practices often makes VMs an easy target for attackers. However, vShield Endpoint provides the offloading of traditional AV from each guest OS to a specialized appliance that runs at the hypervisor level. We'll configure vShield Endpoint and a third-party AV solution in a later chapter.

Getting ready

The ease with which a VM can be provisioned by a user leads to the use of a said machine without the user taking the time to install a proper antivirus software. Ideally, a template will be created and this image will include the requisite security software prior to the actual VM being created. By utilizing such a template, any VM created is secure by default in its initial configuration

How to do it...

In order to install an antivirus software, follow the instructions provided by the particular vendor. Typically, a software installation requires an elevated user permission. A specific example of a firewall configuration is given in the following section.

Configuring the Windows 7 guest OS security

A typical enterprise workstation will be domain joined. In most cases, this workstation will have the built-in firewall disabled unless the infrastructure is highly optimized. If such a case occurs, the firewalls are configured to account for the various applications and unique network settings. The Windows 7 firewall should be turned on by default unless a specific deployment scenario requires unrestricted access to the VM.

Getting ready

In order to proceed with this set of steps, we must be logged in to vSphere Web Client with a user account in the administrators group. There must also be a VM in the inventory to perform the configuration steps.

How to do it...

Perform the following steps:

1. Navigate to the **VMs and Templates** view.
2. Select a VM.
3. Click on **Launch Console** in the **Summary** tab.
4. Log in to the guest Windows 7 operating system.
5. Right-click on the network icon from the lower-right notification area.
6. Select **Open Network and Sharing Center**.
7. Select **Windows Firewall** from the lower-left corner of the network information screen.
8. Verify that Windows Firewall is enabled, as shown in the following screenshot:

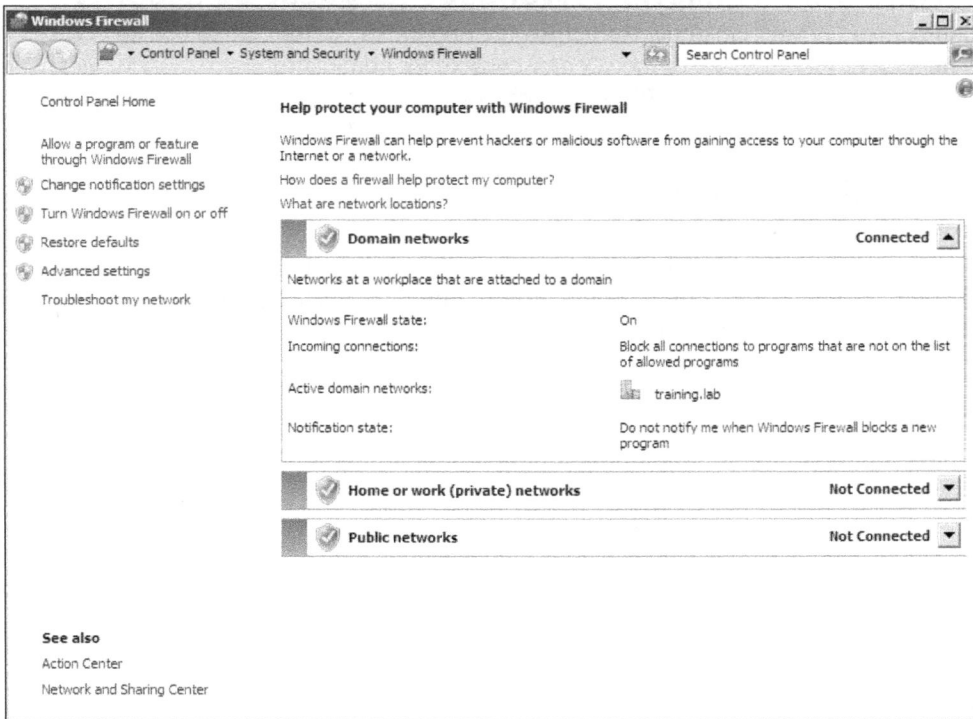

> Windows Firewall can also be enabled and disabled by using the
> `netsh.exe` command via the command line. To enable the firewall, we
> can use `Netsh firewall set opmode enable`, and to disable it,
> we can use `Netsh firewall set opmode disable`.

How it works...

In previous versions of Windows, the firewall functionality was often turned off by users or administrators to cut down on helpdesk calls due to often-blocked applications. The Windows 7 firewall default action notifies the user when a port is being blocked that is required by an application and allows the user to enable the port through the firewall. As you can imagine, it is not a secure by default stance, which is why the firewall is controlled by the domain administrator via a group policy in most cases.

To create a highly secure Windows 7 VM template, start with the Microsoft **Security Compliance Manager** (**SCM**). This tool provides local security policy templates based on best practices to secure not only Windows 7, but also commonly deployed Windows client and server configurations.

Configuring the Windows Server 2008 R2 guest OS security

In addition to a firewall and antivirus on the guest operating system, remote access is likely needed beyond the use of the vCenter console for administrators of the VM. As an example, Windows Server 2008 R2 offers additional security options when establishing a desktop connection.

Getting ready

In order to proceed with this set of steps, we must be logged in to vSphere Web Client with a user account in the administrators group. There also must be a VM in the inventory to perform the configuration steps.

How to do it...

Similar to Windows 7, the Windows Server 2008 R2 Remote Desktop Protocol connection supports **Network Level Authentication** (**NLA**), which is always recommended. Most Windows options will make proper changes to the local firewall policy to enable the desired functionality seen when selecting NLA for remote desktop connections. Perform the following steps to configure NLA:

1. Navigate to the **VMs and Templates** view.
2. Select a VM.
3. Click **Launch Console** in the **Summary** tab.
4. Log in to the guest Windows 2008 R2 operating system.
5. Open the start menu and right-click on the **Computer** object after selecting **Properties**.
6. Select **Remote Settings** from the configuration options on the left-hand side of the screen.
7. Select the NLA option, as shown in the following screenshot:

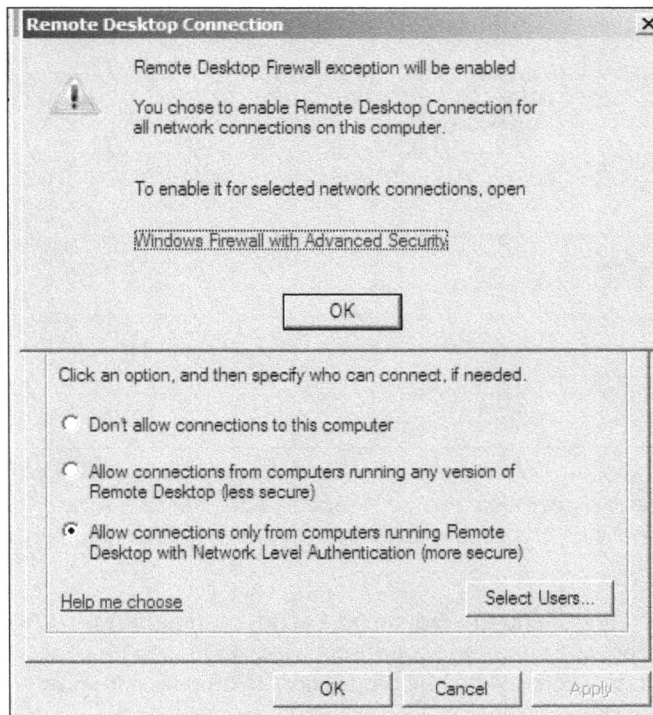

When selecting users for a remote desktop, it is recommended to provide a group of users instead of individual users if at all possible for easy manageability.

How it works...

The NLA setting requires a client that supports it. A user is authenticated prior to being served a logon screen by the server. This reduces the likelihood of a denial of service attack taking down the server.

The server manager provides a quick overview of key security settings, specifically the firewall status and enhanced security configuration, which is on by default. This is shown in the following screenshot:

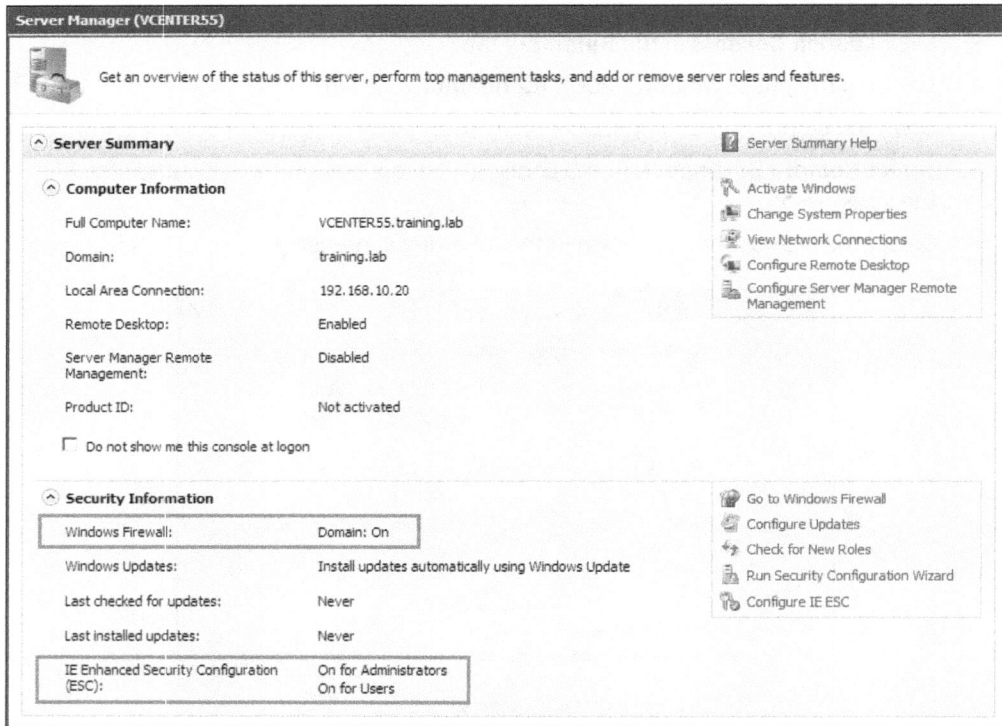

Windows 2008 R2 and higher also include a security configuration wizard that will assist in configuring local policies in a secure manner based on the roles and features installed in the operating system.

Both the host-based firewall and the **Enhanced Security Configuration** (**ESC**) within the Windows server provide separate security controls, which can be used as part of a defense-in-depth strategy to provide multiple barriers to attackers from within or outside the organization boundary.

There's more...

Antivirus software and proper firewall configurations are two of the core methods to keep a VM protected against threats from both virtual and physical networks alike. There are multiple ways to implement both these types of protection, and additional forms of defense should also be implemented as a rule.

Virtual machine antivirus

Basic protection against viruses and malware has become standard in today's modern computing environments. The key differences in the virtual environment include the scheduling of antivirus scans. With physical machines, hardware was separate and concurrent scans occurring at a certain hour were not an issue on the workstation or server. In a virtual environment where resources are shared, concurrent scans can potentially cripple the host given enough load.

Ideally, antivirus can be offloaded to the hypervisor where it is much less resource intensive. vShield Endpoint provides this capability for third-party antivirus vendors. See *Chapter 10, Configuring vShield Endpoint*, for more information on this.

Firewalls

Host-based firewalls are common on most current Windows client and server operating systems. While host-based firewalls are not always necessary and in some cases will generate issues with applications when not configured correctly, they are recommended as a protection layer in the defense-in-depth framework.

The location of the VM must be considered when setting up the firewall. For example, if the VM is connected to both an internal network and a **Demilitarized Zone** (**DMZ**) network, the firewall settings will be very different than a VM on an internal only network behind a firewall. As always, basic risk management should be applied to all the components of the virtual environment.

For a virtual firewall solution, refer to *Chapter 9, Configuring vShield Edge*.

See also

- Find out more about Security Compliance Manager at `http://technet.microsoft.com/en-us/solutionaccelerators/cc835245.aspx`

Guest virtual machine hardening

As a part of the defense-in-depth strategy, the ability to isolate the virtual machine from network threats requires augmentation in the ability to isolate the virtual machine from the possible admin insider threat. vSphere administrators have what equates to physical access to the operating system and the data contained therein.

Getting ready

Each VM communicates with the hypervisor to monitor guests, devices, storage, and tools. This section details several options to verify and set a strong security posture for the virtualization environment and the guest virtual machines in particular. Each of the settings in this section are verified or set under an account included in the administrator account role.

How to do it...

The following tasks provide additional security to the hypervisor, the management infrastructure, and the guest VM. Each task requires administrative access to vSphere Client or vSphere Web Client in order to carry out the task.

Remove unnecessary virtual hardware

When building virtual machines, certain standard hardware is included when the VM is created or cloned. A virtual floppy drive, for example, is of little use to the majority of VMs created in an enterprise. USB, serial, or parallel ports are rarely utilized in VMs.

Ensure that the CD/DVD drives are not connected when not in use. Any route for I/O or connectivity with the VM is a potential attack vector that could be exploited. Perform the following steps for removing unused devices from the VM:

1. Navigate to **Home | vCenter | Hosts and Clusters**.
2. Expand **Datacenter** and **Cluster** (in our example, **Lab Cluster**).
3. Right-click on the desired virtual machine (in our example, **File Server**).
4. Select **Edit Settings...** from the **VM Hardware** section.

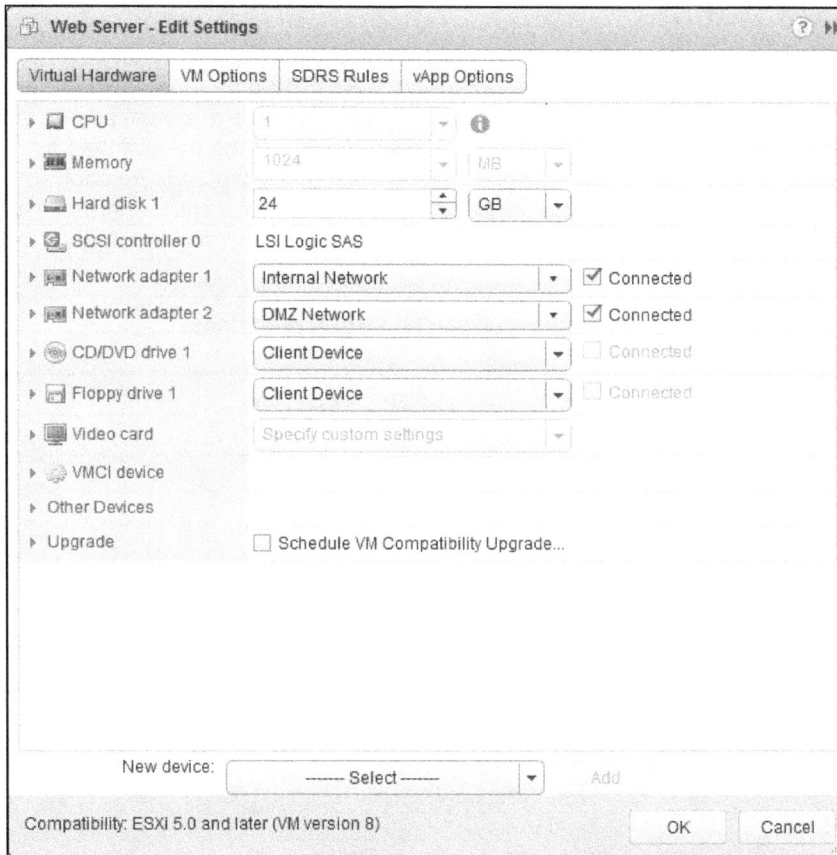

Web Server - Edit Settings

| Virtual Hardware | VM Options | SDRS Rules | vApp Options |

- ▸ 🖳 CPU   1   ▾   ⓘ
- ▸ 🖬 Memory   1024   ▾   MB   ▾
- ▸ 🖴 Hard disk 1   24   ▴▾   GB   ▾
- ▸ 🖳 SCSI controller 0   LSI Logic SAS
- ▸ 🖳 Network adapter 1   Internal Network   ▾   ☑ Connected
- ▸ 🖳 Network adapter 2   DMZ Network   ▾   ☑ Connected
- ▸ 🖳 CD/DVD drive 1   Client Device   ▾   ☐ Connected
- ▸ 🖳 Floppy drive 1   Client Device   ▾   ☐ Connected
- ▸ 🖳 Video card   Specify custom settings   ▾
- ▸ 🖳 VMCI device
- ▸ Other Devices
- ▸ Upgrade   ☐ Schedule VM Compatibility Upgrade...

New device: ------ Select ------   ▾   Add

Compatibility: ESXi 5.0 and later (VM version 8)   OK   Cancel

5. Ensure that unused devices are disconnected; in our example, both floppies and CDs/DVDs are disconnected. Devices can also be permanently removed through configuration parameters.

Unexposed features

Different default parameters are used to create a VM, depending on the tool with which it was created. For example, VMware Workstation and VMware Fusion for Mac have different default parameters than a VM created in vSphere 5.5. In order to ensure the most secure settings for the guest VM, features such as Unity should be disabled by setting the disabled flag to true. Unity is an option when running VMware Fusion on Mac. Since the Unity functionality does not function on vSphere, it should be removed to reduce any potential vulnerabilities that might result from these settings. Perform the following steps for removing unused devices from the VM:

1. Open vSphere Web Client and navigate to **Virtual Machines**.

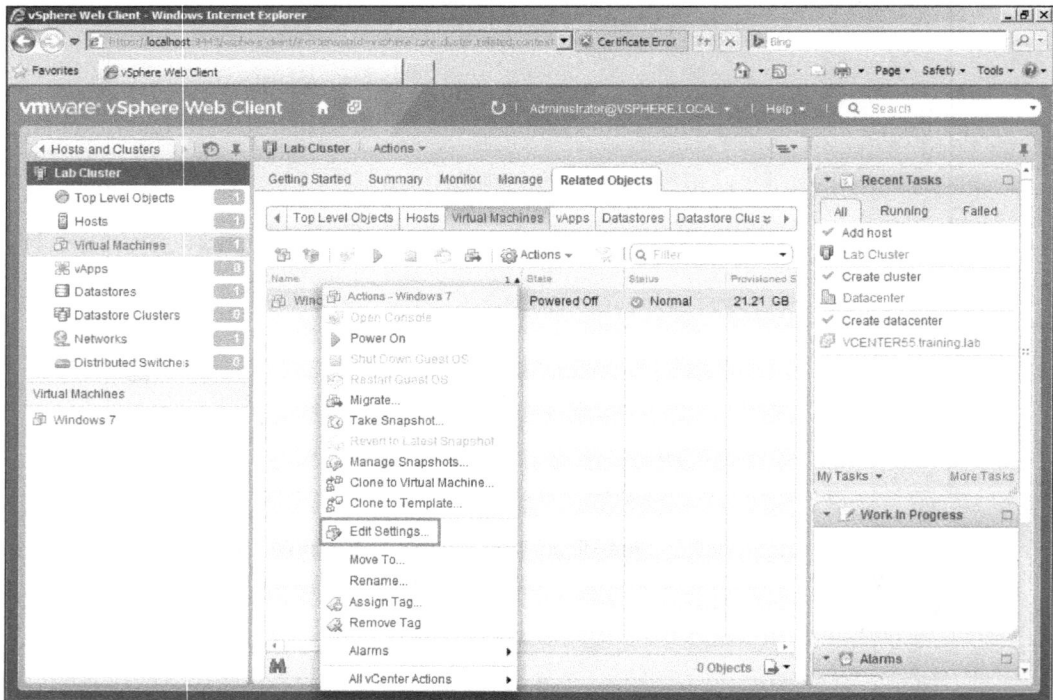

2. Select the virtual machine and right-click on **Edit Settings....**
3. Select **Advanced** and click on **Edit Configuration**.
4. Select **Add Row** to disable Unity.
5. The **isolation.tools.unity.disable** option should be set to **TRUE**.

Configuration Parameters

Modify or add configuration parameters as needed for experimental features or as instructed by technical support. Entries cannot be removed.

Name	Value
ethernet1.pciSlotNumber	34
migrate.hostlog	./Web Server-439acb9d.hlog
ethernet1.filter0.param1	uuid=50241bc2-f5fd-86b0-bf6b-1f67df77b653.001
ethernet1.filter0.name	vshield-dvfilter-module
ethernet1.filter0.onFailure	failOpen
vmware.tools.internalversion	9344
vmware.tools.requiredversion	9344
migrate.hostLogState	none
migrate.migrationId	0
isolation.tools.unity.disable	TRUE

Add Row

OK   Cancel

6. Click on **OK** to save the configuration.

Restricting data between the host and guest

By default, copy and paste operations are disabled between the guest operating system and the console. While the copy-and-paste functionality can be explicitly enabled, it should be kept disabled for the most secure setting.

Clipboard is a functionality that most of us use extensively in our daily work. While an administrator is interacting with a VM within the vCenter console window, this VM has access to the clipboard on the machine in which vSphere Client is running. It is possible, however unlikely, that the VM open in the console could access information previously copied to the clipboard by the administrator such as passwords or other information of a sensitive nature.

Using vSphere Web Client, perform the following steps:

1. Navigate to **Home | vCenter | Hosts and Clusters**.
2. Expand **Datacenter** and the cluster (in our example, **Lab Cluster**).
3. Right-click on the desired virtual machine (in our example, **File Server**).

4. Select **Edit Settings...** from the **VM Hardware** section.

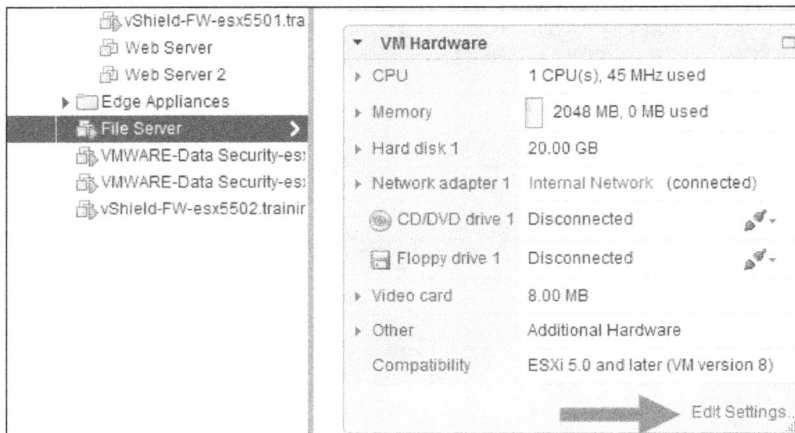

5. Select the **VM Options** tab and select **Configuration Parameters: Edit Configuration**.

6. Click on **Add Row** to insert the following parameters to disable copy and paste.

7. The **isolation.tools.copy.disable** option should be set to **TRUE**.

8. The **isolation.tools.paste.disable** option should be set to **TRUE**.

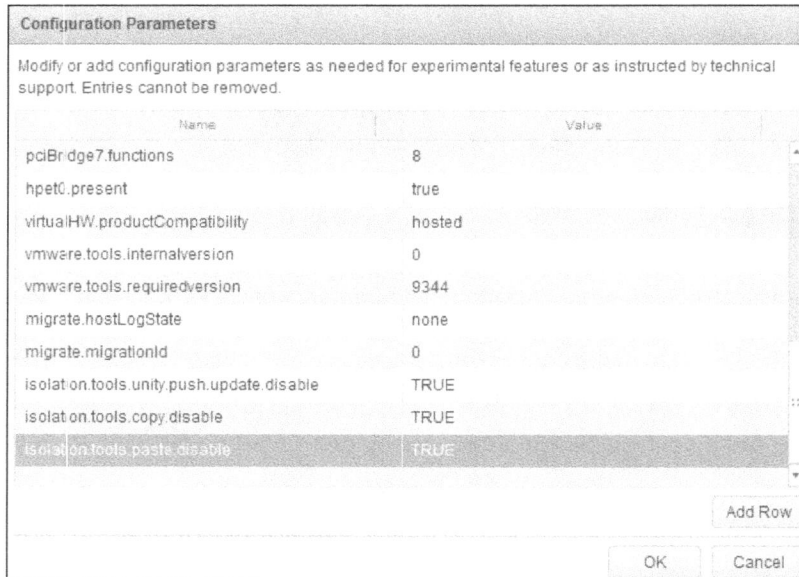

9. Click on **OK** to save the configuration.

Restricting commands

Not all users with access to vCenter necessarily have rights to interact with the VM that they might be managing due to the sensitive nature of the information that resides within that VM. For example, a PeopleSoft or other **Human Resources** (**HR**) system running within a VM will have **Personally Identifiable Information** (**PII**) data in addition to restricted information such as salary information. In this case, the user with permission to administer the VM within vSphere will have no need to access the data in the VM itself.

vSphere provides privilege controls in the form of roles. vSphere's role is to limit access to the guest OS within a VM from the management console. This *no guest* access role acts as a security control, preventing the user associated with the role from gaining access to the data and processes within the VM.

To create a *no guest* access role, log in to vSphere using vSphere Web Client as a user with administrator privileges to vCenter, and then perform the following steps:

1. Select **Administration** and navigate to **Access control | Roles**.
2. Click on **+** to create a role action.

3. Enter **No Guest Access Admin** as **Role Name**.
4. Select **ALL Privileges**.

5. Clear all privileges by navigating to **Virtual machine | Guest Operations**. These three options prevent modifying the guest OS, executing a program within the guest OS, or making queries in the guest OS.

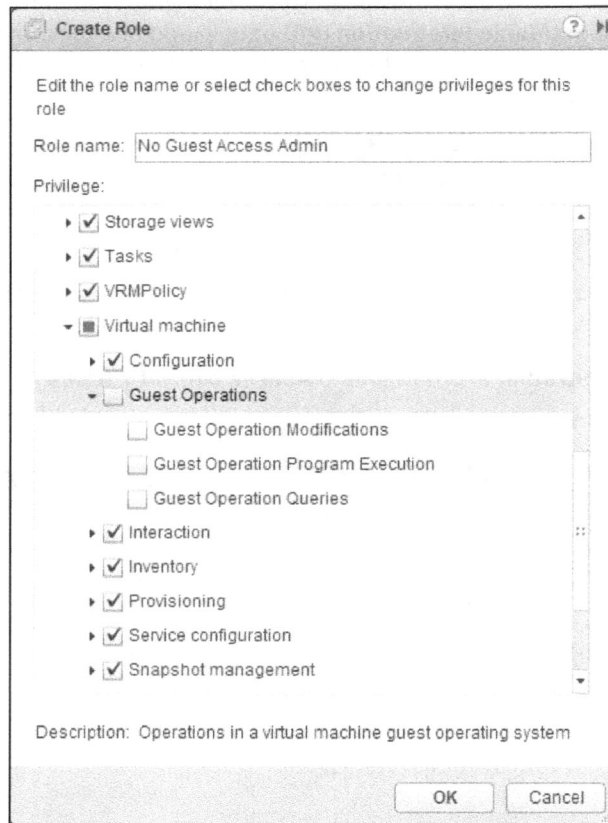

6. Click on **OK** to save the new role.

Limiting the guest OS writes to the host memory

Since the introduction of the buffer overflow vulnerability a la Code Red Worm in 2001, attackers have exploited any system or process that accepts a data flow without the proper check of the validity of data within the flow.

In this recipe, we'll set the size limit of data that can be sent back to the host from VMware Tools. This will ensure that a compromised virtual machine cannot flood the host with data:

1. Navigate to **Home | vCenter | Hosts and Clusters**.

2. Expand **Datacenter** and the cluster (in our example, **Lab Cluster**).

3.   Right-click on the desired virtual machine (in our example, **File Server**).

4.   Select **Edit Settings...** from the **VM Hardware** section.

5.   Select the **VM Options** tab and select **Configuration Parameters: Edit Configuration**.

6.   Add a row to insert the **tools.setInfo.sizeLimit** parameter and set this to **1048576**.

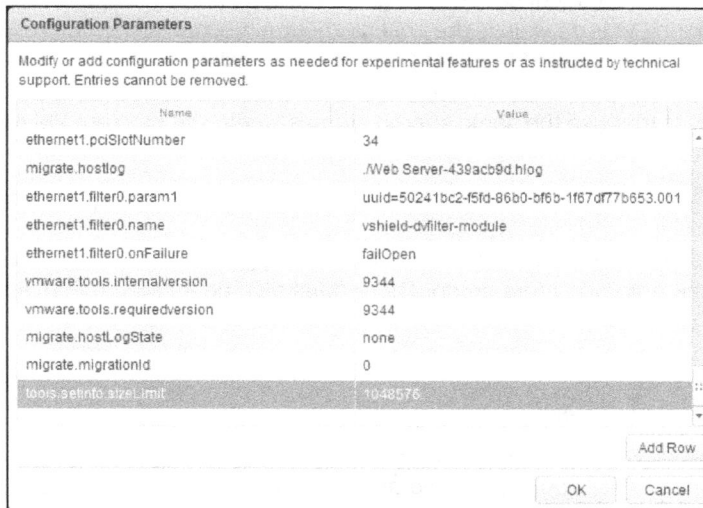

Configuration Parameters	
Modify or add configuration parameters as needed for experimental features or as instructed by technical support. Entries cannot be removed.	
Name	**Value**
ethernet1.pciSlotNumber	34
migrate.hostlog	/Web Server-439acb9d.hlog
ethernet1.filter0.param1	uuid=50241bc2-f5fd-86b0-bf6b-1f67df77b653.001
ethernet1.filter0.name	vshield-dvfilter-module
ethernet1.filter0.onFailure	failOpen
vmware.tools.internalversion	9344
vmware.tools.requiredversion	9344
migrate.hostLogState	none
migrate.migrationId	0
tools.setinfo.sizeLimit	1048576

Add Row

OK   Cancel

7.   Click on **OK** to save the configuration.

How it works...

Each of the settings detailed here are specific examples of an access method between the hypervisor and the VM that is controlled through the vCenter management console. The key point to take away from these settings is a default setup of vCenter that will allow access by the virtualization administrator to the guest operating system within the VM. As mentioned, in the case of HR and finance, VMs that contain PII on employees, customers, partners, and so on, require strict compliance security controls.

Hosting VMs that fall under **Health Insurance Portability and Accountability Act** (**HIPAA**) or **Payment Card Industry** (**PCI**), as an example, requires the types of controls that the settings in the chapter explain. If a rouge virtualization administrator was able to perform guest operations on the payment database server, for instance, they can transfer data in such a way that will not alert the normal security controls hardened against an external attack.

See also

▶   The vSphere 5.5 hardening guide has a comprehensive list of all hardening options available at http://www.vmware.com/security/hardening-guides

Configuring virtual machine resource isolation

Monitoring the guest virtual machine might not seem to have a direct impact on security; however, should a VM spin out of control and go unchecked, it can have severe performance impact on neighboring VMs as well as the host. Without a mechanism to control or contain VMs, the potential to cause a **Denial of Service** (**DoS**) condition exists. In addition, excessive I/O can not only adversely affect the performance of VMs on the same host, but also affect the VMs on any number of hosts that use the same shared storage where the problem VM resides.

Getting ready

In order to proceed with this set of steps, we must be logged in to vSphere Web Client with a user account in the administrators group. There must also be a VM in the inventory to add to a resource pool.

How to do it...

In this recipe, we'll be adding a new resource pool and configuring the values to ensure that the virtual machines in the pool won't have any adverse effect on the compute resources outside the pool. Perform the following steps:

1. Navigate to the **Hosts and Clusters** view.

2. Right-click on the cluster name and select **New Resource Pool...**.

3. The **Create Resource Pool** dialog box shown in the following screenshot will appear. When creating a pool for lab machines, use lower limits for the processor and memory.

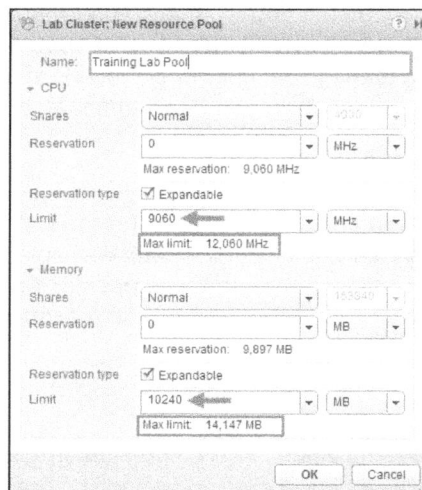

4. Save the settings by clicking on **OK**.

5. Drag existing VMs into the newly created pool to subject them to the lower pool limits.

How it works...

The use of resource pools is highly recommended to put a fence around VMs. So, even if one VM spins out of control, this will only affect this pool of machines and nothing beyond. Even though resource pools don't directly affect system security, this method ensures that critical VMs aren't affected by test or development VMs. As an example, this prevents an entire host from being taken down due to badly behaving VMs. If runaway VMs are allowed to go unchecked, the host can suffer from a denial of service attack based on the consumption of compute resources.

If resource pools are not used, specifying shares and reservations to critical VMs can guarantee that resources are available. Care should be taken when using reservations as these resources will be dedicated to the specified VMs, whether or not they are being consumed, which limits the available resources on the host.

Configuring the standard image templates

One of the benefits of virtualization is the ability to respond quickly to changing business needs and provision virtual machines quickly and efficiently. Test labs and product development might lend themselves to manual VM creation and configuration at the start; however, a formal provisioning process is strongly recommended for production VM generation and provisioning.

Getting ready

In order to proceed with this set of steps, we must be logged in to vSphere Web Client with a user account in the administrators group.

How to do it...

Standard template images that have been properly secured according to the vendor specifications can be customized using the **vSphere Client Guest Customization** wizard shown in the following screenshot:

1. Navigate to the **Home** | **Rules and Profiles** | **Customization Specifications Manager** view.

2. Select **Create a new specification** from the menu bar.

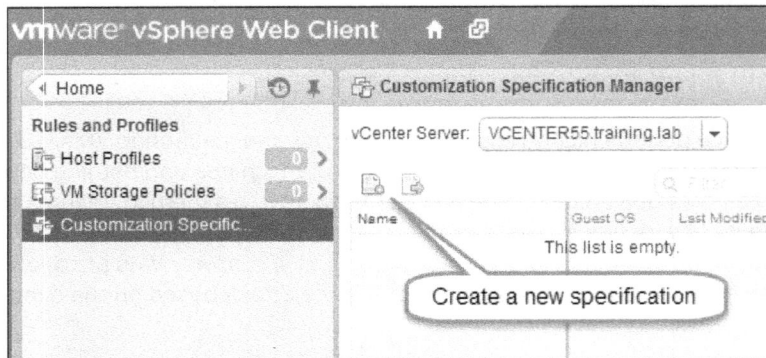

3. Each setting's page allows the customization of guest machines based on the template created from a VM that has already been built.

4. The administrator password is a value that should be recorded and kept in a safe location. This password will become the local machine password for the VM build from the customization file.

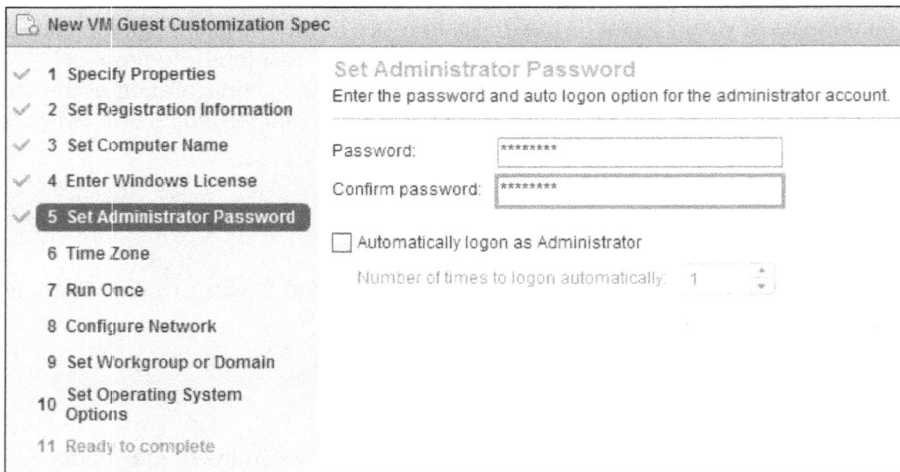

5. Once the customization is complete, the configuration is saved for use in customizing template machines at a later time.

> When applying customizations to Windows, it can take 10 to 20 minutes for the customization to complete, depending on the compute resources available.

How it works...

As a part of the formal provisioning process, templates are used to quickly deploy a baseline image as a new VM. Once the VM has been created, it can be customized accordingly. Templates need to be hardened, patched, and securely configured so that each VM created will have a known initial level of security. Templates can be easily converted into virtual machines so that patches can be applied, for instance, and then converted back to a template form for deployment.

Strict change and configuration control should be applied to the creation and modification of templates in a production environment.

Managing snapshots

Snapshots provide a point-in-time copy of a virtual machine, which can be used to revert to a known working state after changes have been made or applications installed in the case of ThinApp for example. Snapshots are also utilized by some popular backup applications as an effective way to back up a virtual machine without installing a backup software within the virtual machine operating system itself.

User initiated snapshots are not a substitute for proper backup and restore procedures and products. Snapshots can be useful before running updates or an application installation as just in case something goes wrong, a quick rollback can be completed.

Getting ready

In order to proceed with this set of steps, we must be logged in to vSphere Web Client with a user account in the administrators group. There must also be a VM in the inventory to perform the snapshot steps against.

How to do it...

Snapshots are created from either the **Hosts and Clusters** interface or the **VMs and Templates** interface. In this example, we'll use the **Hosts and Clusters** view in vSphere Web Client. Perform the following steps:

1. Navigate to **Home | vCenter | Hosts and Clusters**.
2. Expand **Datacenter** and the cluster (in our example, **Lab Cluster**).
3. Right-click on the desired virtual machine (in our example, **File Server**).

4. Select **Take Snapshot...** from the context menu.

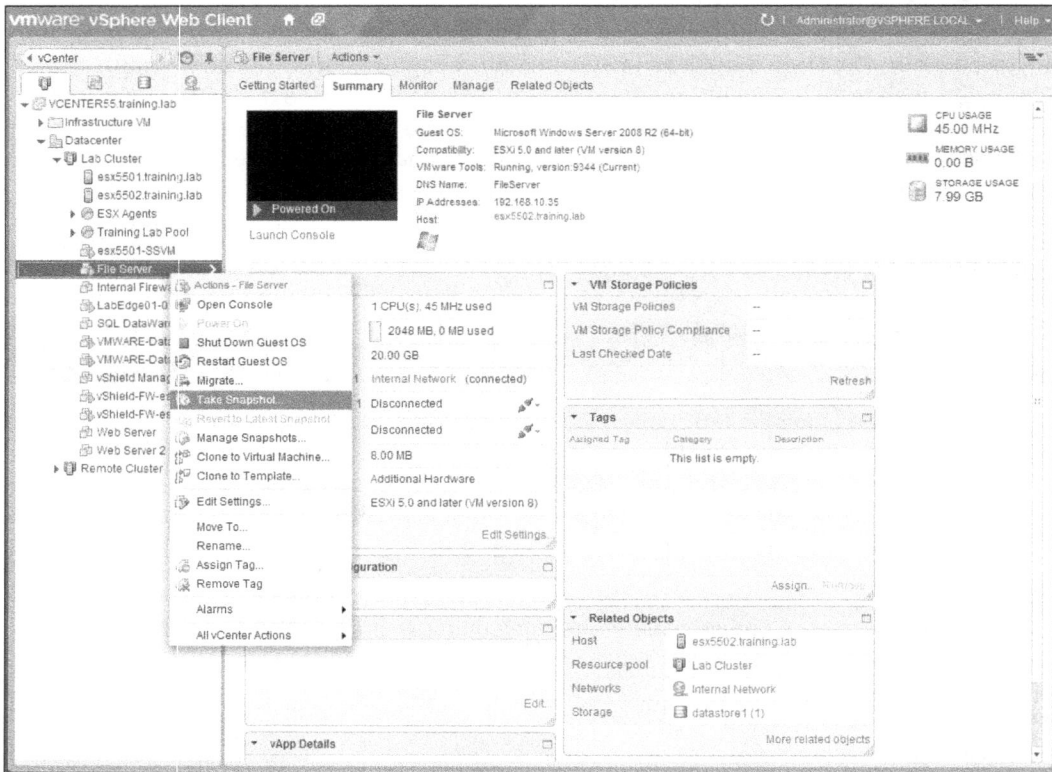

5. Enter descriptive information in **Take VM Snapshot for File Server** including **Name** and **Description**. As a rule of thumb, the more descriptive the better, just in case another administrator needs to take over.

6. Ensure that the option for **Snapshot the virtual machine's memory** is checked to capture the state of the memory as well as the disk.

Take VM Snapshot for File Server

| Name | FileServer_SP1 |

Description | File server pre-sp1 update for rollback if needed Date/Time |

☑ Snapshot the virtual machine's memory

☐ Quiesce guest file system (Needs VMware Tools installed)

OK   Cancel

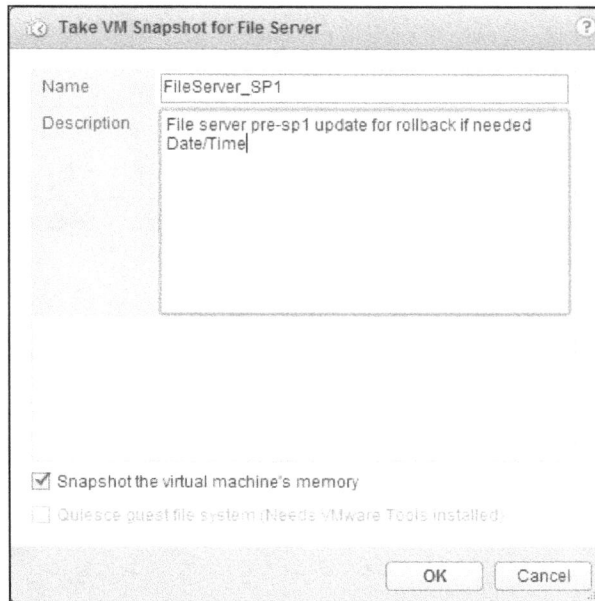

7.   Click on **OK** to initiate the snapshot.

How it works...

Snapshots are stored in the same directory as the virtual disks and contain the following files:

- `Delta.vmdk`: This is generally referred to as child disks
- `.vmsd`: This file contains a database of the virtual machine's snapshot information
- `.vmsn`: These are contents that were in memory at the time of the snapshot

Care should be taken when reverting to snapshots over 30 days old for Windows machines that are domain joined. Domain-joined machines change their machine account password every 30 days. By reverting beyond 30 days, the machine password will no longer match the domain controller and the machine system account will be unable to authenticate it.

Active Directory domain controllers should not be reverted due to the frequent changes made to machine and user accounts.

See also

▶ Domain login fails if snapshot is reverted: `http://kb.vmware.com/kb/1006764`

▶ Read more about backup and restore considerations for virtualized domain controllers at `http://technet.microsoft.com/en-us/library/ virtual_active_directory_domain_controller_virtualization_ hyperv(WS.10).aspx#backup_and_restore_considerations_for_ virtualized_domain_controllers`

4

Configuring User Management

In this chapter, we will cover the following topics:

- ▶ Configuring vCenter Single Sign-On
- ▶ Managing Single Sign-On users with vSphere Web Client
- ▶ Configuring Active Directory integration
- ▶ Managing Active Directory users and groups
- ▶ Assigning permissions
- ▶ Assigning administrative roles

Introduction

With all Enterprise infrastructure products, administrative permissions are paramount to the security of the system, applications, data, and users. Similar to many application systems, VMware offers the ability to manage user and group permissions provided by an external source such as Active Directory or Open LDAP.

In a properly designed system, there should be only rare occasions when the role of a full administrator is required to complete routine tasks. Groups should be created in the supporting directory, which in our case is Active Directory. The use of groups continues to be a wise practice since they are easier to manage than single users and fundamentally provide a more standard mechanism to apply different levels of security to the vSphere environment.

Given the impact, a single misconfigured or mismanaged setting can cause the separation of duties on an enterprise virtualization environment; using proper permissions and roles as a control mechanism is highly recommended.

Configuring vCenter Single Sign-On

Single sign-on has undergone significant changes from Version 5.1. Architectural and operational changes can be reviewed in vSphere publications available at http://www.vmware.com.

Getting ready

In order to proceed, we require access to vSphere Web Client. The client can be run on any modern Windows desktop operating system or server operating system.

> vSphere Web Client requires Adobe Flash, which is not supported on Linux operating systems at this time.

We must be logged into vSphere Web Client with a user account in the administrators group. By default, administrator@vsphere.local is the administrator account for SSO.

How to do it...

In this section, we'll configure Single Sign-On policies:

1. Log in to vSphere Web Client (in our example, at https://vcenter55.training.lab:9443/vsphere-client/).
2. Navigate to the **Administration** view.
3. Expand **Single Sign-On** in the left-hand side pane.
4. Click on the **Configuration** tab in the left-hand side pane.
5. In the main window, click on the **Identify Sources** tab.
6. Verify that **vsphere.local** is present in the source list, as shown in the following screenshot:

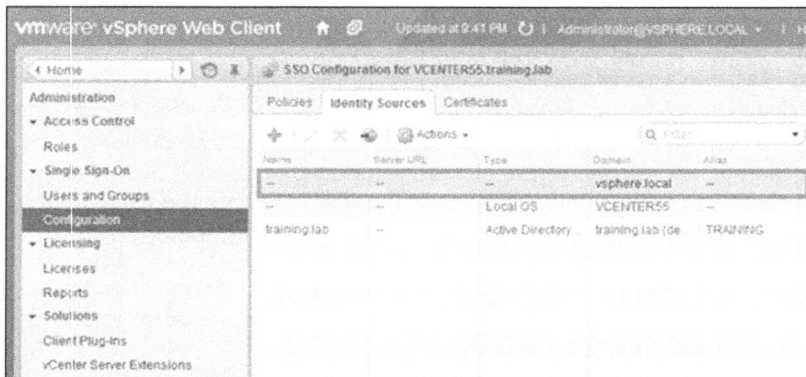

7. Click on the **Policies** tab.

8. Select the **Password Policies** option.

9. Click on **Edit**.

10. Modify **Character requirements**, **Length**, **Maximum lifetime**, and **Restrict re-use** to comply with the current enterprise password policy as closely as possible.

11. Click on **OK** to accept the changes, as shown in the following screenshot:

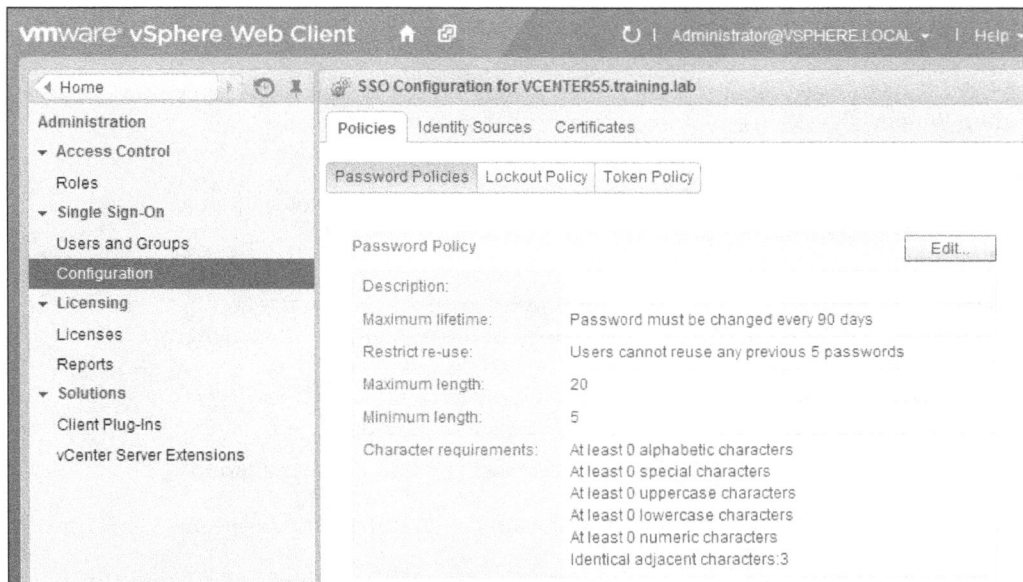

How it works...

Configuring SSO is very similar to configuring an external Active Directory or Open LDAP directory. In essence, SSO is just another directory; in this case, the information is stored in a SQL server database instead of a LDAP-based data structure.

Once a user is validated by the appropriate directory, they are granted a secure token by the **security token service** (**STS**). Once the token is issued, it can be used for the authentication of various vSphere services, such as the inventory service, without being prompted for credentials again.

Managing Single Sign-On users with vSphere Web Client

Single Sign-On users are managed in a similar way to users from other external directories except that these users and groups are specific to the SSO directory within vSphere. Users and groups can be added, modified, and deleted through vSphere Web Client.

Getting ready

In order to proceed, we require access to vSphere Web Client. The client can be run on any modern Windows desktop operating system or server operating system.

> vSphere Web Client requires Adobe Flash, which is not supported on Linux operating systems at this time.

We must be logged into vSphere Web Client with a user account in the administrators group. By default, `administrator@vsphere.local` is the administrator account for SSO.

How to do it...

In this section, we'll cover how to create a new user and add them to a group:

1. Log in to vSphere Web Client (in our example, at `https://vcenter55.training.lab:9443/vsphere-client/`).
2. Navigate to the **Administration** view.
3. Expand **Single Sign-On** in the left-hand side pane.
4. Select **Users and Groups** in the left-hand side pane.
5. In the main window, navigate to the **Users** tab.
6. Click on the **+** symbol to open the **New User** dialog box.
7. Enter the appropriate values to create a new user, as shown in the following screenshot:

New User (?)

Enter values for this user, including the password.

User name: mysso

Password: ******** ℹ

Confirm password: ********

First name: Single

Last name: Sign

Email address: mysso@training.lab

Description: example SSO account

OK   Cancel

Once a user has been added to the `vsphere.local` SSO directory, that user can be added to a group in a similar way.

8. Under **Users and Groups**, click on the **+** symbol in the **Group Members** section, as shown in the following screenshot:

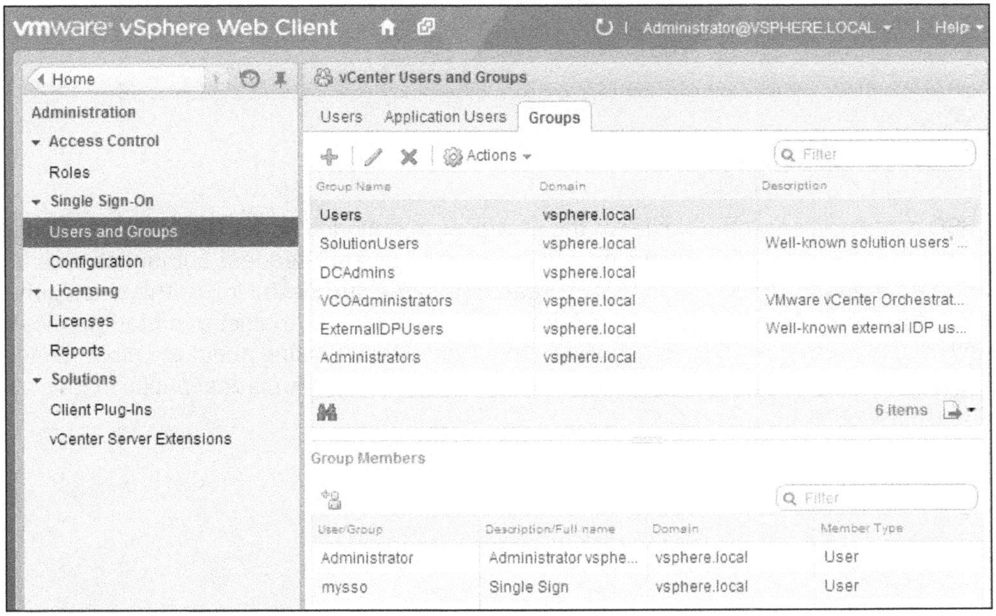

vmware® vSphere Web Client   🏠 📖   ↻ | Administrator@VSPHERE.LOCAL ▾ | Help ▾

◀ Home   👥 vCenter Users and Groups

Administration   Users   Application Users   **Groups**
▼ Access Control
  Roles   ✚ ✏ ✖ ⚙ Actions ▾   🔍 Filter
▼ Single Sign-On   Group Name   Domain   Description
  Users and Groups   **Users**   **vsphere.local**
  Configuration   SolutionUsers   vsphere.local   Well-known solution users'...
▼ Licensing   DCAdmins   vsphere.local
  Licenses   VCOAdministrators   vsphere.local   VMware vCenter Orchestrat...
  Reports   ExternalIDPUsers   vsphere.local   Well-known external IDP us...
▼ Solutions   Administrators   vsphere.local
  Client Plug-Ins
  vCenter Server Extensions 🛆   6 items 📑 ▾

                             Group Members

                             👤⁺   🔍 Filter
                             User/Group   Description/Full name   Domain   Member Type
                             Administrator Administrator vsphe...   vsphere.local   User
                             mysso   Single Sign   vsphere.local   User

9. Select the previously created user from the **Add Principals** dialog box.

10. Click on **OK**, shown as follows:

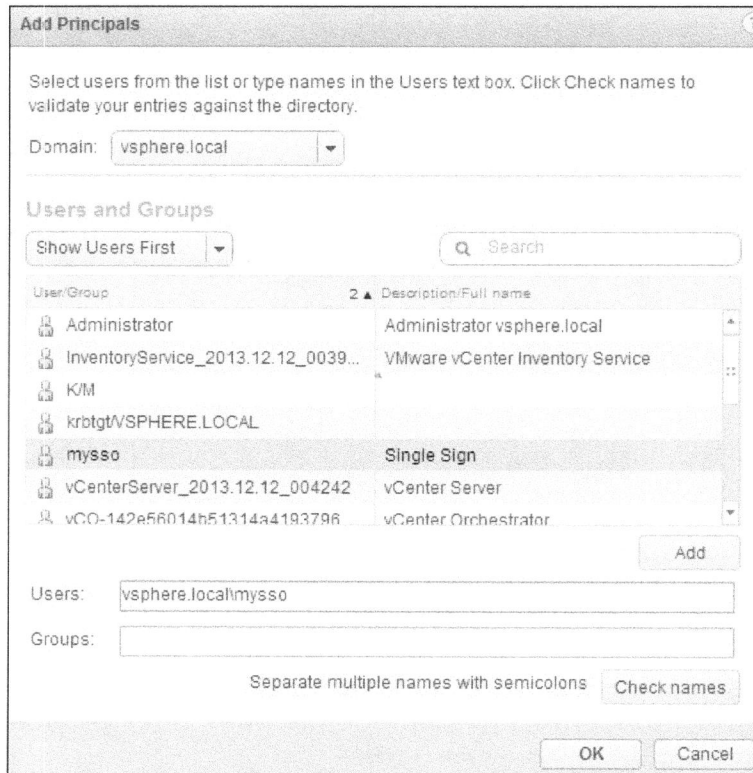

How it works...

The SSO configuration works similar to the previously mentioned Active Directory integration. SSO provides the user with a single login to the system, and subsequent authentications are handled through the secure token that is created from the successful login. The token can be used by a number of systems to allow access to the user without the need to reauthenticate to each disparate system. SSO is especially important when thinking about the cloud and hybrid architectures that span on-premise virtualization environments and public or private cloud environments.

Configuring Active Directory integration

To take advantage of an external identity source such as Active Directory, vCenter must be configured to access the users and groups in the directory.

Getting ready

In order to proceed, we require access to vSphere Web Client. The client can be run on any modern Windows desktop operating system or server operating system.

> vSphere Web Client requires Adobe Flash, which is not supported on Linux operating systems at this time.

We must be logged into the vSphere Web Client with a user account in the administrators group. By default, `administrator@vsphere.local` is the administrator account for SSO.

How to do it...

In this section, we'll add Active Directory as an identity source:

1. Log in to vSphere Web Client (in our example, at `https://vcenter55.training.lab:9443/vsphere-client/`).

2. Navigate to the **Administration** view.

3. Expand **Single Sign-On** in the left-hand side pane.

4. Click on **Configuration** in the left-hand side pane.

5. In the main window, click on the **Identify Sources** tab.

6. Click on the **+** icon to open the **Add identity source** dialog box, as shown in the following screenshot:

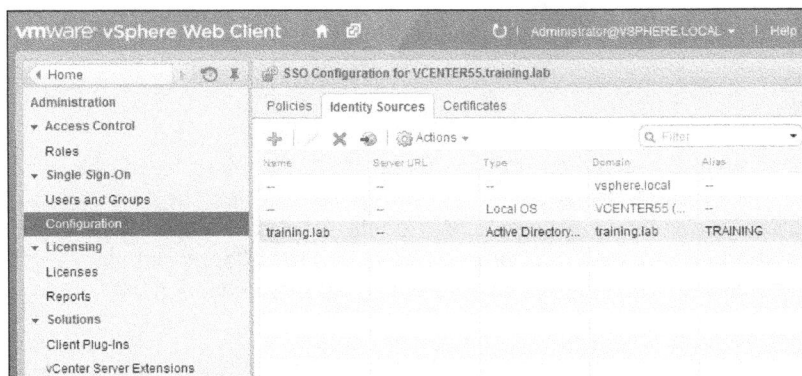

7.   Within the **Add identity source** dialog, perform the following actions:

1.   Select **Active Directory (Integrated Windows Authentication)** as the source type.

2.   Enter **Domain name**.

3.   Accept the default of **Machine Name** for authentication type.

4.   Click on **OK** to accept the changes.

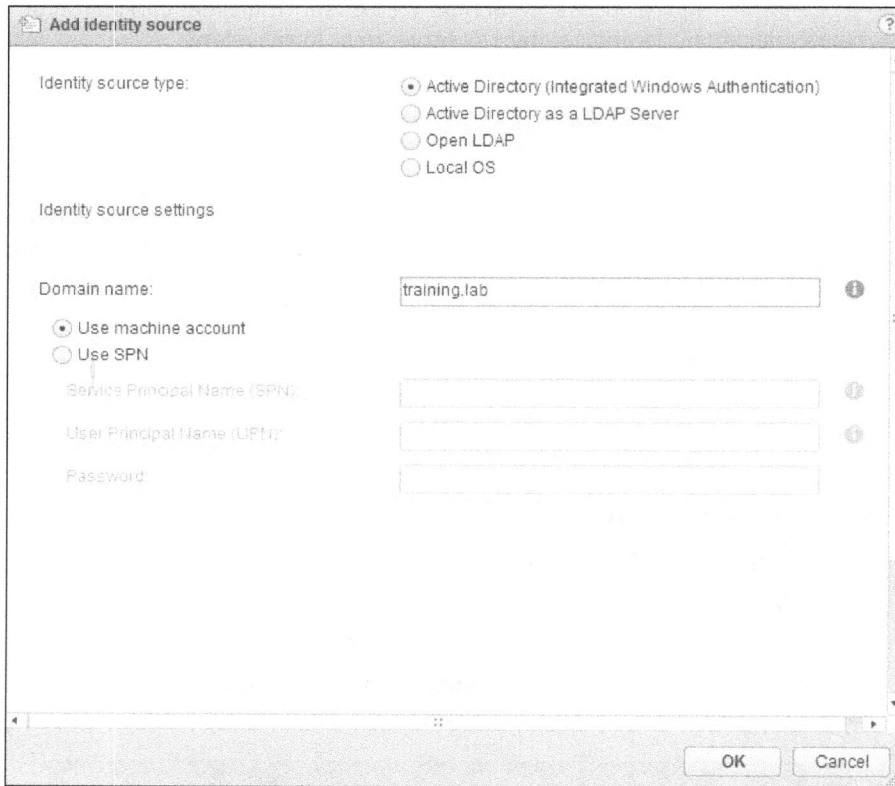

How it works...

vCenter requires an authenticated LDAP connection to Active Directory in order to look up user and group objects. As users are added and removed from groups, they will be assigned proper access to the vCenter environment based on the role or roles to which a group has access. Directory validation occurs at regular intervals based on the vCenter directory's interval setting. The default validation interval in vSphere 5.5 is 1440 seconds.

Ensure that at least one Active Directory domain controller is accessible by a vCenter server, preferably on the same local area network. Wide area connections can impact the directory validation depending on the number of objects in Active Directory.

Managing Active Directory users and groups

The preferred method for managing users and groups that will receive specific permissions through the roles in vCenter is to use **Active Directory Users and Computers** (**ADUC**). By using ADUC, users and groups are subjected to the same provisioning and de-provisioning policies and procedures that are applied to other objects in the Enterprise directory. In addition, the Enterprise password policy will also be applied to user accounts that are used for administrative purposes in the virtual management environment.

As previously mentioned, the use of groups is preferred over assigning individual accounts to roles within vCenter. In this example, we'll be creating a group and adding users to perform a specific task in vCenter.

Getting ready

In order to proceed, we require access to the Active Directory Users and Computers management console and an operational domain controller that was configured in vCenter, in the *Configuring vCenter Single Sign-On* recipe.

> The vCenter server must be configured to use Active Directory as an identity source.

The Active Directory Users and Computers management console is part of the **Remote Server Administration Tools** (**RSAT**) download at http://download.microsoft.com.

How to do it...

In this section, we'll be creating a group and assigning users for a specific task:

1. Launch ADUC from the **Administrative Tools** start menu item.
2. Navigate to the organizational unit created: SDDC.
3. Right-click on **SDDC** and navigate to **New | Group**.

4. Give the group a descriptive name such as VC-TSK-VMOTION, in this example, to grant permission to execute vMotion. Then, click on **OK**, as shown in the following screenshot:

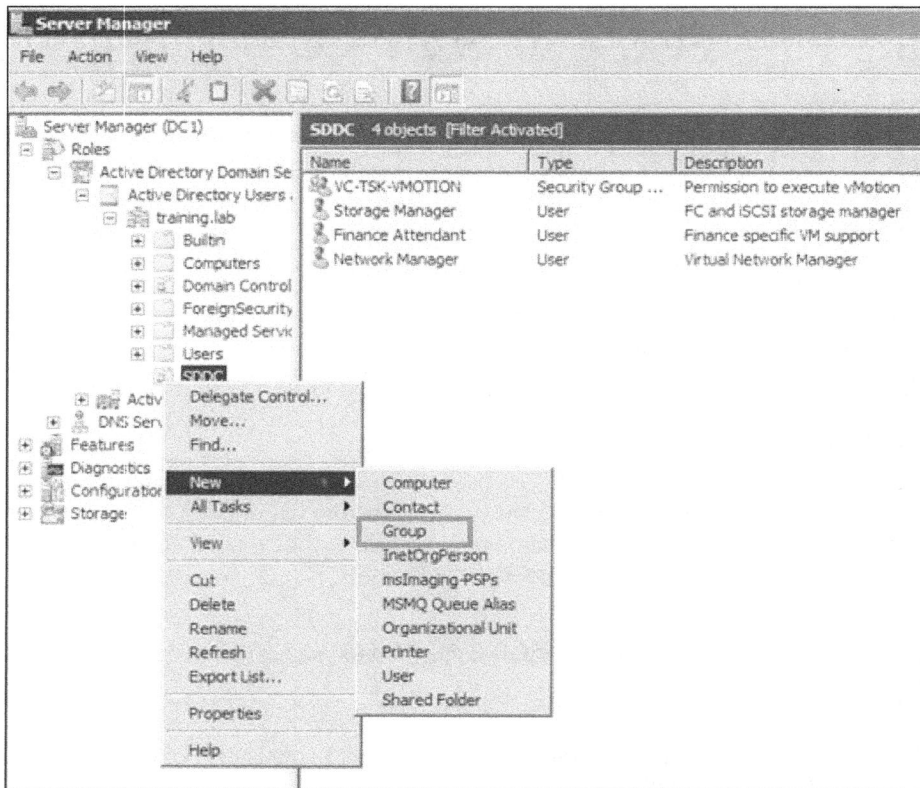

5. Open the newly created group and add a **Description**.

6. Verify that the group type is **Security**, as shown in the following screenshot:

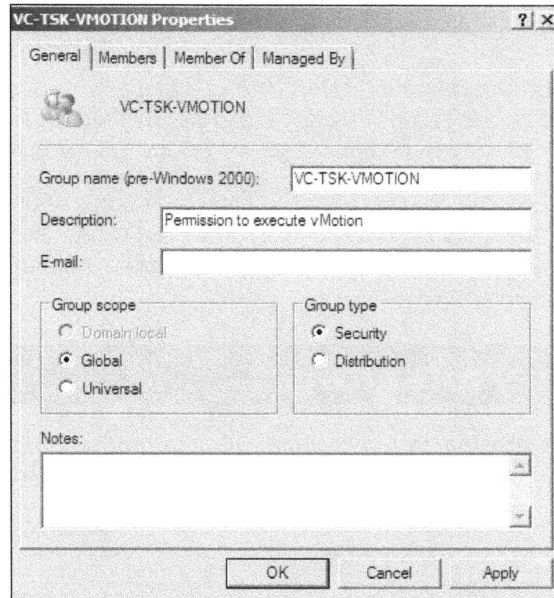

7. Add the appropriate users to the group; in this example, the **Network Manager** and **Storage Manager** users are added, shown as follows:

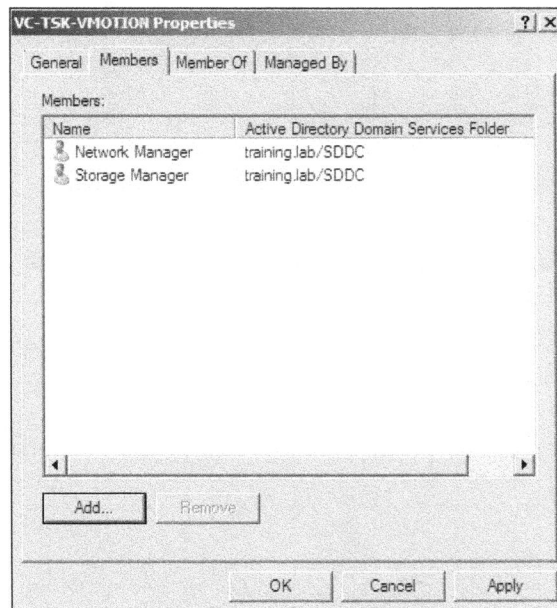

8. Click on **OK** to apply the changes to group membership.

How it works...

Where possible, create an **Organizational Unit** (**OU**) to place all virtualization management accounts and groups within the Active Directory structure. By utilizing an OU structure, additional policies and security can be applied to the groups and/or users if necessary.

Once the permissions and roles are created on vCenter, a majority of user management can take place in Active Directory by simply adding or removing user accounts from defined groups. Utilizing groups ensures that all users in a group have the same permissions and greatly simplifies the administration.

Assigning permissions

Permissions are rights to execute an activity in the vCenter management framework. Roles are a set of multiple permissions required to fulfill a task, such as resource pool management.

Think of a role as a home owner and permissions as access to tasks specific to the home owner role, such as:

- ▶ Access to the structure via a key
- ▶ Access to the electric service
- ▶ Access to the cable or a high-speed connection

Root and vpxuser are considered special users. Beyond the administrator account used to set up the system, all other users and groups must be assigned permissions to complete tasks within vCenter.

Getting ready

In order to proceed, we require access to vSphere Web Client. The client can be run on any modern Windows desktop operating system or server operating system.

> vSphere Web Client requires Adobe Flash, which is not supported on Linux operating systems at this time.

We must be logged into vSphere Web Client with a user account in the administrators group.

How to do it...

A typical task of using vMotion to move a virtual machine from one host to another within a cluster is done by the following permissions:

- ▸ **Resource**: Query vMotion
- ▸ **Resource**: Migrate powered on virtual machine
- ▸ **Resource**: Migrate powered off virtual machine

To utilize the group we created in Active Directory, we'll create a corresponding role in vCenter that has the specific vMotion permissions assigned to it.

Perform the following steps:

1. Navigate to the **Administration** view.
2. Expand **Access Control** in the left-hand side pane.
3. Click on **Roles** in the left-hand side pane.
4. In the main window, select the **+** symbol to create a new role, as shown in the following screenshot:

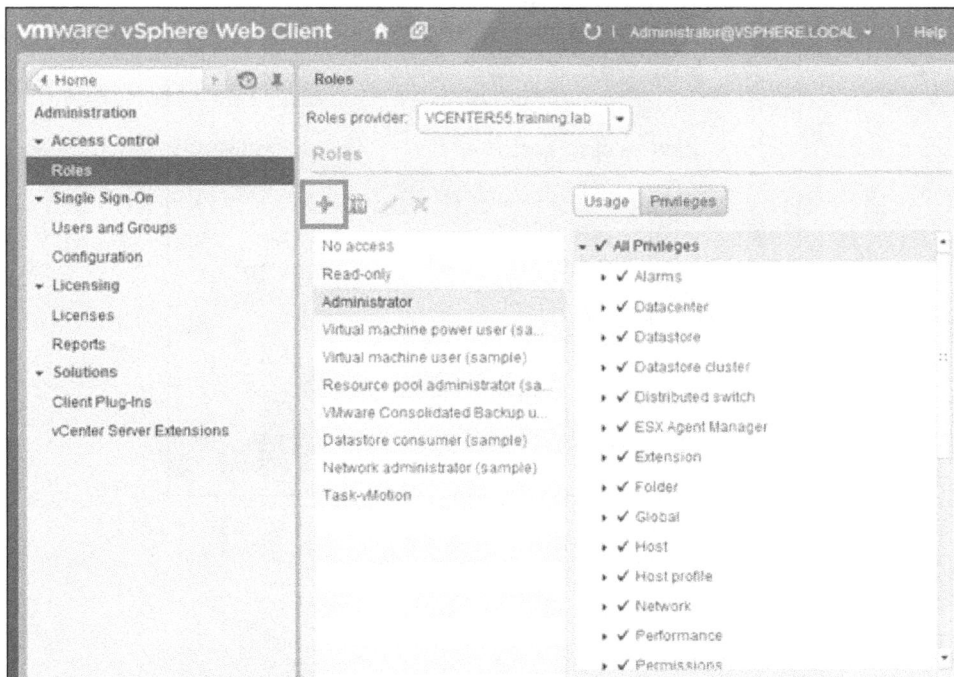

5. Name the role `Task-vMotion`.

6. Expand the **Resource** permission tree.

7. Check the following options:

   ❑ **Assign virtual machine to resource pool**

   ❑ **Migrate powered on virtual machine**

8. Click on **OK**, as shown in the following screenshot:

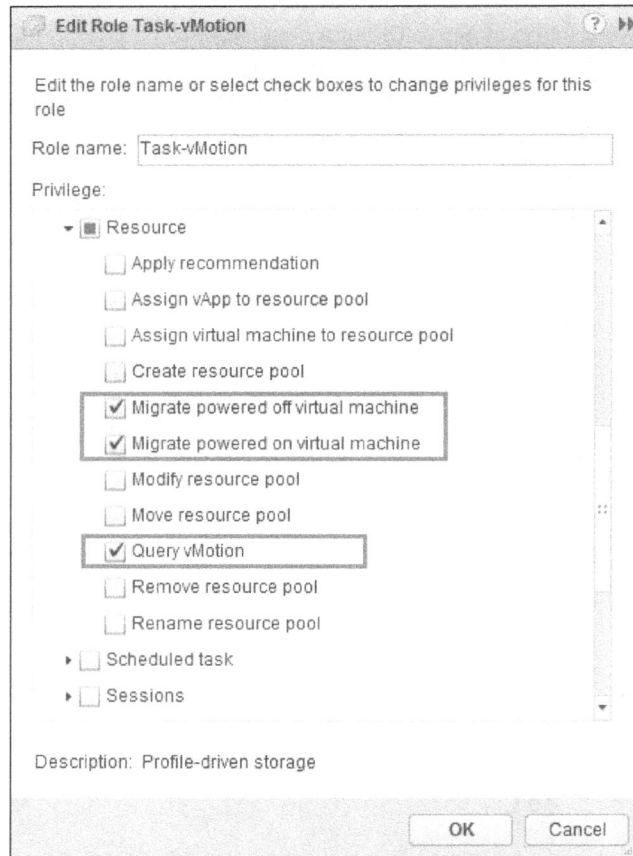

How it works...

Most tasks performed on virtual machines require multiple permissions to one or more objects in the vCenter inventory. Roles provide a mechanism to aggregate specific permissions so that they might be applied to a group of users or possibly specific users on a case-by-case basis.

If a user belongs to two or more groups that have different permissions assigned to the same object and the user itself has a permission defined, the user permission will take precedence over the group permission.

Assigning administrative roles

Roles within vCenter are key to securing the overall virtualization platform not only from outside attacks but from internal attacks and accidental misconfiguration. As pointed out in *Chapter 3, Configuring Virtual Machine Security*, an individual with administrative permissions to a VM can not only manage it but can also log in and extract information from the VM if proper safeguards are not put in place.

The default roles in vCenter are the following:

- No access
- Read-only
- Administrator
- Sample roles

    - Virtual machine power user (sample)
    - Virtual machine user (sample)
    - Resource pool administrator (sample)
    - VMware Consolidated Backup user (sample)
    - Datastore consumer (sample)
    - Network administrator (sample)

Getting ready

In order to proceed, we require access to vSphere Web Client. The client can be run on any modern Windows desktop operating system or server operating system.

> vSphere Web Client requires Adobe Flash, which is not supported on Linux operating systems at this time.

We must be logged into vSphere Web Client with a user account in the administrators group.

How to do it...

Now that we have our Active Directory group and our custom role created with specific permissions assigned to them, we'll assign them to the **Infrastructure VM** folder.

In this section, we'll assign our Active Directory group permissions in vCenter:

1. Navigate to the **vCenter** view.

2. Click on **VMs and Templates** in the left-hand side pane.

3. Select the **Infrastructure VM** folder in the left-hand side pane.

4. In the main window, click on **Permissions** and then select the **+** symbol, as shown in the following screenshot:

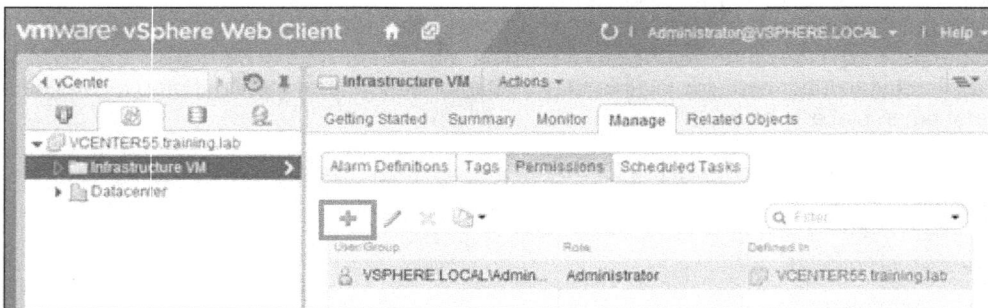

5. Click on **Add** from the **Users and Groups** dialog box.

6. Ensure that **Domain** is pointed to Active Directory.

7. Select the previously created VC-TSK-VMOTION group.

8. Click on **Add**, as shown in the following screenshot:

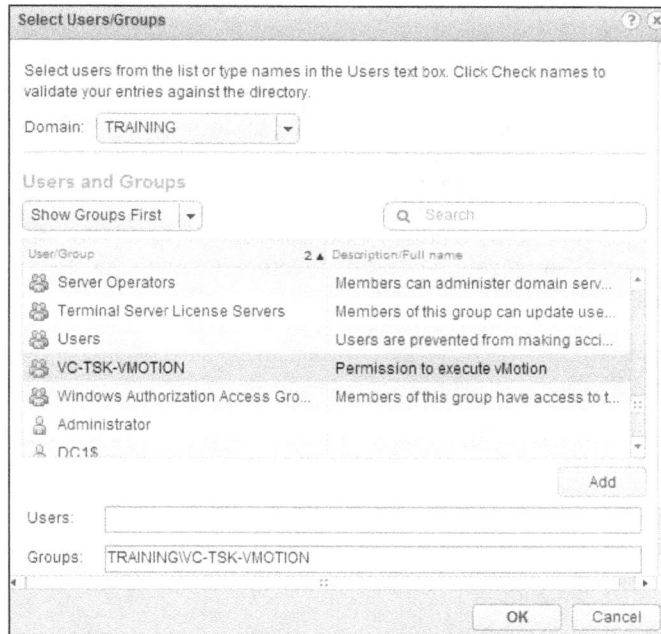

9. Click on **OK**.

10. Select **Task-vMotion** from the dropdown box under **Assigned Role**.

11. Click on **OK**.

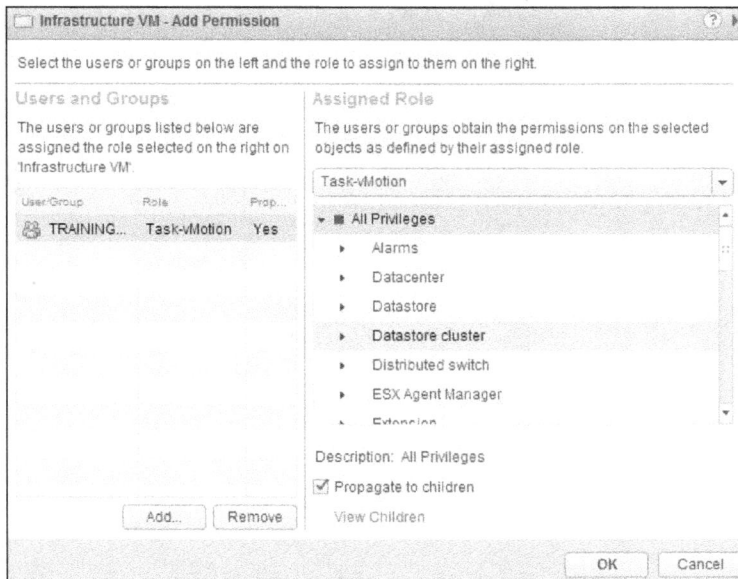

How it works...

Creating a custom role for the task of vMotion is an example of how to implement the separation of duties. By mapping the Active Directory group to the specific role within vCenter, management is greatly simplified and managed simply by adding and removing the proper users and/or groups to the Active Directory group.

This example shows you how some planning and work upfront can help ensure the segregation and compartmentalization of rights to interact with the system in a secure and manageable fashion.

See also

> ► The vSphere 5.5 Hardening Guide at `http://blogs.vmware.com/vsphere/2013/10/vsphere-5-5-hardening-guide-released.html`

5
Configuring Network Security

In this chapter, we will cover the following recipes:

- ▶ Configuring Standard vSwitch security
- ▶ Configuring the port group security
- ▶ Configuring VLANs
- ▶ Creating DMZ networks
- ▶ Providing Distributed vSwitch security options
- ▶ Configuring PVLANs

Introduction

Networking, by its very nature, is insecure by default. The idea was and remains to move information between connected endpoints in the most efficient way through the seven layers of the OSI stack. We've looked at different facets of the vSphere infrastructure and how to secure them against intrusion and administration threats. Improper virtual network design and implementation is a very real threat with high probability when it comes to virtual switch configurations.

One of the primary reasons that contribute to the high likelihood of misconfiguration is the lack of collaboration between the virtual environment administrators and the physical network administrators. While virtual environment administrators tend to understand the virtualizing hardware very well, many come from a *Windows administration* background as opposed to an in-depth networking background.

Physical versus virtual networking teams are often different and don't work with each other. The details are often overlooked when making the connection between the virtual switch environment and the physical switch environment. Most of the functionality problems encountered, let alone security issues, are related to network configurations in particular.

Configuring Standard vSwitch security

The standard vSwitch in a vSphere environment is host-based and provides very flexible configuration options. These options usually suffice in smaller vSphere implementations, especially those businesses that choose to implement the foundation version of vCenter. As we'll discuss in the *Distributed vSwitch security options* recipe of this chapter, making changes to individual host configurations becomes difficult to manage as hosts are added to the datacenter or cluster. We'll be configuring security options on a standard vSwitch in this section at both the switch and the port group level.

Getting ready

In order to proceed, we require access to vSphere Web Client. This client can be run on any modern Windows desktop operating system or server operating system.

> vSphere Web Client requires Adobe Flash, which is not supported on Linux operating systems at this time.

We must be logged in to vSphere Web Client with a user account in the administrators group.

How to do it...

Navigate to the **vCenter** view and then perform the following steps:

1. Expand **Datacenter** from the pane on the left-hand side.
2. Expand **Cluster** under **Datacenter**.
3. Select a valid host from the pane on the left-hand side (in our example, **esx5501.training.lab**).
4. In the main window, click on the **Manage** tab.

5. Select the **Networking** section from the main window.

6. Select **Virtual Switches** from the menu.

7. Click to highlight **vSwitch0**.

8. Click on the pencil icon (shown in the following screenshot) to open the **vSwitch0** settings to edit.

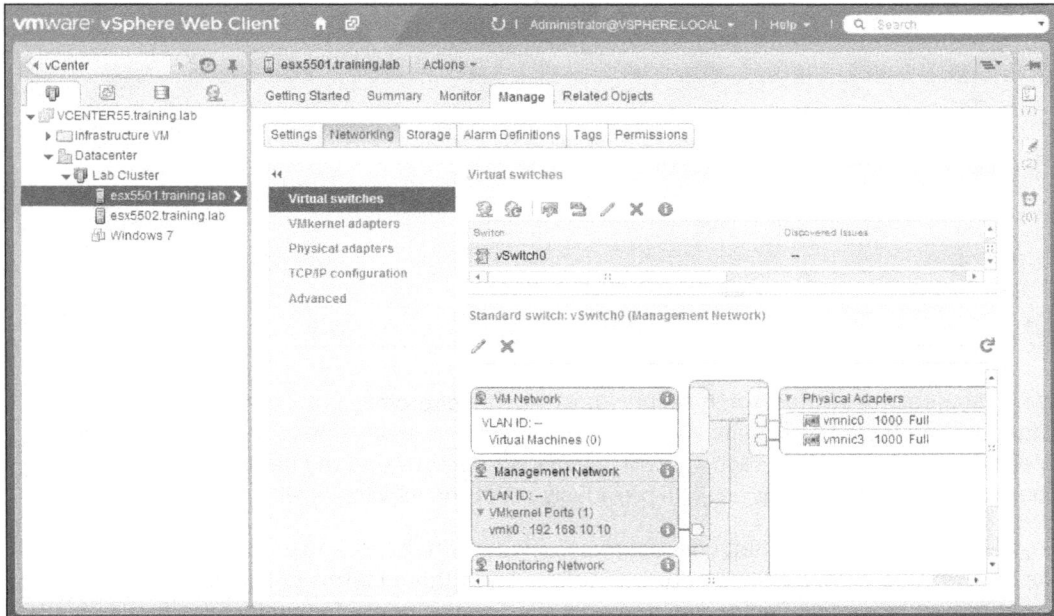

9. Within the **vSwitch0 – Edit Settings** dialog box, as seen in the following screenshot, click on the **Security** menu item.

10. Select the **Reject** option from the drop-down menu for the following settings:

   ❑ **Promiscuous mode**

   ❑ **MAC address changes**

   ❑ **Forged transmits**

11. Click on **OK**.

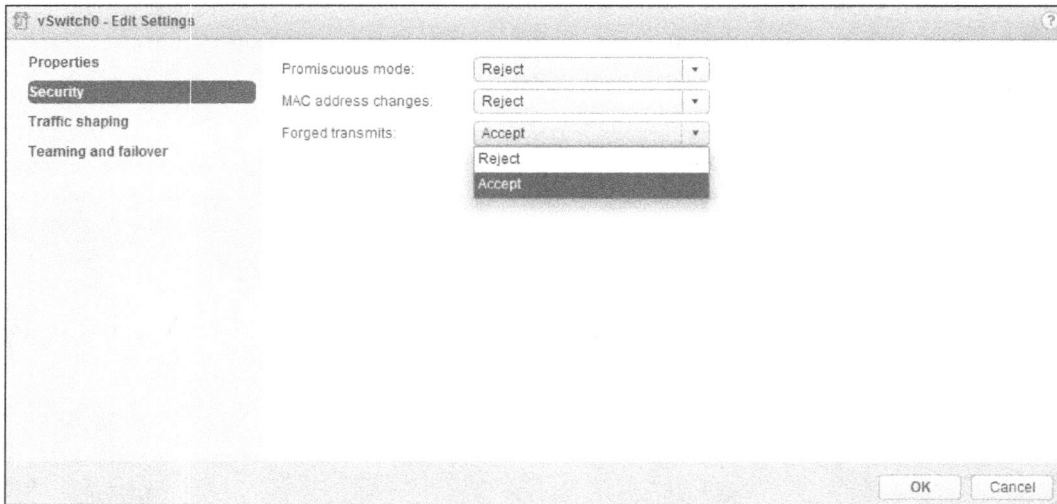

We've now set our virtual switch security policy to reject promiscuous traffic, MAC address changes, and forged transmits. We might later need to override one of these settings for specific traffic. In the next section, we'll discuss port groups and the flexibility to make changes to certain security settings previously set at the vSwitch level.

Segmentation is an important concept maintained in virtual networking design and implementation. Also, isolating network traffic is important in terms of specific usage scenarios and specific vCenter requirements such as the use of fault tolerance and management interfaces to the ESXi hosts.

The following figure shows a port group created specifically for management traffic. The management network port group is shown to be connected directly to the vmnic0 physical network adapter. By default, port groups share all available physical network adapters connected to the vSwitch. In instances such as iSCSI, a port group is mapped (connected) to a specific physical adapter and does not share traffic with other port groups or physical adapters.

How it works...

A vSwitch is a virtual implementation of a physical layer 2 switch, and as such includes options found on common physical layer 2 switches. Layer 2 refers to the data link layer of the OSI model with security policies that include **Promiscuous mode**, **MAC address changes**, and **Forged transmits**:

- ▶ **Promiscuous mode**: This setting allows a virtual machine to listen to or receive a l traffic observed on that particular network. This is an insecure method of operation that allows the adapter operating in promiscuous mode to potentially view traffic that is destined for other virtual machines or network endpoints.

- ▶ **MAC address changes**: When this option is set to **Reject**, requests made to change the initial MAC address from the initial value to a different effective value are denied. One situation where the **MAC address changes** option will be set to **Accept** is when using some load balancing software such as Microsoft Network Load Balancing specifically in the unicast mode. In this case, multiple virtual network adapters share the same MAC address for the virtual IP address that provides load balancing.

- ▶ **Forged Transmits**: This setting affects outbound traffic transmitted from the virtual machine. If the guest operating system MAC address does not match the virtual machine's effective MAC address, the packet is dropped by the ESXi host. The guest operating system has no knowledge that these packets are being dropped by the host.

The earlier versions of vCenter had different default settings for **MAC address changes** and **Forged transmits** that should be verified prior to upgrading to vSphere 5.5 to ensure expected behavior post upgrade. The default settings are shown in the following table:

Default setting	vSphere 5 and earlier	vSphere 5.1 and newer
Promiscuous mode	Reject	Reject
MAC address changes	Accept	Reject
Forged transmit	Accept	Reject

Configuring the port group security

Port groups provide different types of functionalities in the vSphere environment. For example, a VMkernel port group can be used for fault tolerance logging, IP storage, and vMotion. Another type of port group is a **virtual machine** (**VM**) network type. Multiple VM networks are used to segment traffic into different trust zones such as internal (trusted) and external (untrusted).

Getting ready

In order to proceed, we require access to vSphere Web Client. This client can be run on any modern Windows desktop operating system or server operating system.

> vSphere Web Client requires Adobe Flash, which is not supported on Linux operating systems at this time.

We must be logged in to vSphere Web Client with a user account in the administrators group.

How to do it...

Navigate to the **vCenter** view and then perform the following steps:

1. Expand **Datacenter** from the pane on the left-hand side.
2. Expand **Cluster** from the pane on the left-hand side.
3. Select a valid host from the pane on the left-hand side (in our example, **esx5501.training.lab**).
4. In the main window, select the **Manage** tab.
5. Select the **Networking** section from the main window.
6. Select **Virtual Switches** from the menu.
7. Highlight **vSwitch0**.

8. Select the **Management Network** port group.

9. Click on the pencil icon to open the **Management Network** settings to edit.

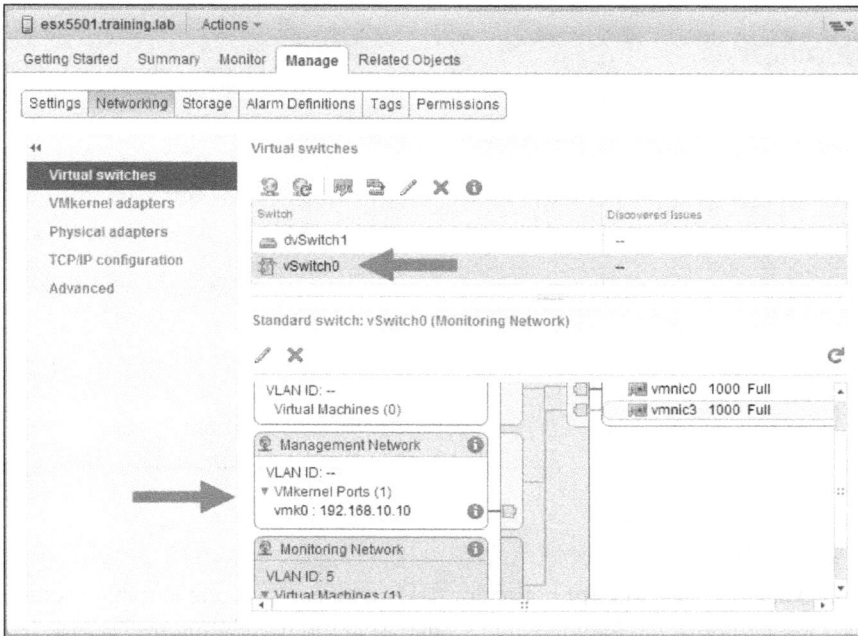

Within the **Monitoring Network – Edit Settings** dialog box, execute the following steps:

1. Highlight the **Security** menu item.

2. Select the **Reject** options for the following settings:
   - **Forged transmits**
   - **MAC address changes**

3. Select the **Accept** option for the **Promiscuous mode** setting.

4. Click on **OK**.

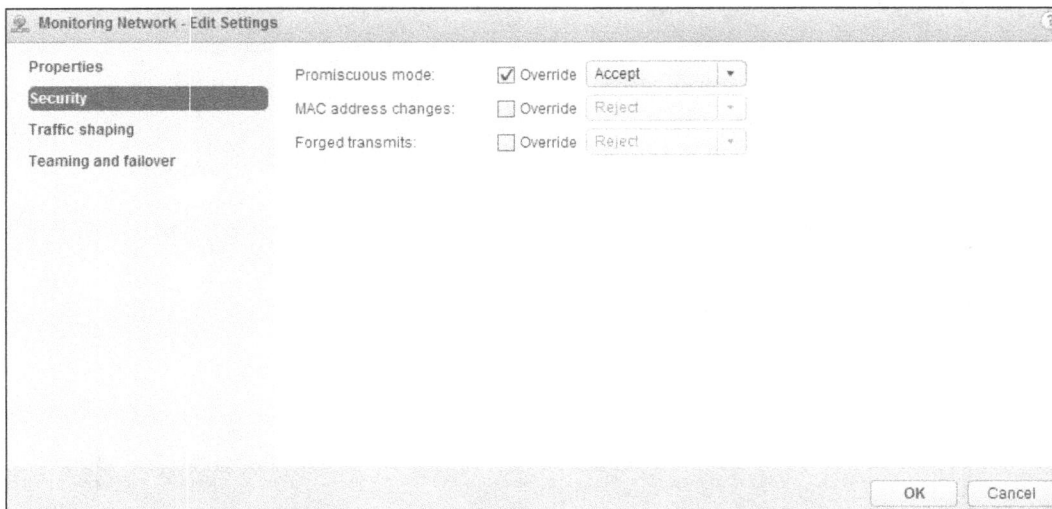

How it works...

The reason we selected the **Accept** option for the promiscuous mode is to allow our sniffer that runs on the Windows 7 machine to get attached to the monitoring port group. By allowing the sniffer to run on the monitoring port group, we are able to see all web traffic passing over the port group. This port group setting overrides the vSwitch setting we configured earlier. In other words, only the virtual machines that are attached to the monitoring network port group have the ability to utilize the promiscuous mode. Any other virtual machines in separate port groups connected to the vSwitch will inherit the vSwitch security settings, unless they are overridden by the port group security settings.

Configuring VLANs

Virtual Local Area Networks (**VLANs**) are a mechanism to segment network traffic without using a separate physical port or network connection. VMware VLANs conform to IEEE standards of specific tagging that allows routing of packets only to ports on a given VLAN.

VLANs are frequently used to segment physical networks to reduce broadcast traffic and limit traffic to a certain number of endpoints. As an example, the finance or HR department might employ a VLAN to segment their network traffic from the rest of the network. VLANs can also improve security by virtual segmentation; however, there are methods to jump from one VLAN to another, which means VLANs provide pretty good security but not complete segregation. If complete segmentation is required, then physical network isolation should be implemented.

VLANs use 802.1q tags to tag the traffic for a specific VLAN. VLAN IDs can be assigned between 1 and 4094. A VLAN of tag 0 indicates that no VLAN tagging is being used. VLAN 4095 is a special VLAN ID that allows all VLAN traffic through a specified port.

There are three types of VLAN tagging supported by vSphere 5.5:

- **External Switch Tagging (EST)**: This is analogous to VLAN 0 where the traffic belongs to a VLAN that is configured externally to the VMware environment and no special rules are applied.

- **Virtual Switch Tagging (VST)**: This is the tagging in which the virtual switch or port group tags the traffic with a specific VLAN ID. This is similar to EST for the physical switch.

- **Virtual Guest Tagging (VGT)**: Here, the VLAN ID is set to 4095 at the switch or port group, which allows all tagged traffic to reach the virtual machines that are set up to send and receive the tagged VLAN traffic.

Getting ready

In order to proceed, we require access to vSphere Web Client. This client can be run on any modern Windows desktop operating system or server operating system.

> vSphere Web Client requires Adobe Flash, which is not supported on Linux operating systems at this time.

We must be logged in to vSphere Web Client with a user account in the administrators group.

How to do it...

To set the VLAN property on a port group, a new port group can be created or an existing port group can be modified.

Navigate to the **Hosts** view and perform the following steps:

1. Select **Networks** from the pane on the left-hand side.
2. Select the **Manage** tab from the main window.
3. In the main window, select the **Networking** menu item.
4. Select **Virtual switches** from the main window on the left-side menu.

5. Select **vSwitch1** from the **Virtual switches** list.

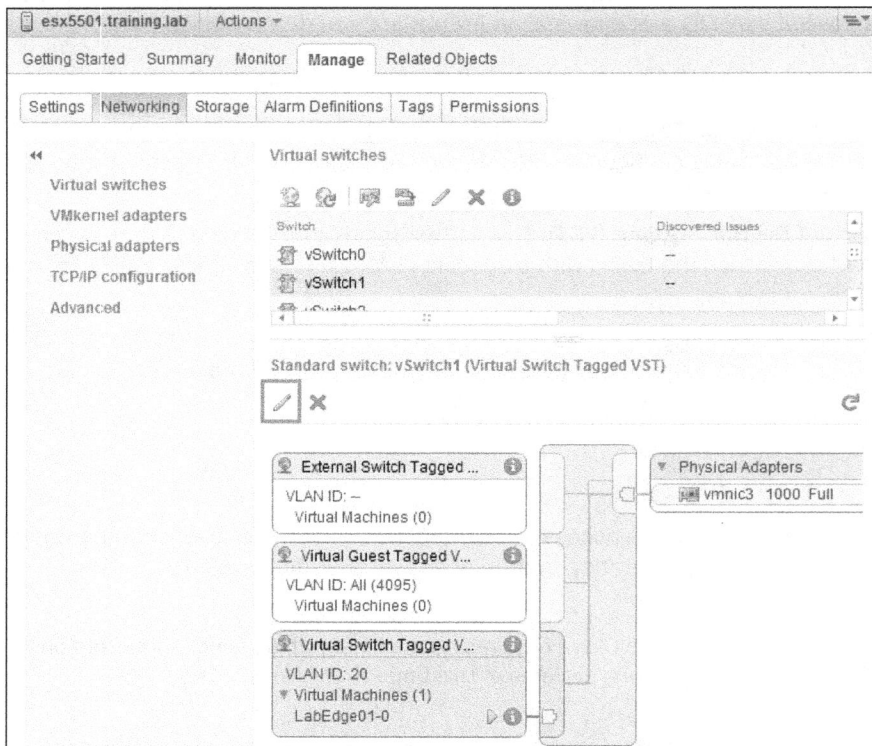

6. To modify the VLAN setting, select the **Virtual Switch Tagged VST** port group.
7. Click on the pencil icon to edit.
8. Highlight **Properties**.
9. Select **VLAN ID** to see the available values.

Virtual Switch Tagged VST - Edit Settings   ?

Properties	Network label:	Virtual Switch Tagged VST
Security	VLAN ID:	20 ▾
Traffic shaping		
Teaming and failover		

OK   Cancel

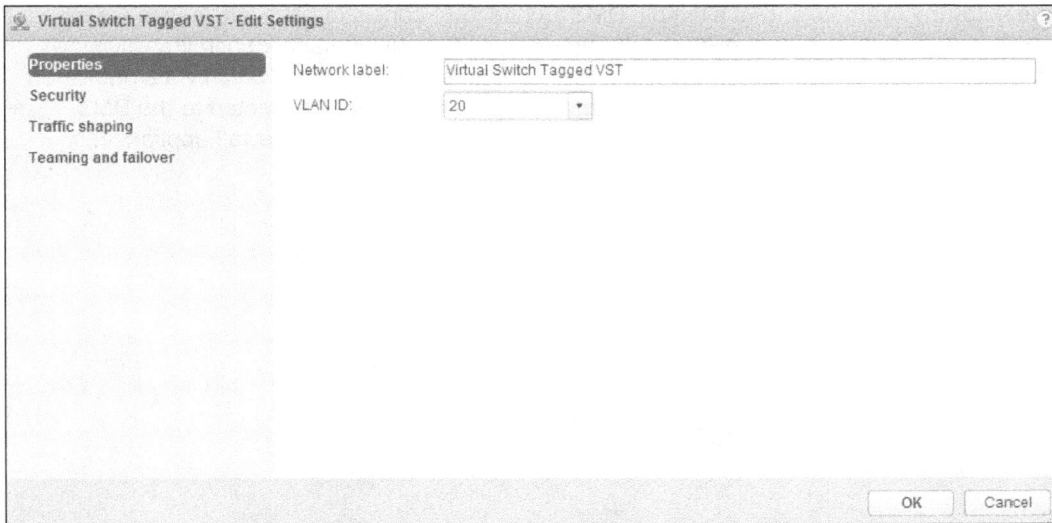

10. Click on **Cancel** to close the port group properties.

How it works...

Each of the VLAN tagging schemes provides flexibility and interoperability with the existing physical network switches. Understanding how tagging works and what VLANs are being used by physical network connections in the ESXi host is critical in configuring the vSwitches and port groups properly.

The VGT method seems to be the least utilized in production virtual infrastructures since it requires each virtual machine to be configured to accept the VLAN tagged traffic. In addition, the configuration of multiple virtual machines' VLAN IDs is a much greater management burden than configuring the VLAN at either the virtual or physical switch.

Creating DMZ networks

The term **Demilitarized Zone** (**DMZ**) is commonly used to describe a zone in a network with a certain level of trust that is lower compared to the internal or private network. DMZ is sometimes referred to as a semi-trusted zone in which web servers are most commonly placed, published, or exposed to the Internet or an untrusted network.

With the virtualization technology available today, it is not only possible, but also practical to build a DMZ architecture strictly using virtual elements. In order to build a pilot or proof of concept for an Internet-facing application, the requisition of physical servers, network switches, and firewalls is no longer necessary. Now, that same environment can be implemented on a single physical host as an example.

The following example shows a simple DMZ architecture consisting of a single web server, an internal firewall virtual appliance, and an external firewall appliance. Each firewall is connected to its own vSwitch, which is in turn connected to a physical switch via a dedicated physical network card present in the ESXi host. The web server is connected to the DMZ vSwitch, which is also connected to a dedicated vNIC in each virtual firewall appliance.

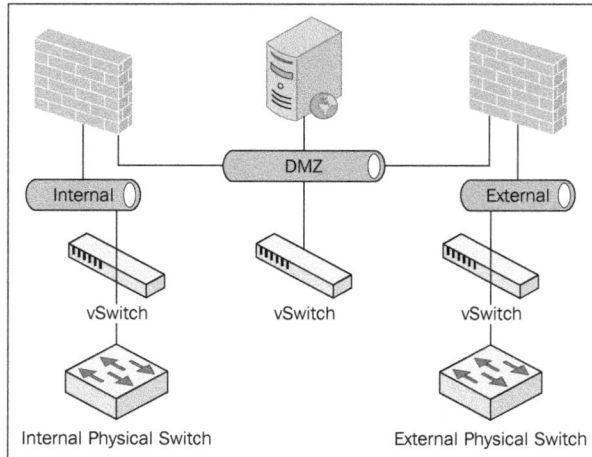

Getting ready

In order to proceed, we require access to vSphere Web Client. This client can be run on any modern Windows desktop operating system or server operating system.

> vSphere Web Client requires Adobe Flash, which is not supported on Linux operating systems at this time.

We must be logged in to vSphere Web Client with a user account in the administrators group. For this example, we'll log in as the SSO administrator or `administrator@vsphere.local`. The training\administrator account can also be used.

How to do it...

In order to implement the design shown previously, we must first ensure that our physical network adapters are connected to the proper physical network segments: one internal or private and the other external or public. Once the proper physical connectivity is confirmed, the virtual network segmentation can be completed.

To complete the virtual DMZ network configuration, in this example, we'll be using three standard vSwitches that are configured within the ESXi host network's container: **esx5501.training.lab**.

Navigate to the **Hosts** view and perform the following steps:

1. Select **Networks** from the pane on the left-hand side.
2. Select the **Manage** tab from the main window.
3. In the main window, select the **Networking** menu item.
4. Select **Virtual switches** from the main window on the left-side menu.
5. Create a vSwitch using the globe icon with a port group named **External Network** connected to a physical NIC.

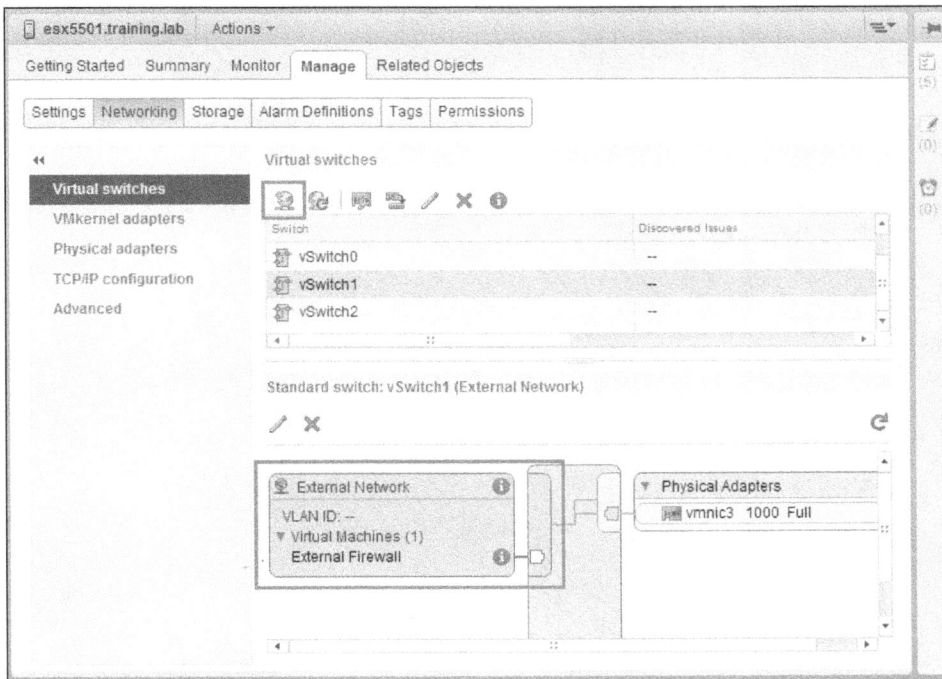

6. Repeat the process to create a vSwitch, and create a port group named **Internal Network**.

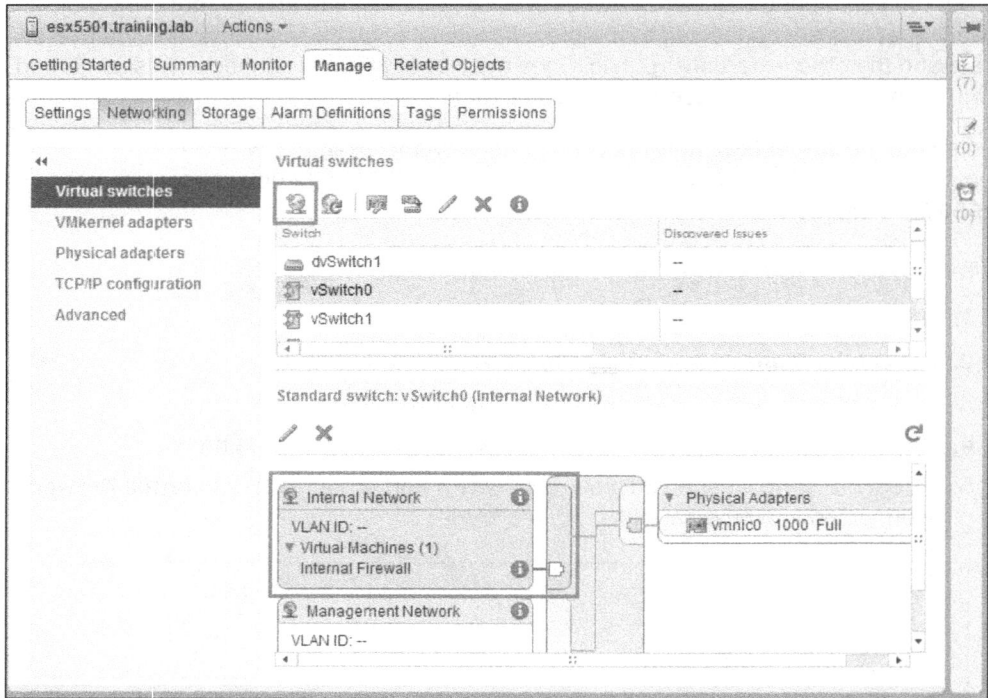

7. Create a third vSwitch with a port group of **DMZ Network,** but don't connect it to a physical network adapter.

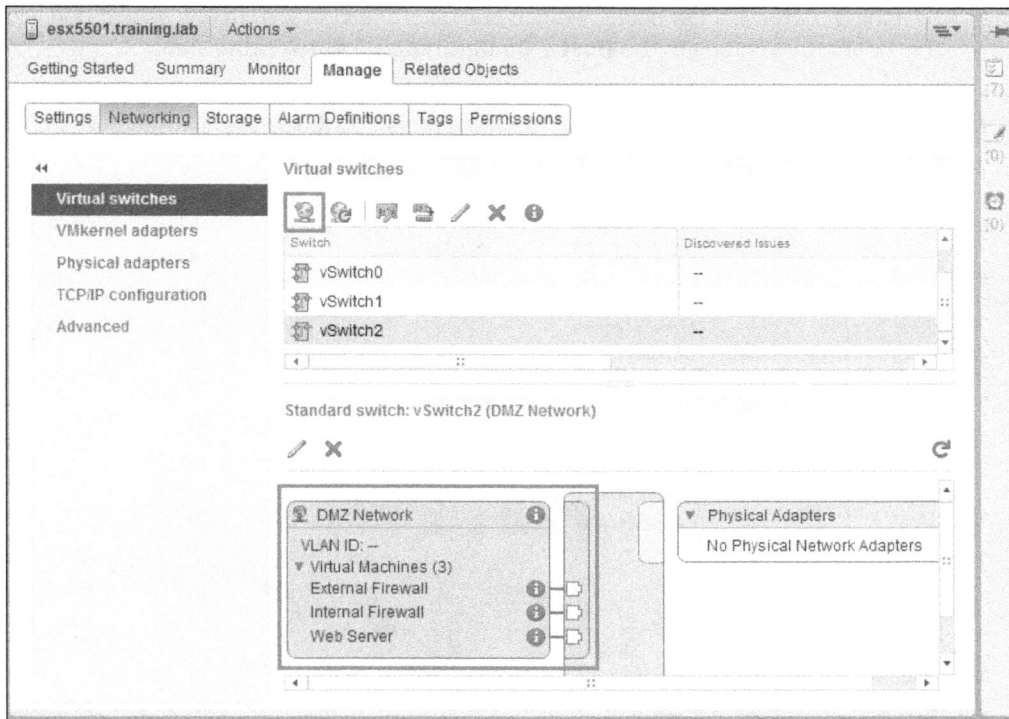

8. Assign the **Web Server**, **Internal Firewall**, and **External Firewall** virtual machines to the port groups, as shown in the preceding figure.

9. Switching to the vCenter client, we can see all of the virtual switches associated with this host by navigating to the **Host | Configuration | Networking** view.

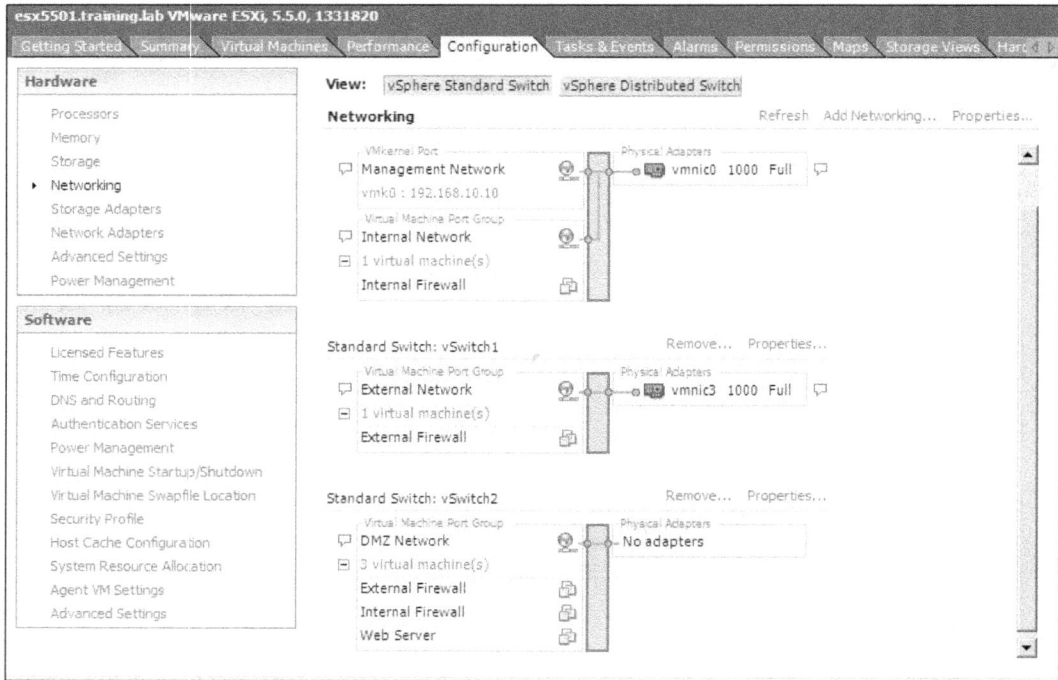

10. Select the **Maps** tab and then click on the **VM to Network** display option to display a graphic of the DMZ network connectivity.

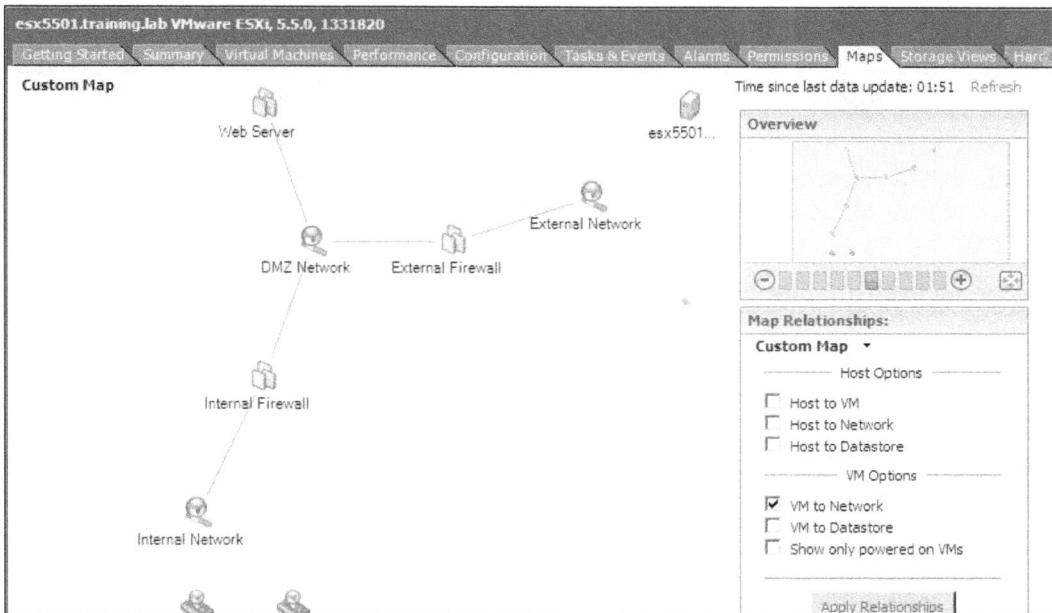

How it works...

To properly protect the private network from the public network, each physical network connection is assigned to a separate vSwitch. Traffic between vSwitches is isolated until a network path is created between the virtual switches. In addition to a public virtual switch and a private virtual switch, we've added a third DMZ virtual switch that is responsible for passing traffic within the DMZ security zone.

Our firewall virtual machines in this case are mulithomed and will have a virtual NIC or leg on the DMZ network and another leg on either the public vSwitch or the private vSwitch. The web server and application server in our example are connected to the DMZ network via the DMZ virtual switch.

The resulting logical connections between the virtual machines, port groups, vSwitches, and physical adapters match the logical diagram we started with defining single-host DMZ architecture.

In essence, we've created three distinct security zones on a single host and are able to pass the appropriate traffic between the public and private networks as specified by the firewall rules put in place.

Providing Distributed vSwitch security options

The standard vSwitch security options are also applicable to the distributed vSwitch; however, the distributed vSwitch provides for more complex and resilient network architecture. With specific regards to security, the distributed vSwitch provides a private VLAN option, which will be covered in the next section.

The **Virtual Switch Tagging** (**VST**) in standard vSwitches is known as **VLAN Trunking** in the distributed vSwitch configuration.

Getting ready

In order to proceed, we require access to vSphere Web Client. This client can be run on any modern Windows desktop operating system or server operating system.

> vSphere Web Client requires Adobe Flash, which is not supported on Linux operating systems at this time.

We must be logged in to vSphere Web Client with a user account in the administrators group.

How to do it...

Navigate to the **Hosts** view and perform the following steps:

1. Expand **Networks** from the pane on the left-hand side.
2. Select **dvPortGroup** from the pane on the left-hand side.
3. In the main window, select the **Manage** tab.
4. Select the **Settings** menu item.
5. Select **Policies** from the main window on the left-hand side menu.
6. Note the VLAN type.
7. Click on the **Edit...** button.

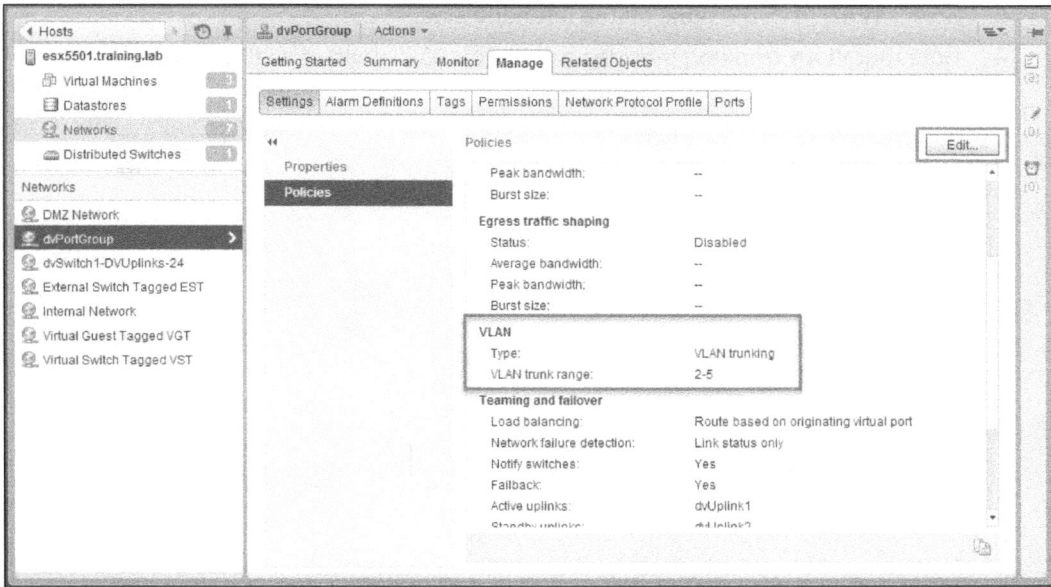

Within the **dvPortGroup – Edit Settings** dialog box, perform the following steps:

1. Select **Security** from the pane on the left-hand side.
2. Note that all the options are set to **Reject** by default.

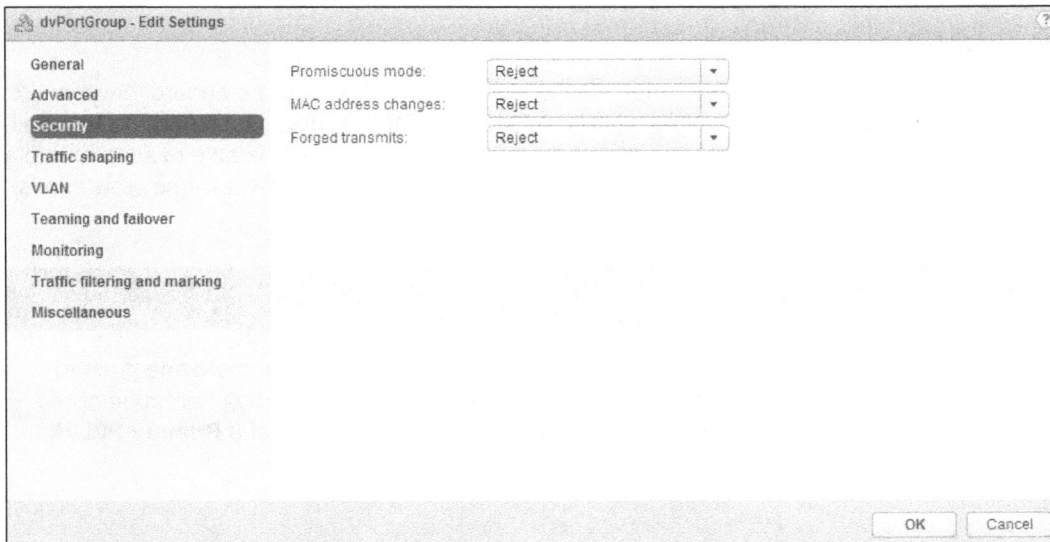

3. Select **VLAN** from the pane on the left-hand side.

4. Note that **VLAN trunking** provides a range of IDs instead of all IDs as in the standard vSwitch.

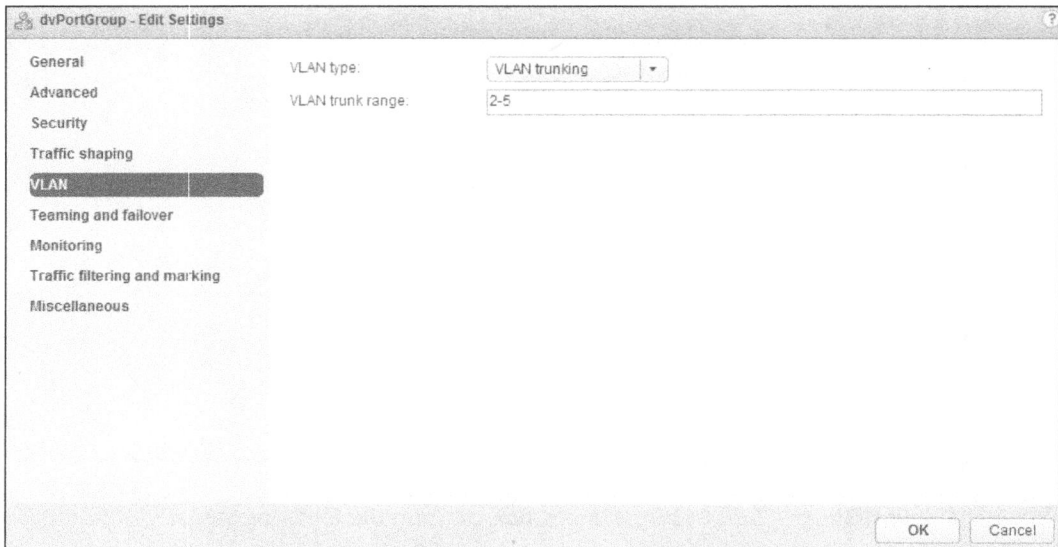

5. Click on **Cancel**.

How it works...

From a security perspective, distributed vSwitches work the same way a standard vSwitch does. There are a few differences as mentioned in the **VLAN trunking** option and the **Private VLAN** option. Distributed vSwitches present a single logical switch that is able to span multiple ESXi hosts. This simplifies configuration and management as virtual server farms grow and is key in private cloud implementations.

Configuring PVLANs

Private VLANs are an extension to the concept of VLANs, which allow for more fine-grained management of traffic between virtual machines. A **Private VLAN** adds segmentation of the logical broadcast domain, creating private groups. A PVLAN comprises of a **Primary PVLAN** and **Secondary PVLANs**.

Getting ready

In order to proceed, we require access to vSphere Web Client. This client can be run on any modern Windows desktop operating system or server operating system.

> vSphere Web Client requires Adobe Flash, which is not supported on Linux operating systems at this time.

We must be logged in to vSphere Web Client with a user account in the administrators group.

There must be at least one distributed virtual switch configured in the datacenter in order to create a PVLAN.

How to do it...

Navigate to the **Hosts** view and perform the following steps:

1. Expand **Distributed Switches** from the pane on the left-hand side.
2. Select **dvSwitch1** from the pane on the left-hand side.
3. In the main window, select the **Manage** tab.
4. Select the **Settings** menu item.
5. Select **Private VLAN** from the main window on the left-hand side menu.
6. Click on the **Edit...** button.

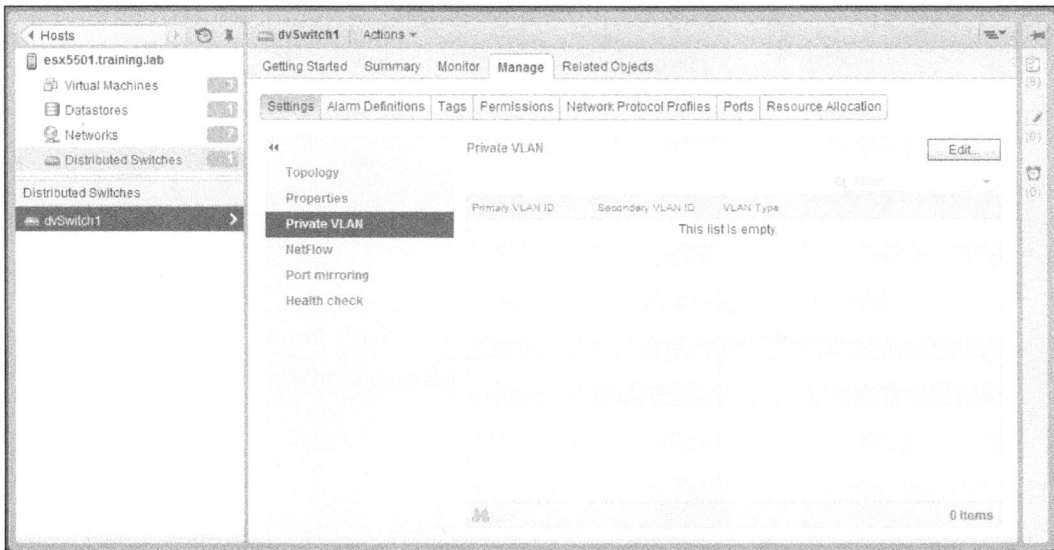

Since our list is empty, we need to create PVLAN primary and secondary IDs. To do this perform the following steps:

1. Within **dvSwitch1 – Edit Private VLAN Settings**, select **Add** from the pane on the left-hand side. This will add a **Primary ID** of **1**.

2. Select **Add** from the pane on the right-hand side two consecutive times. Two additional secondary IDs will be added.

3. Select the second entry under secondary IDs and change the ID to **10** and the type to **Community**.

4. Select the third entry under secondary IDs and change the ID to **100** and the type to **Isolated.**

5. Click on **OK** to close.

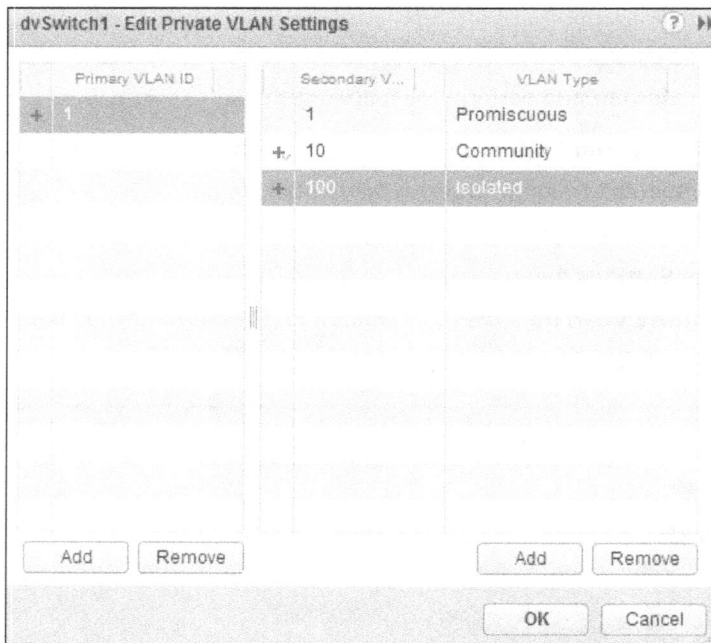

6. The Private VLAN is configured and can now be added to the distributed switch through the **VLAN Type** option we previously set to **VLAN trunking**.

7. Once the **VLAN Type** option is set to **Private VLAN,** the secondary IDs are available to select.

8. Select **Isolated** under the **Private VLAN ID** dropdown.

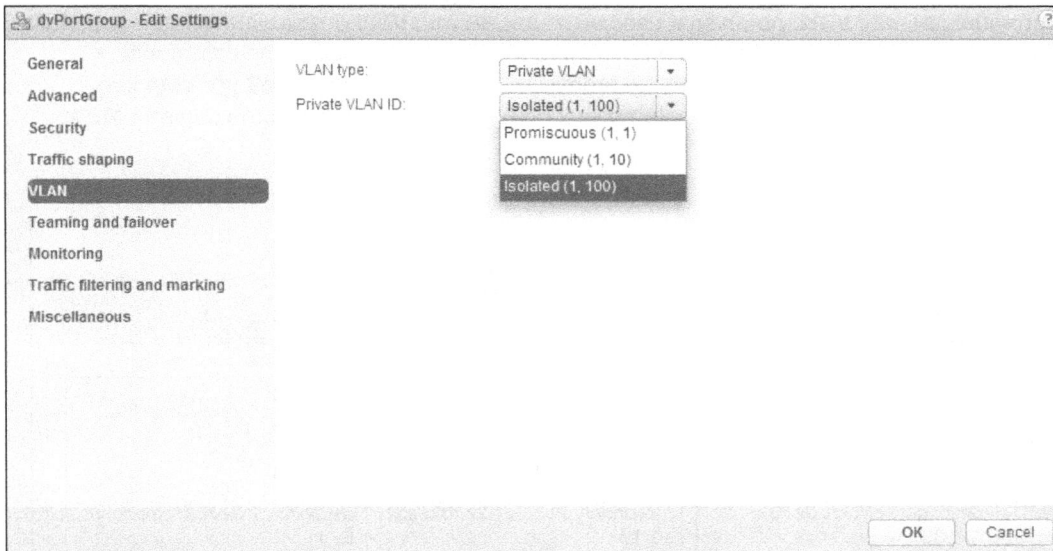

9. Click on **OK** to close.

How it works...

The primary PVLAN serves as a container for secondary PVLANs. There are three types of secondary PVLANs:

- ▸ **Promiscuous**: This port type can send and receive traffic to any other secondary PVLAN in the same primary PVLAN

- ▸ **Community**: This port type can send and receive traffic to any other port within the same secondary PVLAN or to and from the promiscuous PVLAN in the same primary PVLAN

- ▸ **Isolated**: This port type can only send and receive traffic from the promiscuous PVLAN

In our example, we've created a PVLAN with a primary ID of 1 and created additional secondary PVLANs. The Community PVLAN with a secondary ID of 10 can communicate with any other secondary set as **Community**. The isolated secondary PVLAN with a secondary ID of 100 can only communicate with the promiscuous secondary PVLAN with an ID of 1.

In another example, if **VM1** was on Secondary PVLAN 101 and wanted to communicate with **VM2,** it cannot because they are both on an isolated secondary PVLAN. Likewise, **VM2** cannot communicate with **VM1**; however, it can communicate with **VM5** on the promiscuous secondary PVLAN. Lastly, **VM3** and **VM4** can communicate with each other within the community secondary PVLAN as well as **VM5** in the promiscuous PVLAN. Neither **VM3** nor **VM4** can communicate with any VM in the isolated secondary PVLAN as shown by the denied **VM3** to **VM2** connection.

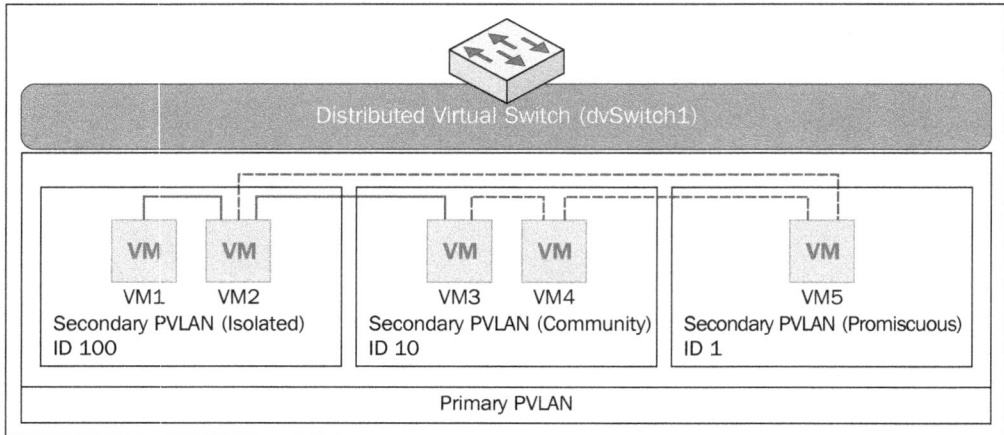

See also

▶ Private VLAN overview: `http://kb.vmware.com/selfservice/microsites/` `search.do?language=en_US&cmd=displayKC&externalId=1010691`

6
Configuring Storage Security

In this chapter, we will cover the following recipes:

- ▶ Configuring network isolation
- ▶ Configuring iSCSI security
- ▶ Configuring Header and Data Digest

Introduction

Shared storage is very common in any small to enterprise deployment of ESXi and vCenter that requires high availability. The key here is the use of vCenter and functionality including **High Availability (HA), vMotion, Storage vMotion, Fault Tolerance (FT)**, and **Distributed Resource Scheduler (DRS)**. For implementations that do not take advantage of high availability, shared storage offers minimal benefits.

vSphere offers several mechanisms. From a pure VMware perspective, there are several opportunities to secure IP-based communication between the hosts and the **storage area network (SAN)** or **network-attached storage (NAS)** in the form of authentication. Beyond specific settings within vCenter, there are best practices to be followed in network configurations to isolate and segment storage traffic.

It should be noted that assumptions are made in this section with regard to storage networking. Although network architecture guidance is beyond the scope of this cookbook, providing a highly available storage network that is free from **Single Points of Failure (SPoF)** is always a best practice.

Fibre Channel storage is primarily secured through fiber switches and connected SAN configurations. There are no specific security settings within vCenter as there are for iSCSI connections.

Configuring network isolation

As a rule, all storage traffic, regardless of the medium or protocol used, should be isolated from any and all management or client network traffic. The IP network segmentation should employ separate physical switches where possible. If a shared physical switch is used, then a VLAN should be used to isolate the iSCSI traffic from all other network traffic on the network. **IP Security** (**IPSEC**) is currently not supported for IPv4 iSCSI traffic.

We'll configure a separate vSwitch for iSCSI traffic, which is always the preferred method to isolate storage traffic and prevent commingling with management and VM network traffic.

Getting ready

In order to proceed, we require access to vSphere Web Client. The client can be run on any modern Windows desktop operating system or server operating system.

> vSphere Web Client requires Adobe Flash, which is not supported on Linux operating systems at this time.

We must be logged in to vSphere Web Client with a user account in the administrators group.

How to do it...

In this section, we'll create and configure a new virtual switch by performing the following steps:

1. Launch vSphere Web Client using an account with administrative privileges.
2. Navigate to the **vCenter Home** view.
3. Select **Hosts** under **Inventory Lists** from the pane on the left-hand side.
4. Select a valid host from the pane on the left-hand side (in our example **esx5501.training.lab**).
5. In the main window, select the **Manage** tab and then select **Networking** to display the current virtual switches on the host.
6. Select the world icon to add the host networking.

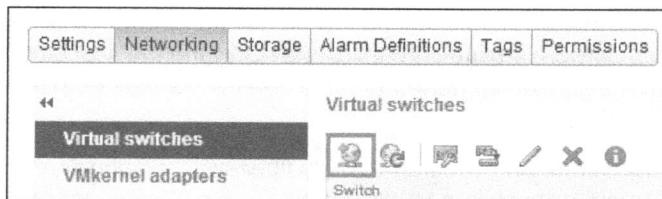

7. Select the **VMkernel Network Adapter** connection type, as shown in the following screenshot:

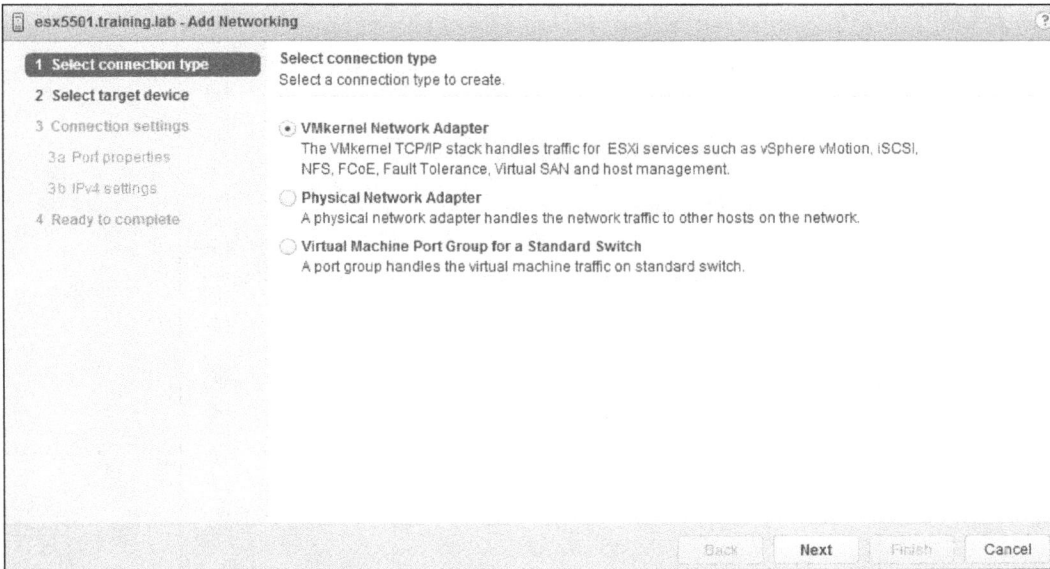

8. Click on **Next**.

9. Select the **New standard switch** target device, as shown in the following screenshot:

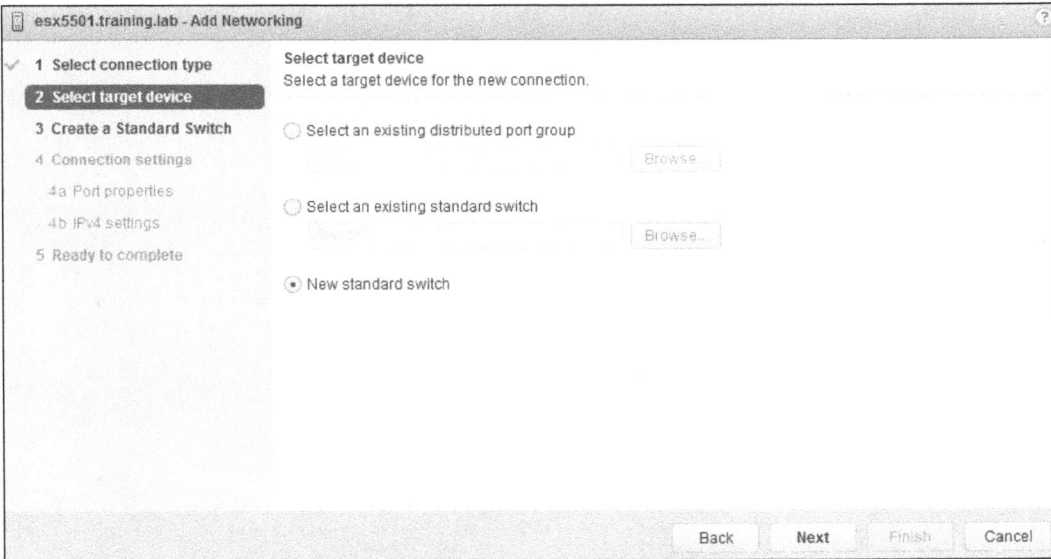

10. Click on **Next**.

11. Click on **+** to add an unused adapter and select the adapter.

12. Click on **OK**.

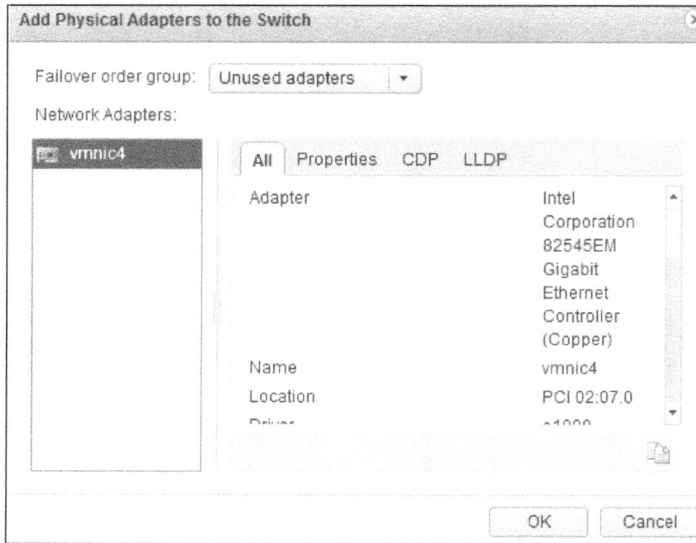

13. Verify that the new adapter is added under the **Active adapters** section.

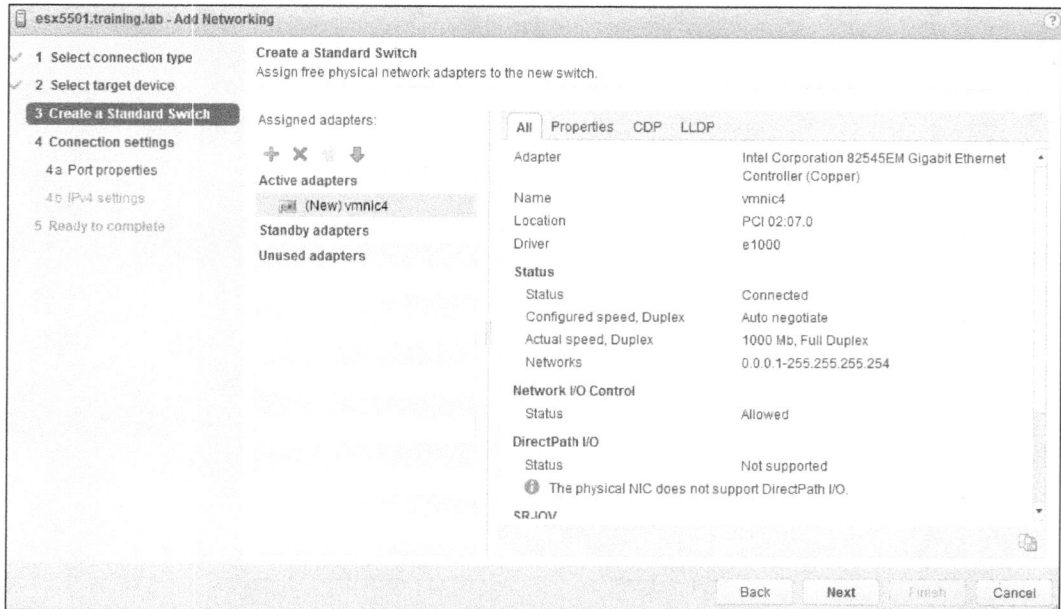

14. Click on **Next**.

15. Customize **Network label** (in our example, iSCSI).

16. Set the appropriate **VLAN ID** (in our example, 20).

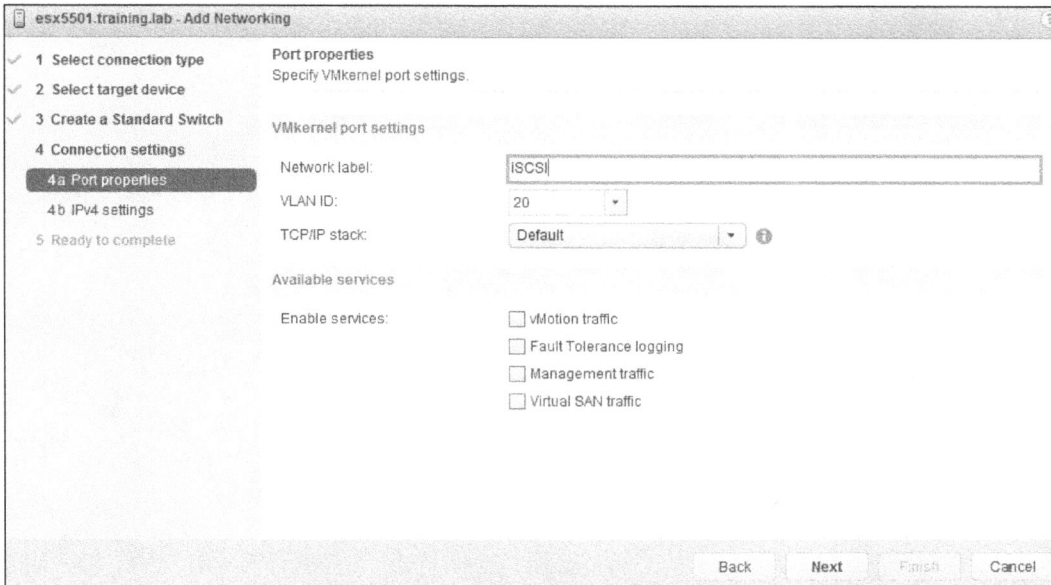

17. Click on **Next**.

18. Configure **IPv4 settings** and enter the appropriate static IP information.

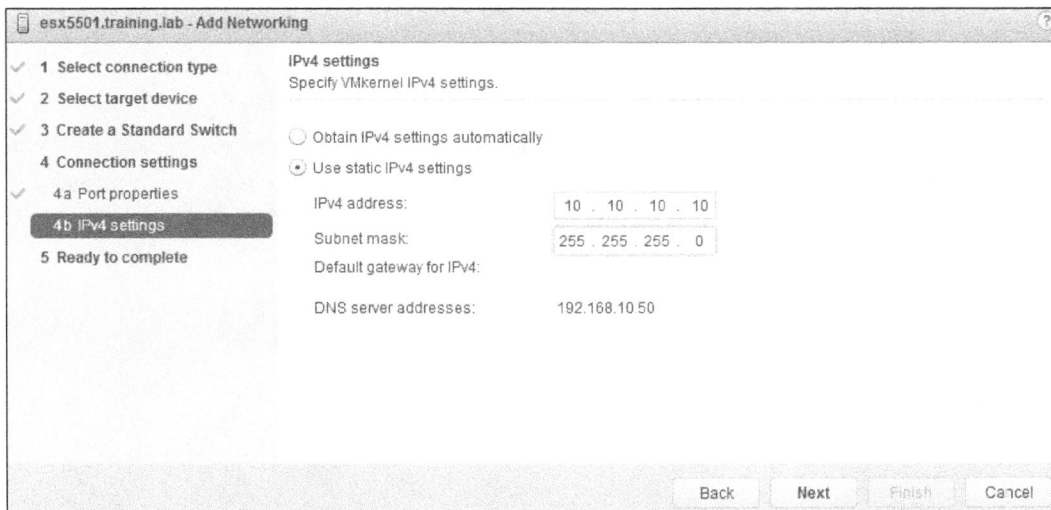

19. Click on **Next**.

20. Review the vSwitch information.

21. Click on **Finish**.

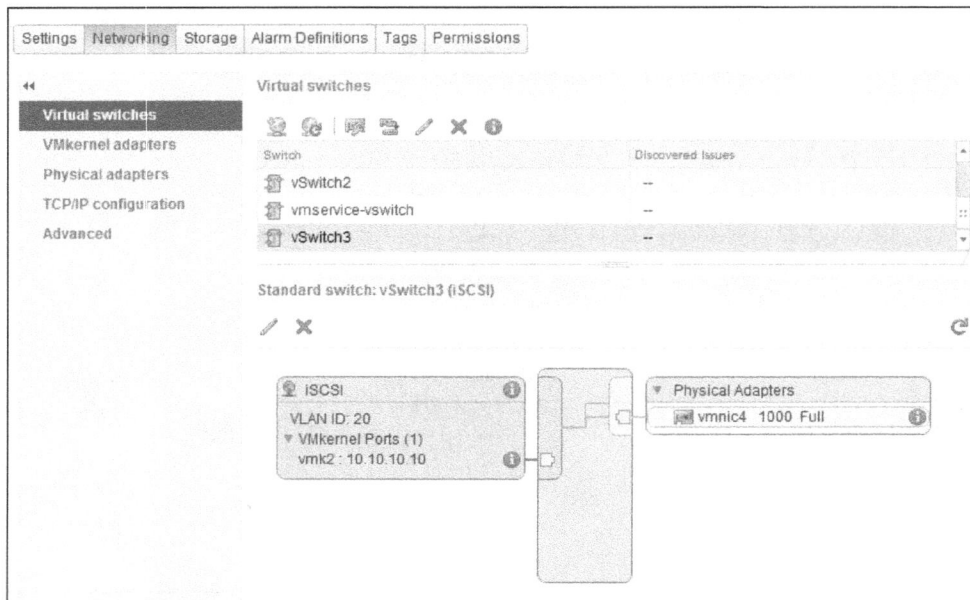

How it works...

By creating a separate vSwitch, we are assured that the iSCSI traffic will remain separated from normal production traffic to virtual machines or management traffic to the host. In our example, we have further segmented this traffic by using a separate physical NIC, which is a better option to extend the isolation to the physical network layer. If a dedicated physical NIC is not available, then VLANs can be used to separate this traffic.

This example used a standard vSwitch; however, in a more complex environment, with many ESXi hosts, a distributed vSwitch is preferable for ease of management.

Configuring iSCSI security

One major risk with enabling iSCSI storage is the ease at which it can be deployed and configured in an unsecure fashion. Not so long ago, the enterprise storage was primarily based on the Fibre Channel technology and used almost exclusively for any infrastructure supporting mission critical business applications. Today, iSCSI provides a cost-effective alternative to smaller businesses to implement shared storage supporting a VMware cluster, for example.

All iSCSI network traffic should always be segmented from all other network traffic on a separate subnet. In addition to segmentation, authentication between the ESXi host and the SAN or NAS is recommended to guard against man in the middle attacks. An additional layer of security in the form of authentication between the host (initiator) and the target (SAN or NAS) known as **Challenge Handshake Authentication Protocol** (**CHAP**) is recommended.

Getting ready

In order to proceed, we require access to vSphere Web Client. This client can be run on any modern Windows desktop operating system or server operating system.

[vSphere Web Client requires Adobe Flash, which is not supported on Linux operating systems at this time.]

We must be logged in to vSphere Web Client with a user account in the administrators group. In addition, the host must have been previously configured to use either a hardware or software iSCSI initiator in order to see the iSCSI authentication options within vCenter.

How to do it...

In this section, we'll configure iSCSI authentication by performing the following steps:

1. Launch vSphere Web Client using an account with administrative privileges.
2. Navigate to the **vCenter Home** view.
3. Select **Hosts** under **Inventory Lists** from the pane on the left-hand side.
4. Select a valid host from the pane on the left-hand side (in our example **esx5501.training.lab**).
5. In the main window, select the **Manage** tab and then select **Storage** to display the host storage information.

6. Select **Storage Adapters** from the left-hand side menu in the main window that shows the iSCSI adapter.

> 💡 If the iSCSI Software Adapter shows a **Disabled** status, it must be enabled by selecting the **Enable** option.

7. Select the **iSCSI Software Adapter** (in our example, we use the **vmhba33** adapter with the **iSCSI** type).

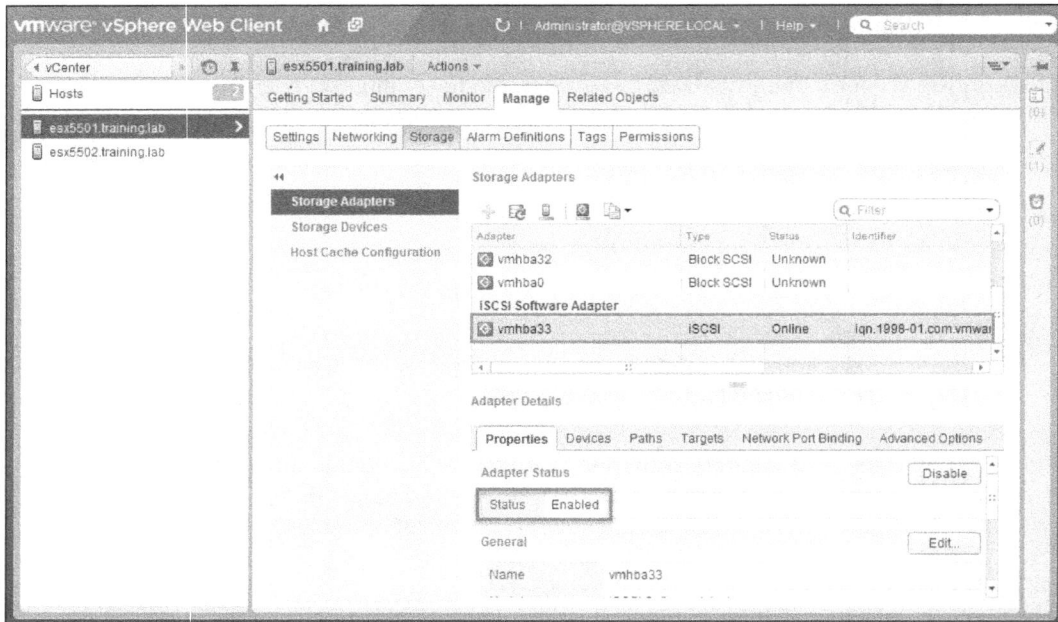

8. Within the **Adapter Details | Properties** tab, scroll down through the properties until the **Authentication** heading is visible.

9. Click on the **Edit** button to open the authentication options for the iSCSI adapter.

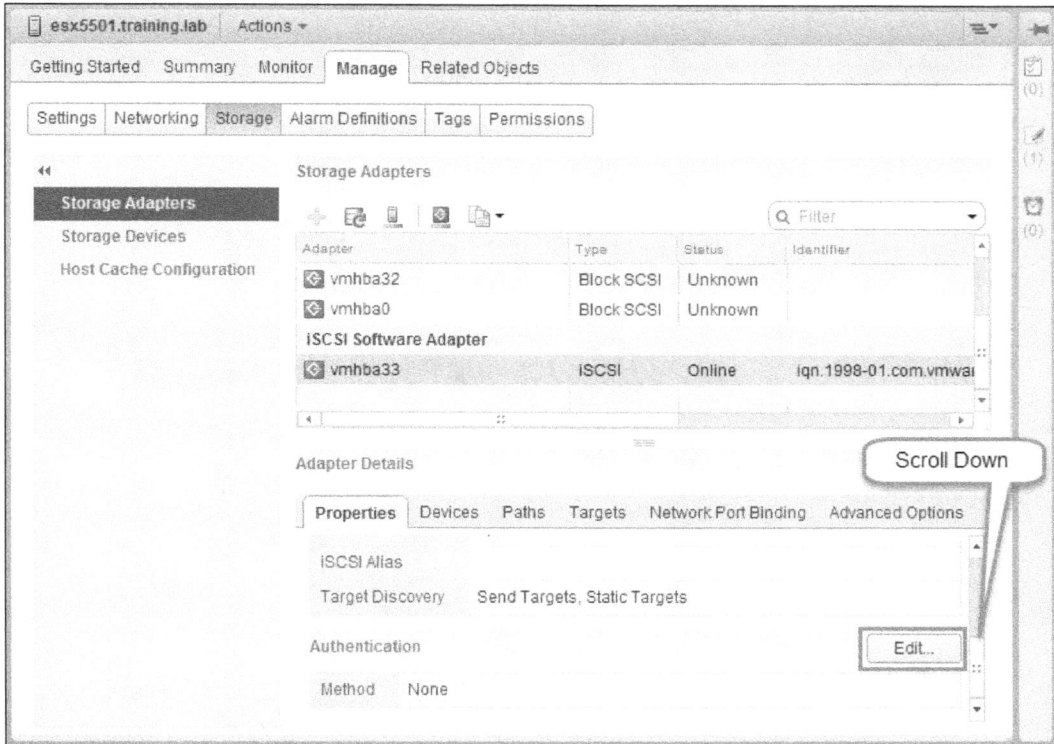

10. Within the **Edit Authentication** dialog box, there are five options for authentication. Select the **Use bidirectional CHAP** option, which sets the authentication to its highest setting.

11. Once **Use bidirectional CHAP** is selected, a name and secret phrase or key must be entered for both the incoming and outgoing initiator.

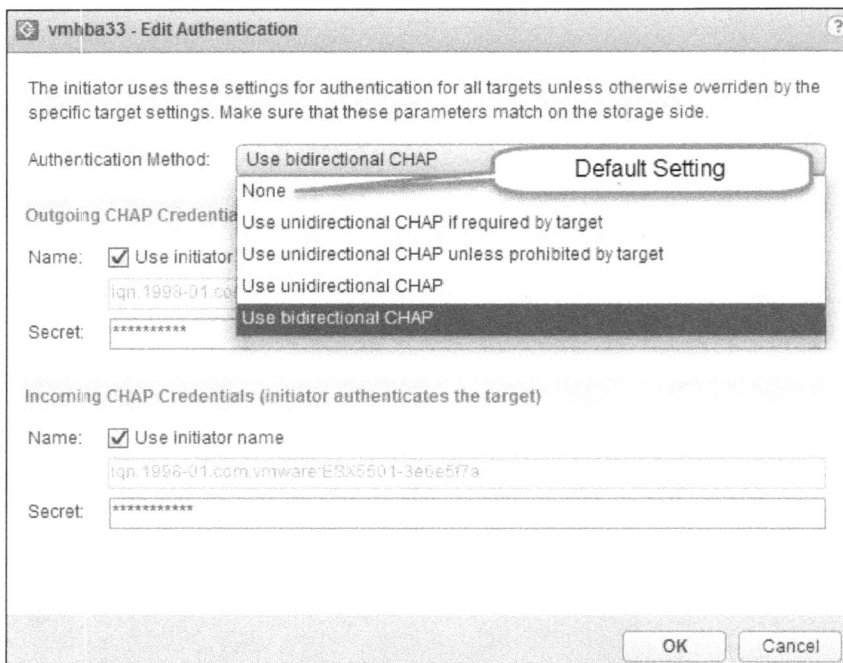

12. Click on **OK** to save the configuration.

> When CHAP authentication fails, errors will be generated in the ESXi host system log. Typical error codes are 201 (Authentication Failure) and 202 (Authorization Failure). A full list of error codes is available at `http://kb.vmware.com/selfservice/microsites/search.do?language=en_US&cmd=displayKC&externalId=2012171`.

How it works...

vSphere requires a special kind of virtual network connection in order to connect to the iSCSI storage known as a **VMkernel Network Adapter**. This port group is typically created on a standard vSwitch. This iSCSI port provides TCP/IP connectivity to storage provisioned on a SAN or NAS device. While it is a best practice to segment this storage traffic from a normal IP network traffic, this does not always take place in all deployments.

Authentication by means of CHAP requires the target, initiator, or both parties to prove their identity through passphrase authentication. The most commonly used option is for the initiator to provide credentials to the target so that the target confirms that the initiator is permitted to access the target device (storage). Implementing bidirectional authentication requires both the target and initiator to authenticate with one another and provides the most robust form of security between the host and the SAN or NAS storage. Some storage vendors do not support bidirectional CHAP authentication, so check with your vendor before you attempt to implement any form of CHAP. Incorrect configuration of CHAP authentication can lead to the storage becoming unavailable to an individual host or a group of host machines.

The various authentication options are as follows:

- **None**: No authentication is attempted between the host and the target.
- **Use unidirectional CHAP if required by target**: CHAP is used if required by the target device. A particular target or storage system might require CHAP, while another target might prohibit such authentication depending on the environment providing storage to the ESXi host servers.
- **Use unidirectional CHAP unless prohibited by target**: CHAP is used unless specifically prohibited by a target device.
- **Use unidirectional CHAP**: Without regard to the configuration of the target device, CHAP is to be used by the initiator to authenticate.
- **Use bidirectional CHAP**: Both the initiator and the target must successfully authenticate for traffic to pass between the host and the shared storage.

> Some form of unidirectional CHAP should always be used as a best practice to ensure that rouge host initiators cannot connect to the shared storage target without proper authorization and authentication.

Configuring Header and Data Digest

Two advanced options are available for an iSCSI connection to provide additional security to the data connection between the VMware ESXi host and the SAN or NAS storage. Header and digest integrity checks do what one might expect: they verify the integrity of the packet header or data by using a checksum operation. The digest checksum requires compute cycles to complete and will adversely affect performance of the host. The only exception to this performance issue is the use of Intel Nehalem processors, which provide additional capabilities to offload the digest calculations and reduce the performance impact to the host system.

Header and Data Digest are not widely used in production systems due to the performance impact weighed against the gain in security provided by the integrity check method. There is no need for this type of integrity check; however, the use of this level of security should correspond to a condition called out in risk assessment or specific compliance requirement related to data integrity.

The security control from these settings will likely only be valued in a situation where there is a moderate to high risk of packets being tampered within transit between the initiator and the target systems. Proper network planning and segmentation in addition to CHAP authentication should minimize the need for the use of header or data digest settings.

Getting ready

In order to proceed, we require access to vSphere Web Client. This client can be run on any modern Windows desktop operating system or server operating system.

> vSphere Web Client requires Adobe Flash, which is not supported on Linux operating systems at this time.

We must be logged in to vSphere Web Client with a user account in the administrators group. In addition, the host must have been previously configured to use either a hardware or software iSCSI initiator in order to see the iSCSI authentication options within vCenter.

How to do it...

In this section, we'll configure the header integrity settings by performing the following steps:

1. Launch vSphere Web Client using an account with administrative privileges.
2. Navigate to the **vCenter Home** view.
3. Select **Hosts** under **Inventory Lists** from the pane on the left-hand side.

4. Select a valid host from the pane on the left-hand side (in our example **esx5501.training.lab**).

5. In the main window, select the **Manage** tab and then select **Storage** to display the host storage information.

6. Select **Storage Adapters** from the left-hand side menu in the main window that will show the iSCSI adapter.

7. Select (highlight) the **iSCSI** from the adapter list.

8. Within the **Adapter Details**, select the **Advanced Options** tab.

9. Click on the **Edit...** button.

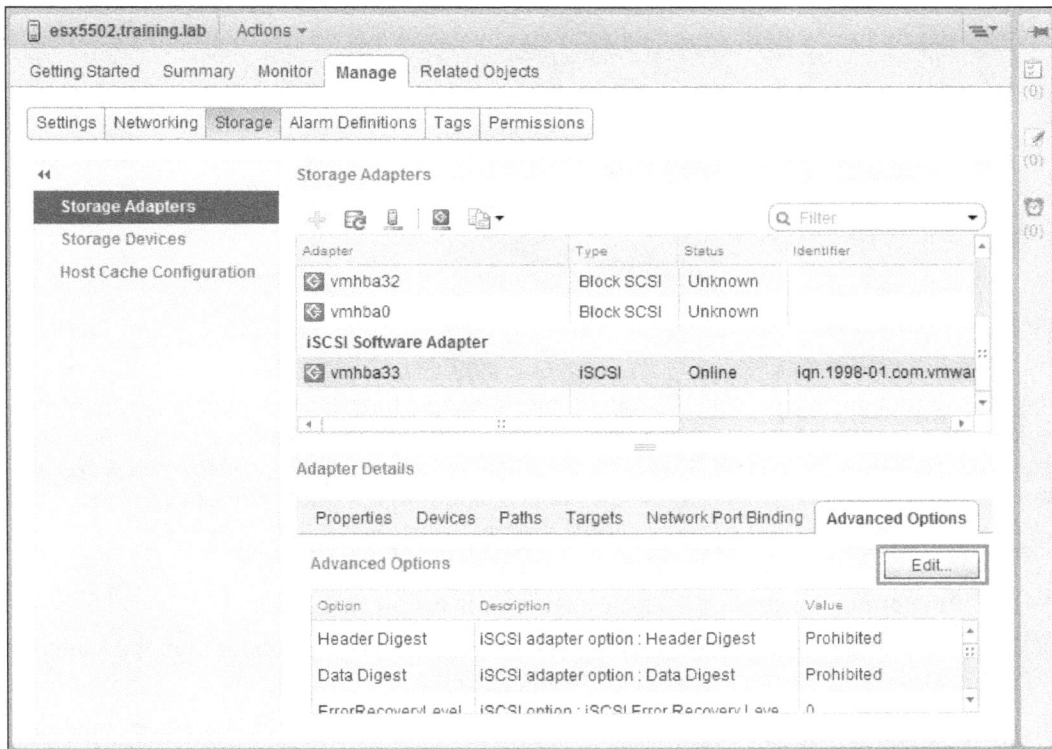

10. Once the **Advanced Options** dialog opens, the first two options displayed are **Header Digest** and **Data Digest**.

11. Select the **Header Digest** option and change the value to **Required**, as shown in the following screenshot.

12. Select **Data Digest** and note the possible values: **Prohibited**, **Discouraged**, **Preferred**, and **Required**.

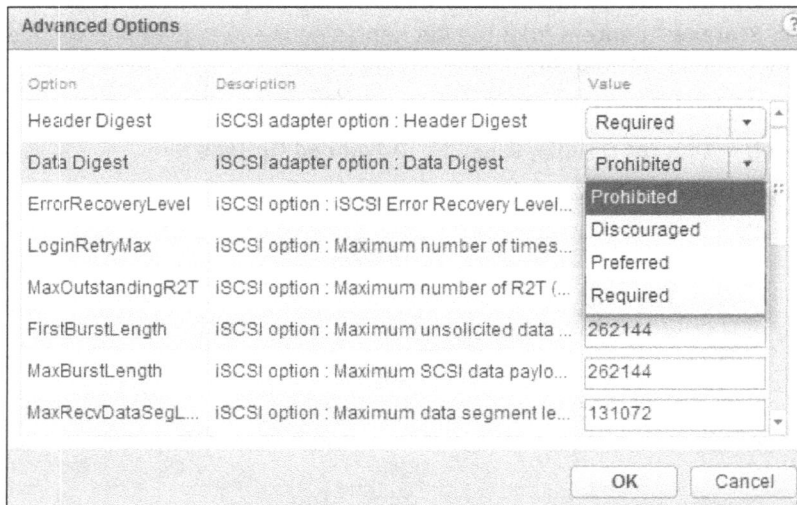

13. Click on **OK**.

Advanced Options		?
Option	Description	Value
Header Digest	iSCSI adapter option : Header Digest	Required ▼
Data Digest	iSCSI adapter option : Data Digest	Prohibited ▼
ErrorRecoveryLevel	iSCSI option : iSCSI Error Recovery Level...	Prohibited
LoginRetryMax	iSCSI option : Maximum number of times...	Discouraged
MaxOutstandingR2T	iSCSI option : Maximum number of R2T (...	Preferred
		Required
FirstBurstLength	iSCSI option : Maximum unsolicited data ...	262144
MaxBurstLength	iSCSI option : Maximum SCSI data paylo...	262144
MaxRecvDataSegL...	iSCSI option : Maximum data segment le...	131072
		OK Cancel

How it works...

The iSCSI digest options present the opportunity to enable further data security by means of verifying the integrity of the IP information. Both Header and Data Digest methods should be used with care as they incur additional computational overhead when implemented. Keep in mind that TCP/IP by definition is a reliable protocol and will retransmit dropped packets.

The various options for both header digest and data digest are as follows:

- ▶ **Prohibited**: Digest checksum calculations will not be used at all
- ▶ **Discouraged**: The target controls the digest checksum calculations, and the initiator requests a preference to disable the digest setting
- ▶ **Preferred**: The target controls the digest checksum calculations, and the initiator requests a preference to enable the digest setting
- ▶ **Required**: Digest checksum calculations will always be used

There's more...

Now we want to discuss the Fibre Channel security configuration with you. Here are some details that are helpful for further reference and understanding.

Configuring the Fibre Channel security

The Fibre Channel is a closed system when compared to other storage protocols such as iSCSI. The fibre mesh extending between the ESXi **Host Bus Adapter** (**HBA**), **Fibre Channel** (**FC**) switch, and **SAN Small Form-Factor Pluggable** (**SFPs**) allows storage traffic only and does not require additional segmentation from production TCP/IP network traffic.

Fibre Channel uses zones and **World Wide Names** (**WWNs**) to configure the mesh allowing the proper hosts to access the proper **Logical Unit Numbers** (**LUNs**) presented on the proper SAN. This allows a path or paths between a set of hosts and single or multiple SANs presenting the appropriate LUNs to ESXi for configuration as datastores.

The configuration for Fibre Channel networking is done outside vCenter at the host HBA, FC switch, and SAN level. An example zone as viewed by a FC switch interface is shown in the following screenshot:

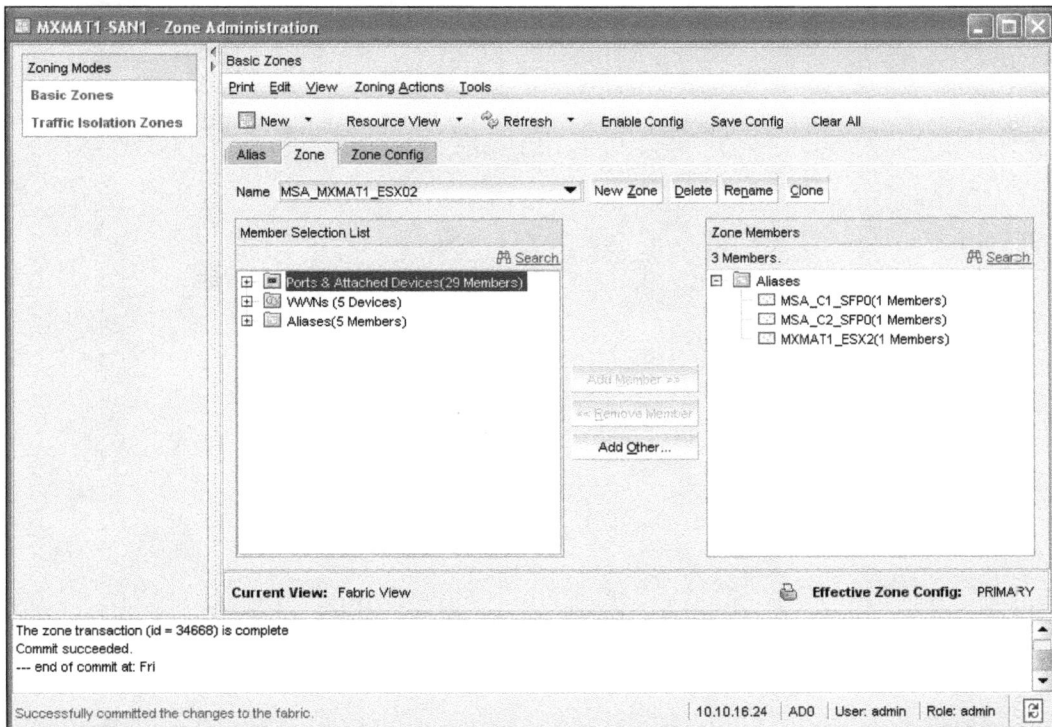

See also

▸ For more information on WWN zoning, visit `http://www.sansecurity.com/san-security-faq.shtml`.

▸ For more information on fibre channel SAN fabric, visit `http://www.brocade.com/solutions-technology/technology/san-fabric-technology/index.page`

▸ For more information on fibre channel technologies, visit `http://www.snia.org/`.

7
Configuring vShield Manager

In this chapter, we will cover the following recipes:

- ► Installing vShield Manager OVA
- ► Configuring vShield Manager settings
- ► Adding vShield licensing to vCenter
- ► Configuring SSL security for Web Manager
- ► Configuring Single Sign-On
- ► Configuring user accounts and roles
- ► Configuring services and service groups

Introduction

The vShield suite comprises of several components that provide additional security to the standard vCenter managed environment. These virtual appliances are aimed at protecting against attacks, misconfiguration, and misuse while achieving and maintaining compliance of the virtual datacenter.

vShield currently comprises of the following components:

- ► vShield App
- ► vShield Edge
- ► vShield Endpoint
- ► vShield Data Security

vShield Manager is a prerequisite virtual appliance required to manage each of these components on a single vCenter Server. Multiple instances of vShield App, vShield Edge, vShield Endpoint, and vShield Data Security can be managed from a single vShield Manager appliance. Installing and configuring vShield is a multistep process that needs be followed in order to ensure correct functionality.

vShield Manager can be thought of as mission control for all the security components in the vShield suite. This control and management includes monitoring and distributing configuration changes to instances of the components.

Installing vShield Manager OVA

vShield manager is the management component of the vShield suite and must be installed and configured before any other component of the suite is installed. The manager is packaged as a virtual appliance and must be downloaded and installed through vCenter.

Getting ready

Since vShield Manager is a preconfigured virtual appliance, certain conditions must be met prior to the installation of the appliance. These conditions are as follows:

- ▶ vCenter 5.5 must be installed.
- ▶ Each host managed by vCenter must be ESXi 5.1 or higher.
- ▶ VMs to be protected by vShield Endpoint or vShield Data Security must have a minimum virtual hardware Version 7. Versions 8 through 10 are also supported.
- ▶ Ensure the DNS resolution is functioning correctly.
- ▶ Confirm that the user account has permission to add and power on virtual machine within vCenter.
- ▶ Ensure access to the datastore where the virtual appliance will reside.
- ▶ Enable cookies on the browser used to manage vShield Manager.
- ▶ Ensure that port 443 (HTTPS) is accessible from vCenter and the ESXi host where the vShield Manager will be deployed.

Throughout this book, we have utilized vSphere Web Client to set our configuration information. In the vShield chapters, we'll be using the traditional vSphere Client along with the vShield Manager Web console. In order to use both these tools, the following conditions must be met:

- ▶ The vShield Manager plugin must be enabled within the vSphere Client
- ▶ The current version of Adobe Flash Player must be installed in the browser that is used to connect to the vShield Manager Web console

How to do it...

In this section, we'll download and install the vShield Manager virtual appliance by performing the following steps:

1. Download the vShield Manager OVA file from VMware and place it on a file share accessible to the vCenter server, preferably on a local disk accessible to the vSphere client.

> The OVA file can be found at: `https://my.vmware.com/web/vmware/details?productId=351&downloadGroup=VCNS550A_GA#custom_iso`.

2. Launch vSphere Client using an account with administrative privileges.
3. Navigate to the **vCenter Home** view.
4. Select **Hosts and Clusters** from **Inventory**.
5. Highlight **Datacenter** from the pane on the left-hand side.
6. Navigate to **File | Deploy OVF Template...**.

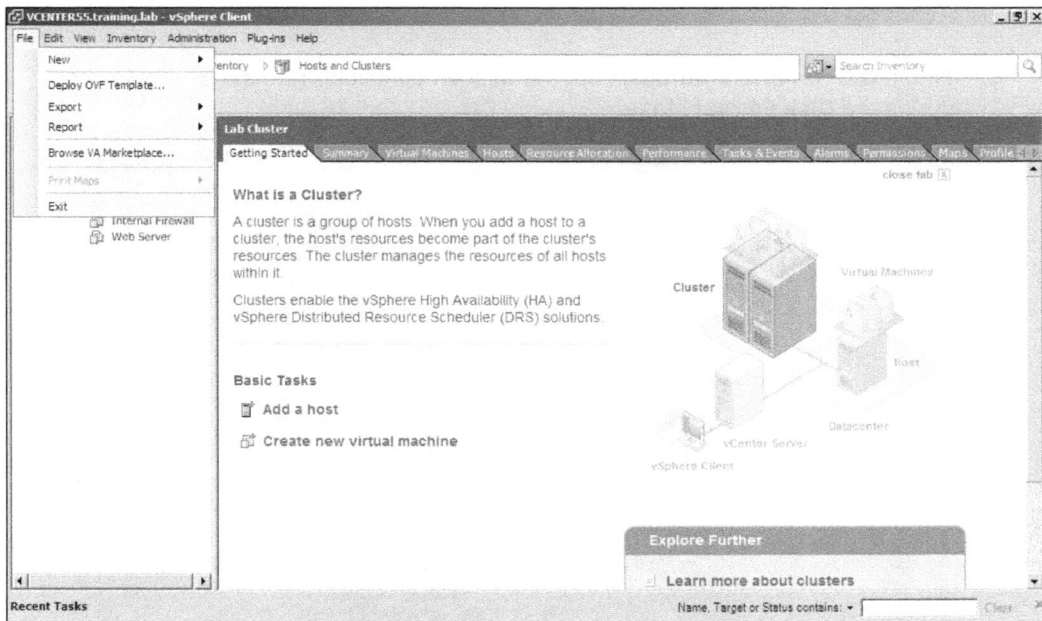

7. Enter the file path or URL where the OVA file resides, as shown in the
    following screenshot:

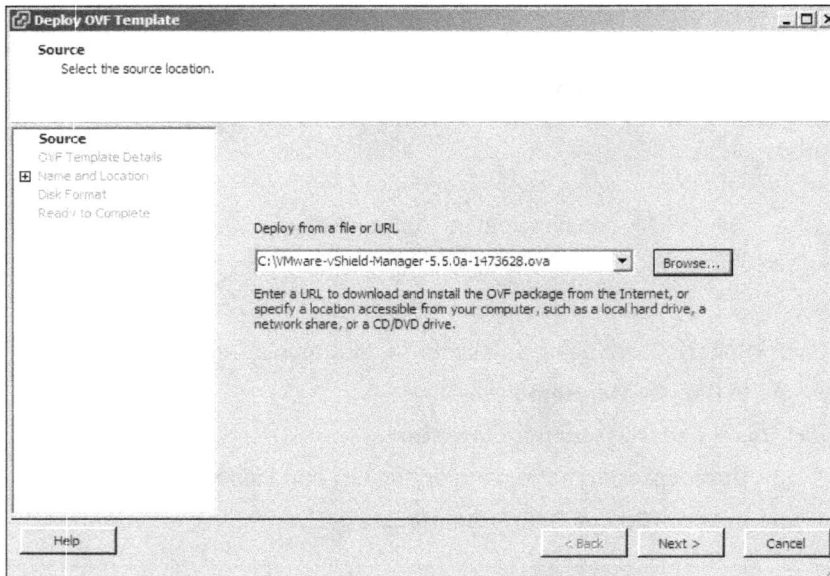

8. Within **OVF Template Details,** note the **Size on disk** field. This will be important
    during the **Disk Format** stage.

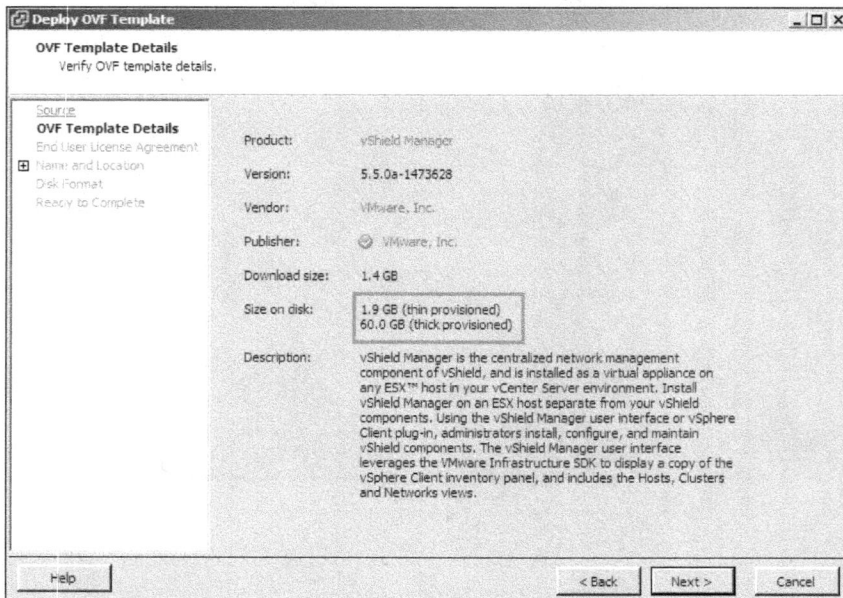

9. Click on **Next**.

10. Accept the License Agreement on the screen that follows.

11. Click on **Next**.

12. Accept the default name place in proper a inventory location, as shown in the following screenshot:

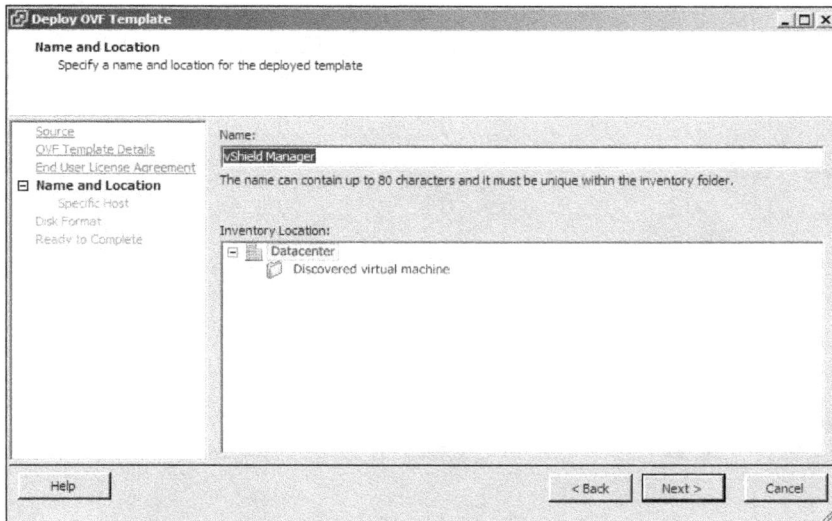

13. Click on **Next**.

14. Select a valid host name for the virtual appliance.

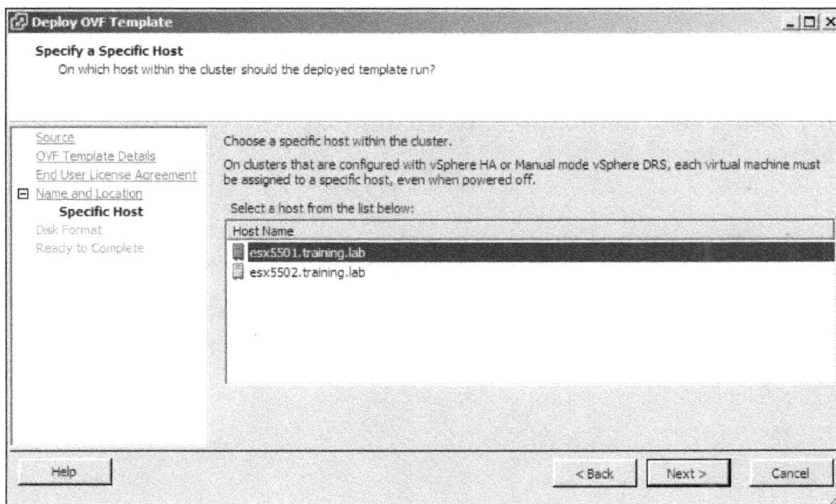

15. Click on **Next**.

16. Select a datastore and the **Thin Provision** disk format.

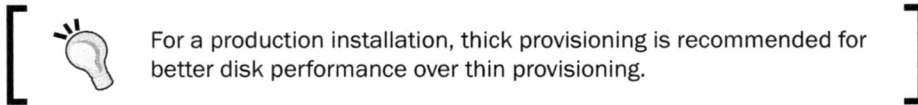

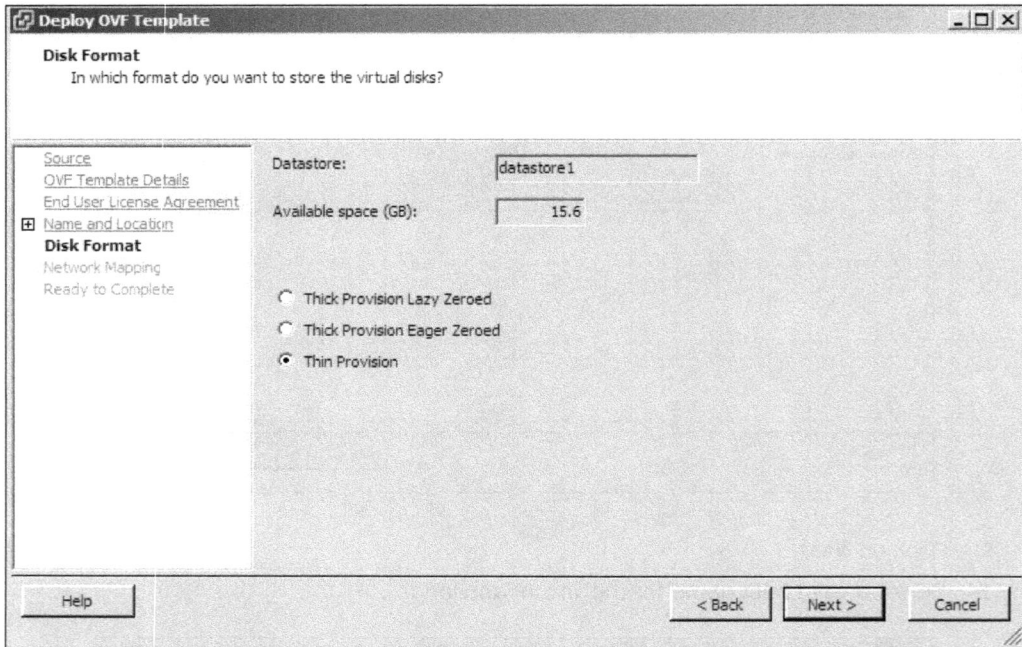

> For a production installation, thick provisioning is recommended for better disk performance over thin provisioning.

Deploy OVF Template — □ ×

Disk Format
In which format do you want to store the virtual disks?

Source	
OVF Template Details	
End User License Agreement	
Name and Location	
Disk Format	
Network Mapping	
Ready to Complete	

Datastore: `datastore1`

Available space (GB): `15.6`

○ Thick Provision Lazy Zeroed
○ Thick Provision Eager Zeroed
● Thin Provision

Help < Back Next > Cancel

---

17. Click on **Next**.

18. Select **Destination Networks – Internal Network** to allow access to virtual machines in the inventory.

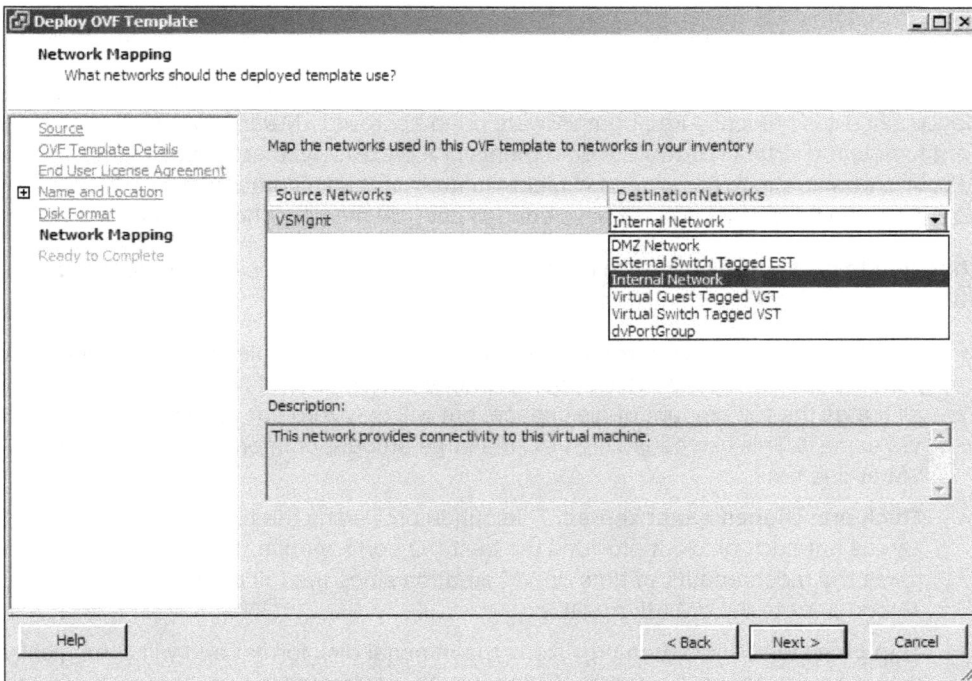

19. Click on **Next**.

> For more complex deployments that segment command and control servers from appliances vShield Manager should be assigned to the command and control network segment.

20. Review the information and click on **Finish** on the next screen to provision the appliance. This will take several minutes.

21. Click on **Close** in the **Deployment Completed Successfully** dialog box.

How it works...

The OVF template is basically a prepackaged virtual machine that is referred to as a Virtual Appliance since it is preconfigured from VMware or an approved VMware partner. It is always prudent to note the virtual hardware requirements of a prepackaged appliance before installing it into your environment. In the case of vShield Manager, it is configured to require 8 GB of RAM to start. If a given ESXi host does not have enough physical memory, the appliance will not start.

Another area to note is the options to configure the disk format of the virtual appliance. There are three options:

> ▶ **Thick provisioned lazy zeroed**: This option provisions the full disk extent, but does not zero out each block. This option provides better I/O performance. The lazy option allocates the full amount of disk space, but will only zero out each block prior to the VM using it. This can cause high I/O if a large amount of information is written to the VM at one time.

> ▶ **Thick provisioned eager zeroed**: This option provisions the full disk extent and zeroes out each block. It provides the best I/O performance. The eager zeroed option takes the most amount of time on VM creation since the full amount of disk space is zeroed prior to the VM utilizing it.

> ▶ **Thin provision**: This option provisions the minimal disk format and will dynamically grow as more space is needed. During growth, performance is impacted. It provides good I/O performance. This option is used increasingly today, as most enterprise class storage can compensate for the performance hit normally found in dynamically growing a VM disk.

In a test or proof of concept environment, a lower amount of RAM and a thin provisioned disk format is acceptable for a trial situation. Recommendations for production are the default amount of RAM and a thick provisioned disk format for the reasons noted previously.

Configuring vShield Manager settings

Once the vShield Manager virtual appliance has been provisioned and powered on, it is ready for initial configuration. The initial setup of networking information is done at the command line. Once this is complete, all subsequent configuration is completed through the Web console.

Getting ready

In order to proceed, we require access to the vShield web console. The client can be run on any modern Windows or Mac desktop operating system or server operating system.

[⟨note⟩ The vShield web console requires Adobe Flash, which is not supported on Linux operating systems at this time.]

How to do it...

To verify that the OVA is correctly provisioned, we'll power it on and check the settings by performing the following steps:

1. Open the vSphere web client and log in with administrative privileges.
2. Navigate to **vCenter** | **Virtual Machines** | **vShield Manager**.
3. Right-click on **vShield Manager** and select **Power On.**

4. Note the auto-configured IP address of **169.254.202.114** highlighted in the preceding screenshot.

> If the vShield Manager appliance is brought up on a network with no DHCP services, it will use an autoconfig 169 address and will not be accessible by a web browser.

Next, we'll set the basic IP information on the appliance so we can access it from the web interface by performing the following steps:

1. Select the **Launch Console** hyperlink.

2. Log in as `admin` with `default` as the password.

3. Type `enable` to switch from **user mode** to **executive mode**, as done on a router or switch. The password here is `default`.

4. Type `setup` to enter the configuration mode.

5. Enter a valid IP Address (in our example, `192.168.10.100`).

6. Enter a valid subnet mask (in our example, `255.255.255.0`).

7. Enter a valid default gateway (in our example, `192.168.10.1`).

8. Enter a valid primary DNS IP (in our example, `192.168.10.50`).

9. Enter a valid secondary DNS IP (in our example, `<empty>`).

10. Enter a valid DNS domain search list (in our example, `training.lab`).

11. Press the *Y* key when asked if you want to save the new configuration.

12. When asked if you want to reboot now, press the *Y* key.

```
Manager login: admin
Password:
Manager> enable
Password:
Manager# setup

Use CTRL-D to abort configuration dialog at any prompt.
Default settings are in square brackets '[]'.

IP Address (A.B.C.D): 192.168.10.100
Subnet Mask (A.B.C.D): 255.255.255.0
Default gateway (A.B.C.D): 192.168.10.1
Primary DNS IP (A.B.C.D): 192.168.10.50
Secondary DNS IP (A.B.C.D):
Warning: Secondary DNS not set.
DNS domain search list (space separated): training.lab
Old configuration will be lost, and system needs to be rebooted
Do you want to save new configuration (y/[n]): y
Do you want to reboot now (y/[n]): _
```

To configure the general settings of the vShield Manager, we must first log in to the web console. Ensure the virtual appliance that was previously installed is running and the IP address assigned is accessible from your workstation. Now we'll continue to configuring the vShield Manager through the web interface:

1. Open a web browser (in our example we're using Internet Explorer 10).

2. Enter the IP address just configured into the web browser address field (in our case, `192.168.10.100`).

> In most cases, a dialog box will present a warning due to an untrusted certificate. Ignore this warning as we will assign proper certificates later in the lesson.

3. Log in through the web browser with the username `admin` and the password `default`. Then click on **Login**. This is shown in the following screenshot:

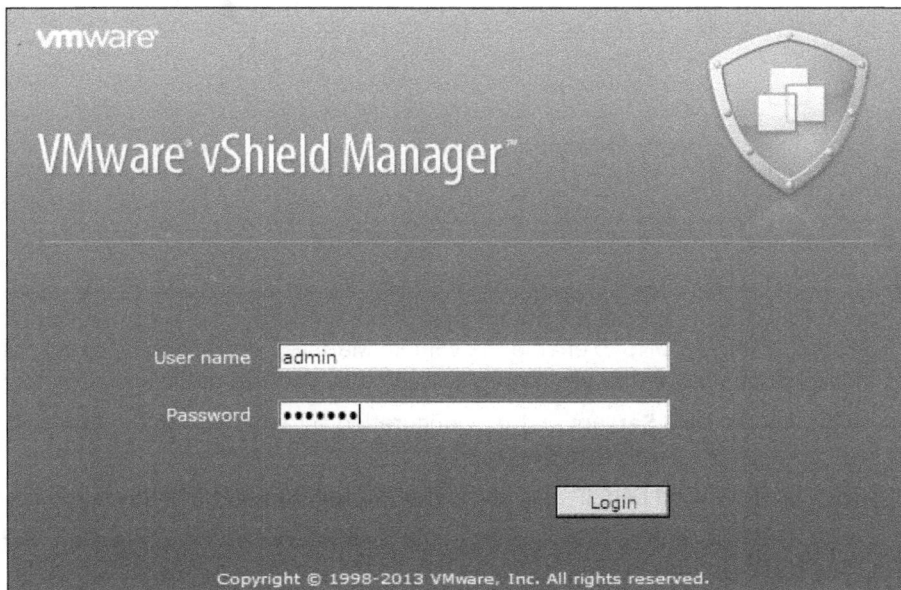

4. Ensure the **Settings & Reports** leaf is selected from the pane on the left-hand side and the **Configuration** tab is selected in the main screen, as shown in the following screenshot:

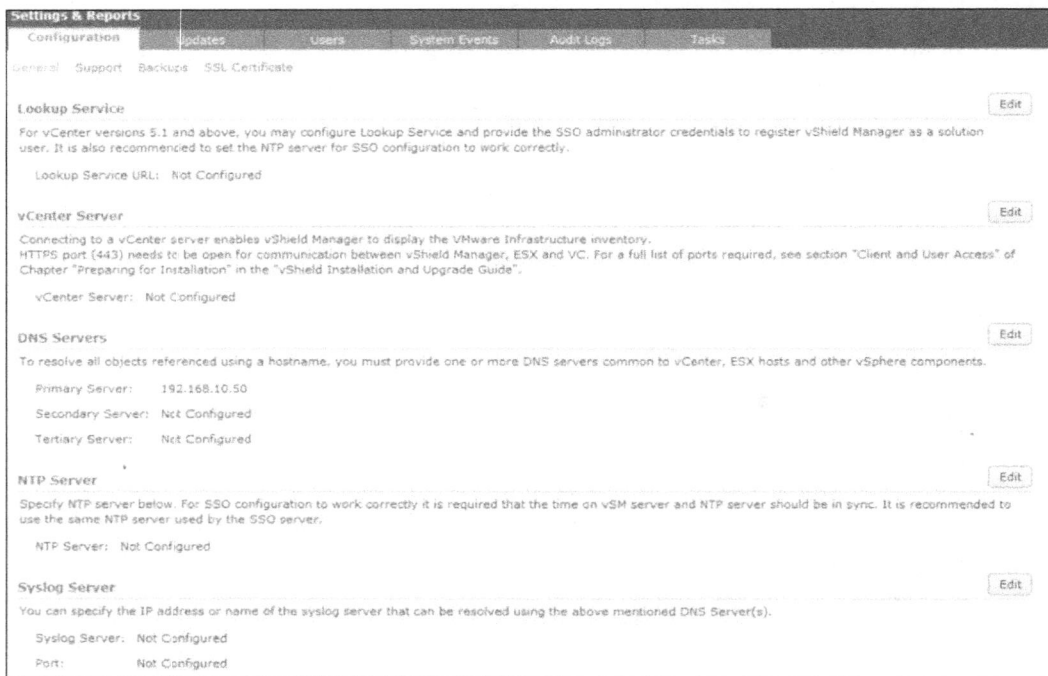

5. We'll first configure DNS to enable the vShield Manager virtual appliance to properly resolve host names in the environment. To do this, perform the following steps:

1. Locate **DNS Servers** on the configuration screen. Click on the **Edit** button associated with **DNS Servers**.

2. Enter a valid DNS IP address in the **Primary Server** field; this is required.

3. Enter additional DNS servers in the **Secondary Server** and **Tertiary Server** fields if available.

> A primary and secondary DNS server is recommended for name resolution fault tolerance.

DNS Server Information ✕

Specify one or more DNS servers common to vCenter, ESX hosts and other vSphere components to resolve all objects that are referenced by hostname.

Primary Server: ＊ 192.168.10.50

Secondary Server:

Tertiary Server:

OK   Cancel

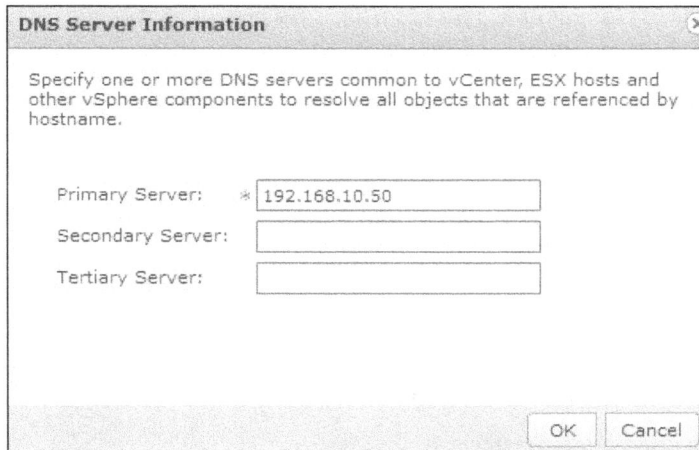

6. Click on **OK** to save the settings and close the window.

Next, we'll configure NTP by adding a reliable time source by performing the following steps

1. Locate **NTP Server** on the configuration screen and click on the **Edit** button associated with **NTP Server**.

2. Enter either an internal NTP server or a public NTP server such as `tick.usno.navy.mil`.

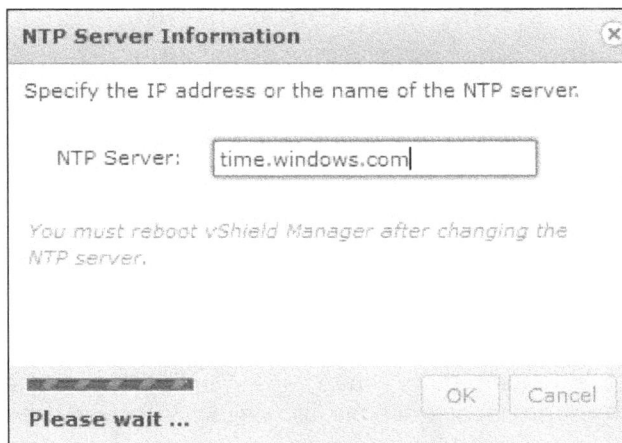

NTP Server Information ✕

Specify the IP address or the name of the NTP server.

NTP Server: time.windows.com

You must reboot vShield Manager after changing the NTP server.

OK   Cancel

Please wait ...

3. Click on **OK** to save the settings and close the window.

4. Reboot vShield Manager.

5. Once vShield Manager has rebooted, log in as previously directed and navigate to the **Settings & Reports | Configuration** tab.

6. Locate **vCenter Server** on the configuration screen and click on the **Edit** button associated with **vCenter Server.**

7. Enter the vCenter Server IP address (in our example: `192.168.10.20`).

8. Enter either the Active Directory account of the vCenter administrator or the Single Sign-on vCenter **Administrator Username**.

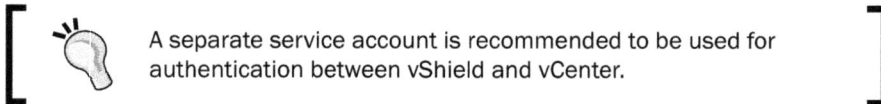

> A separate service account is recommended to be used for authentication between vShield and vCenter.

9. Enter the appropriate **Password**.

10. Ensure that **Assign vShield 'Enterprise Administrator' role to this user** is checked.

---

vCenter Server Information   ⊗

Specify the hostname or the IP address of the vCenter server and provide the administrator credentials to connect.

vShield Manager will be registered as an extension to the vCenter server.

Changing the vCenter address may result in unpredictable behavior. Please update only if you change IP of your current vCenter Server.

vCenter Server:	* `192.168.10.20`
Administrator Username:	* `administrator@vsphere.local`
Password:	* `***********`

☑ Assign vShield 'Enterprise Administrator' role to this user

☐ Modify plug-in script download location (May be required for NAT environments)

vShield Manager IP: [   ]   Port: [   ]

                                                        [OK] [Cancel]

---

11. Click on **OK** to save the settings and close the window. Since we haven't set up certificates yet, it is normal to see the following **Security warning** dialog box:

Security warning

Unable to verify the authenticity of host
192.168.10.20.

The SHA1 thumbprint of the certificate is:

2E:7B:FA:95:FA:92:D6:DC:C5:0C:9B:BA:AF:1
0:9F:C2:28:71:11:52

Do you wish to connect anyway?

Choose "Yes" if you trust the host.

Choose "No" to abort the connection to the host
at this time.

Yes   No

12. Click on **Yes** to confirm the connection.

Once the vCenter has been added successfully, the left-hand side pane of the vShield Manager Web console will be populated with the vCenter information for **Datacenter**, **Cluster**, **Hosts**, and **Virtual Machines**.

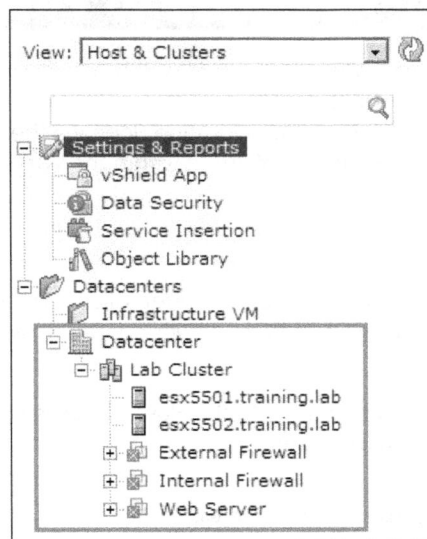

View: Host & Clusters

- Settings & Reports
  - vShield App
  - Data Security
  - Service Insertion
  - Object Library
- Datacenters
  - Infrastructure VM
  - Datacenter
    - Lab Cluster
      - esx5501.training.lab
      - esx5502.training.lab
      - External Firewall
      - Internal Firewall
      - Web Server

How it works...

The general configuration section of the vShield Manger web console contains four key settings, which enable the virtual appliance to interact with the vCenter implementation. The key settings we've configured in this section include setting target information for the following target information:

- ▶ **DNS Servers**: The host name resolution is required for vShield Manager to interact with both the ESXi host servers and the virtual machines that will be protected. DNS servers should be available on the subnet where the vShield Manager Management IP address resides.

- ▶ **NTP Server**: Correct time stamps are key to the proper functionality of the vShield infrastructure. The NTP server specified should be reliable and accurate since many virtualized environments experience time drift when an accurate time server is not available.

- ▶ **vCenter Server**: The vCenter server information is required for vShield Manager to interact, send, and receive information to vCenter. This connection information also allows the traditional vSphere Client to interact through the plugin functionality availability within vCenter.

Adding vShield licensing to vCenter

Similar to other VMware products, vShield Manager will run in the evaluation mode for 60 days before it ceases to function. vShield is somewhat unique in a way that the basic configuration is done in the web interface with further configuration done via the vCenter plugin. Unlike VMware View, the license information is configured within the vCenter Licensing area.

Getting Started

In order to proceed, we require access to vSphere Web Client. The client can be run on any modern Windows desktop operating system or server operating system.

[vSphere Web Client requires Adobe Flash, which is not supported on Linux operating systems at this time.]

We must be logged into the vSphere Web Client with a user account in the administrators group.

How to do it...

Perform the following steps:

1. Navigate to the **vCenter Home** view.
2. Select **Administration** from the pane on the left-hand side.
3. Select **Licenses** from the pane on the left-hand side.
4. Navigate to the **Solutions** tab.
5. Select **Assign License Key...**.

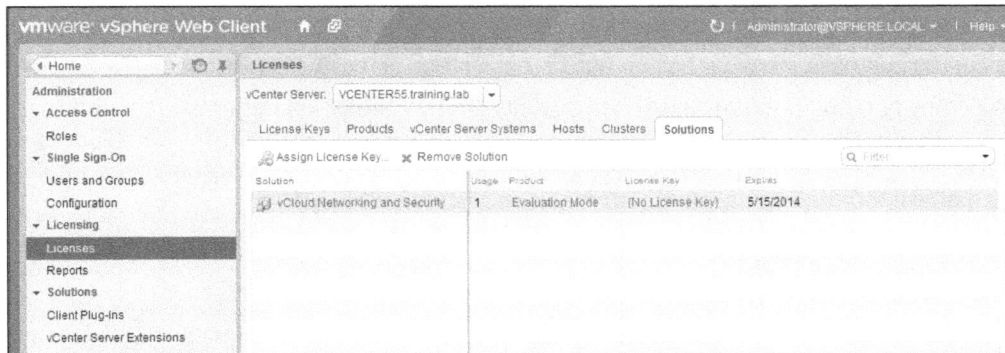

6. Select **Assign a new license key** from the drop-down list box.
7. Enter a valid license key.

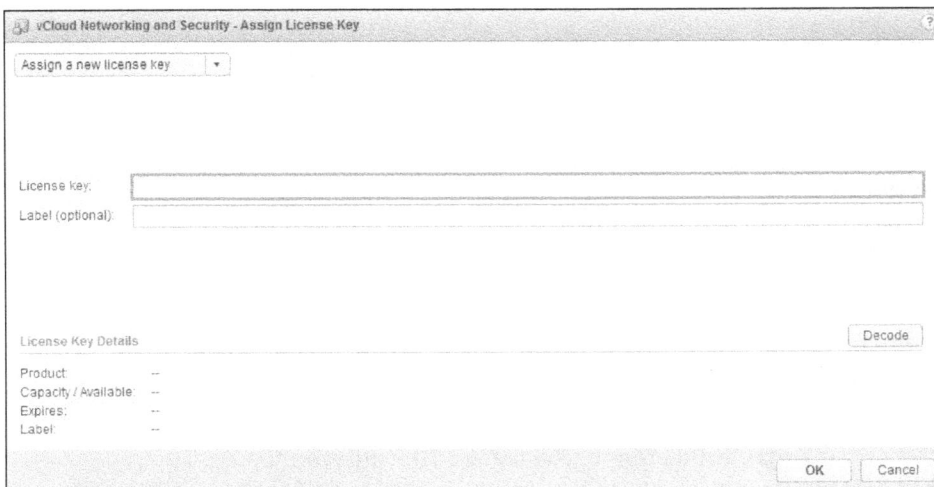

8. Click on **OK** to save the settings and close the window.

How it works...

Similar to vCenter licenses and ESXi host licenses, the vShield licensing information is managed within vCenter. The licensing information can be managed through either vSphere Client or vSphere Web Client. The licensing information is stored in the database used by vCenter, which can vary based on the size of the deployment and the database vendor selected.

> If a license key is not entered within 60 days, the application will no longer function.

Configuring SSL Security for Web Manager

Certificates play an important role in the security of any vCenter implementation and this extends to other applications and components such as vShield Manager. The configuration tools in the vShield Manager web console allows for the request and import of standard X.509 certificates generated by an internal or public certificate authority.

Getting ready

In order to proceed, we require access to vShield Web Console. This client can be run on any modern Windows or Mac desktop operating system or server operating system.

> vShield Web Console requires Adobe Flash, which is not supported on Linux operating systems at this time.

Ensure the account used for login has administrative rights to vShield Manager.

How to do it...

Perform the following steps:

1. Navigate to the **Settings & Reports | Configuration** within vShield Manager.
2. Select **SSL Certificate**.
3. Enter information into the following required fields:
   - **Common Name**: A name describing the certificate.
   - **Organization Unit**: The responsible department making the request.
   - **Organization Name**: The name of the organization.

❑ **Country Code**: The country where the certificate will be installed.

❑ **Key Algorithm**: The default setting is DSA which is a weak cipher. Select **RSA** as the algorithm instead.

The key algorithm and size relate to the complexity of the encryption used to create the certificate. In our example, we're using a 2048 key length with a RSA asymmetric algorithm, which is more difficult to crack than a 1024 key length using a DSA asymmetric algorithm.

❑ **Key Size**: Once the algorithm is changed, new key lengths will become available. Select **2048** as the key size.

Settings & Reports

Configuration	Updates	Users	System Events	Audit Logs	Tasks

General   Support   Backups   SSL Certificate   Networking

▽ Generate Certificate Signing Request

Certificate signing request(CSR) is used to apply for certificate from an authority of your choice. Fill out the form to generate one.

* Common Name:	vShield Manager
* Organization Unit:	IT Security
* Organization Name:	Training Lab
City Name:	
State Name:	
* Country Code:	US
Key Algorithm:	○ DSA ● RSA
Key Size:	2048 ▾

Generate

4. Select **Generate** to create and save the certificate request.

5. Click the **Download generated certificate** button and save the request to a location where it can be submitted to the proper certificate authority for issuance:

Settings & Reports

Configuration	Updates	Users	System Events	Audit Logs	Tasks

Certificate Signing Request is generated successfully   ✕

General   Support   Backups   SSL Certificate   Networking

▷ Generate Certificate Signing Request   ➡ Download generated certificate

6. After the request has been fulfilled by the CA, the certificate can be imported through the same **SSL Certificate** configuration page.

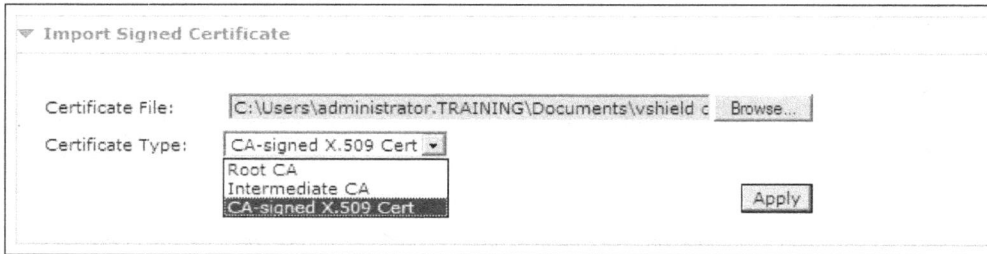

```
▼ Import Signed Certificate

  Certificate File:   C:\Users\administrator.TRAINING\Documents\vshield c   Browse...

  Certificate Type:   CA-signed X.509 Cert ▾
                      Root CA
                      Intermediate CA                           Apply
                      CA-signed X.509 Cert
```

7. Browse to the location where the issued certificate file is located.

8. Import the certificate that was issued by the CA as type **CA-signed X.509 Cert**.

9. Click on **Apply** to save changes and close.

How it works...

The standard for public key certificates is X.509 and these certificates are used for authentication and encryption, depending on the application. In the case of vShield Manager, the certificate is used to validate or trust the requested server or service.

Each vCenter generates a new self-signed certificate when it is installed. A self-signed certificate is valid but not trusted. In other words, there is no chain of trust that can be validated by the requesting party, which in this case is vShield Manager.

Certificates must be issued from a trusted source and a source that the requestor also trusts for certificate warnings to disappear. The trusted source can either be an internal CA managed by the organization or a public CA such as Verisign.

Configuring vCenter certificates will be covered in *Chapter 12, Configuring vSphere Certificates*.

Configuring Single Sign-On

Single Sign-On allows user and group account access across products so that a valid user in vCenter can be given access to vShield Manager without having to create a new user in vShield Manager for every user or group that requires access.

Getting ready

In order to proceed, we require the same prerequisites as in the *Configuring vShield Manager Settings* recipe earlier in this chapter.

How to do it...

Perform the following steps:

1. Navigate to **Settings & Reports | Configuration** within vShield Manager.

2. Locate **Lookup Service** on the configuration screen and click on the **Edit** button associated with **Lookup Service**.

3. Check the option for **Configure Lookup Service**.

4. Enter the vCenter Server IP address (`192.168.10.20` in our example).

5. Enter either the **SSO Administrator Username** created during the vCenter installation in its **Universal Principal Name** (**UPN**) format (in our example, `administrator@vsphere.local`).

6. Enter the appropriate password.

> Do not change the default port of 7444 unless a custom port was set up for SSO when vCenter was installed. If a custom port was used, this number should match the SSO port number.

Lookup Service Information

☑ Configure Lookup Service
Specify the IP address or name of the server which hosts the lookup service.

Lookup Service Host:	`192.168.10.20`
Port:	`7444`
Lookup Service URL:	`https://192.168.10.20:7444/lookupservice/sdk`
SSO Administrator Username:	`administrator@vsphere.local`
Password:	`***********`

OK   Cancel

7. Click on **OK** to save changes and close the window.

If an initialization error occurs similar to the following notification, the most likely cause is that the system clock on the vShield Manager virtual appliance is out of sync with the vCenter server. Ensure NTP is configured and working for both vShield and vCenter.

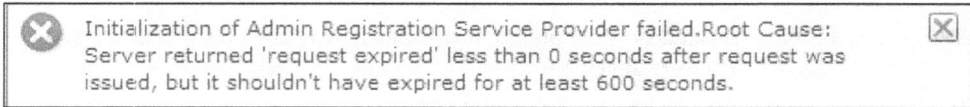

> ❌ Initialization of Admin Registration Service Provider failed.Root Cause: Server returned 'request expired' less than 0 seconds after request was issued, but it shouldn't have expired for at least 600 seconds. ⊠

How it works...

In vSphere version 5.1 and higher, applications can register with SSO as a solution user. This configuration allows, as the name implies, Single Sign-On capabilities across vCenter and solutions that are approved to integrate with vSphere. During the vCenter installation of the SSO component, a web address was configured. This allows solutions such as vShield Manager the capability to look up SSO credentials from a secure HTTP site. In our example, the lookup service URL is `https://192.168.10.20:7444/lookupservice/sdk`.

Configuring user accounts and roles

The addition of solutions such as vShield Manager need not carry with them increased management burden typically associated with a security or additional solution. In this section, we'll add our Active Directory based administrator account to a role within vShield Manager to demonstrate the SSO capabilities to authenticate users from other identity directories.

Getting ready

In order to proceed, we require access to vShield Web Console. This client can be run on any modern Windows or Mac desktop operating system or server operating system.

> vShield Web Console requires Adobe Flash, which is not supported on Linux operating systems at this time.

Ensure the account used for login has administrative rights to vShield Manager.

How to do it...

Perform the following steps:

1. Navigate to the **Settings & Reports | Users** area within vShield Manager.

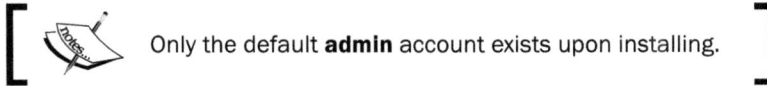

> ✎ Only the default **admin** account exists upon installing.

2. Click on **Add**.

		You are logged in as a System Administrator		Logged in as: admin	
Settings & Reports					
Configuration	Updates	Users	System Events	Audit Logs	Tasks

Add · Edit · Delete · Change Role · Actions ▾

User ▲	Origin	Role	Status	Access Scope
admin	Local	System Administrator	Enabled	Global

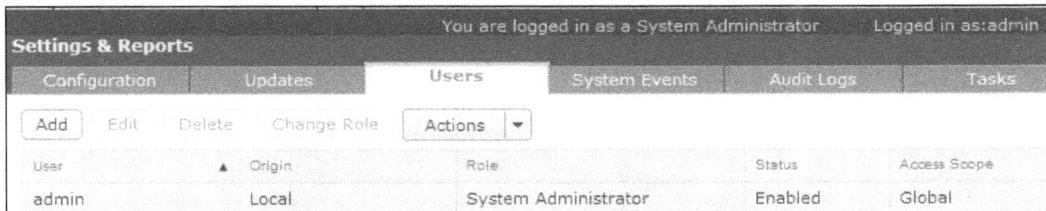

3. Select **Specify a vCenter user** (in our example `training\administrator`).

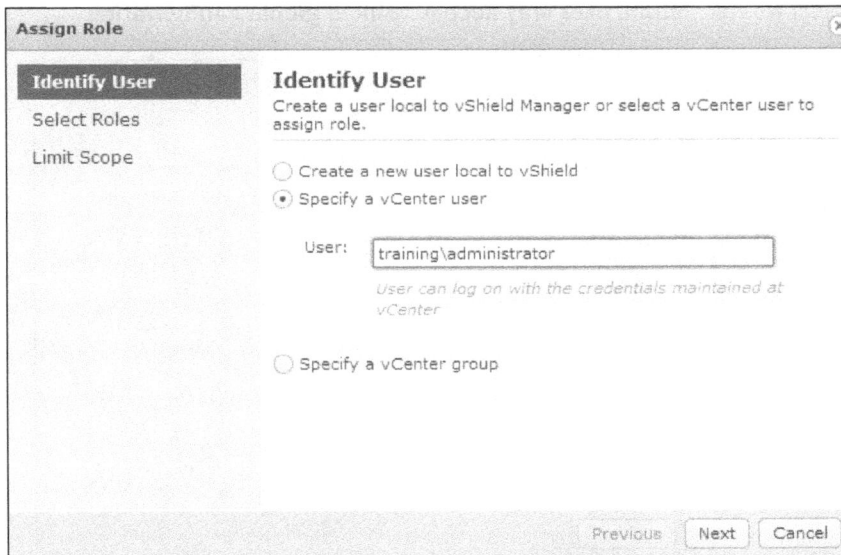

Assign Role ⊗

Identify User

Select Roles

Limit Scope

Identify User

Create a user local to vShield Manager or select a vCenter user to assign role.

○ Create a new user local to vShield
◉ Specify a vCenter user

User: `training\administrator`

User can log on with the credentials maintained at vCenter

○ Specify a vCenter group

Previous · Next · Cancel

4. Click on **Next** to continue.

5. Select **Enterprise Administrator** as the vShield role.

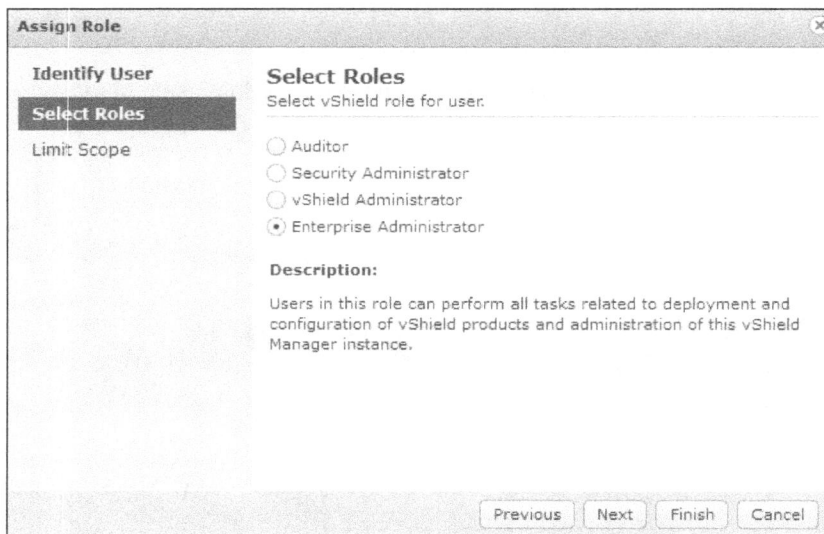

6. Click on **Next** to continue.

7. Select **No restriction, user may access vShield global configuration**.

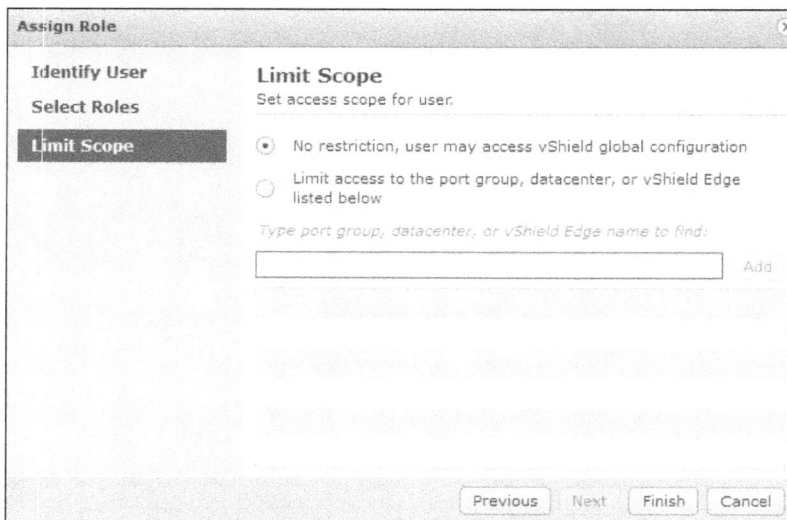

8. Click on **Finish** to save changes and close the window.

How it works...

To ensure that users with the proper authorization have access to the appropriate information, delegation can be used to grant applicable rights. In our example, we've granted the vCenter administrator account, based in Active Directory, rights as an enterprise or global vShield Manager Administrator.

The default roles have the following rights:

- **Auditor:** This is the ability to view system settings, events, auditing, and report information with read only permission
- **Security Administrator:** This is the ability to configure security compliance policies and view reporting and auditing information
- **vShield Administrator:** This is the ability to perform all tasks related to deployment and management of the vShield Manager instance
- **Enterprise Administrator:** This is the ability to perform all tasks related to deployment and configuration of vShield products

This can easily be an Active Directory group for auditors or groups that have specific rights to manage certain services or application security groups. The auditor group might require *read only* rights for example. The value in this ability to provide sign-on based on a centralized identity directory means less management of separate accounts and rights, which also lowers the risk of system misconfiguration.

Configuring services and service groups

Services in vShield are defined as a protocol/port combination. A common service example is DNS, which is defined as the protocol UDP and the port 53 or UDP:53. In our example, we'll group services required for web traffic into a security group that includes our existing web server.

Getting ready

In order to proceed, we require access to vShield Web Console. The client can be run on any modern Windows or Mac desktop operating system or server operating system.

> vShield Web Console requires Adobe Flash, which is not supported on Linux operating systems at this time.

Ensure the account used to log in has administrative rights to vShield Manager.

How to do it...

Groups can be created after the vCenter server has been added to the vShield Manager configuration by performing the following steps:

1. Navigate to the **Datacenters | Datacenter** area within vShield Manager.

2. Select the **General** tab.

3. Select the **Grouping** menu.

4. Click on the **+** icon and then select **Security Group**

   Groups can consist of IP addresses, MAC addresses, or security groups.

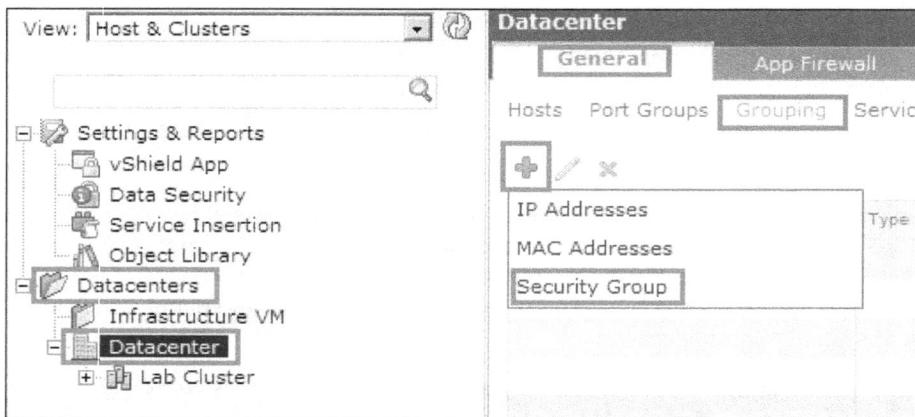

5. Give the **Security Group** a name, in our example, we'll call it **Public Web Server**.

6. The members of the group include the following:

   ❑ **Web Server**: This is a member type of virtual machine

   ❑ **DMZ Network**: This is a member type of network

   ❑ **Lab Cluster**: This is a member type of cluster

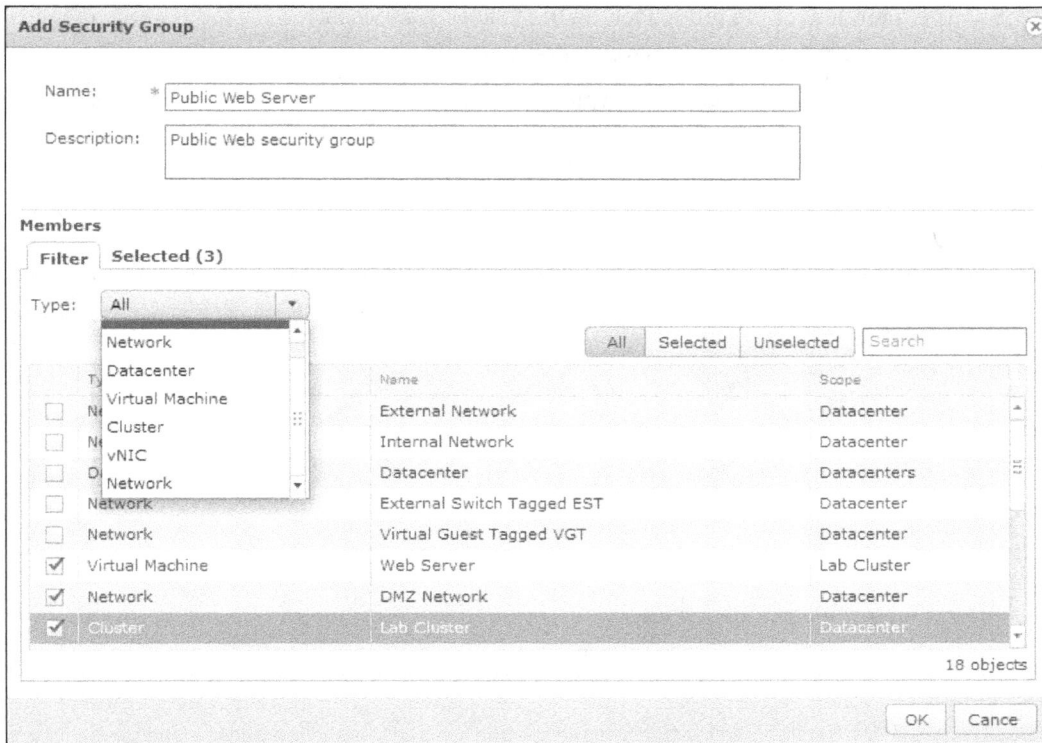

7. Click on **OK** to save the changes and close the window.

Likewise, services can be grouped together to be used later in firewall rules by performing the following steps:

1. Navigate to the **Datacenter | General** tab.
2. Select the **Services** menu.
3. Select the **+** icon and then **Service Group**.
4. Give the **Service Group** a name (in our example, we'll call it **Public Web Services**).

5. The members of the group include the following services:

   ❑ **HTTP**: This is for unencrypted web traffic

   ❑ **HTTPS**: This is for encrypted web traffic

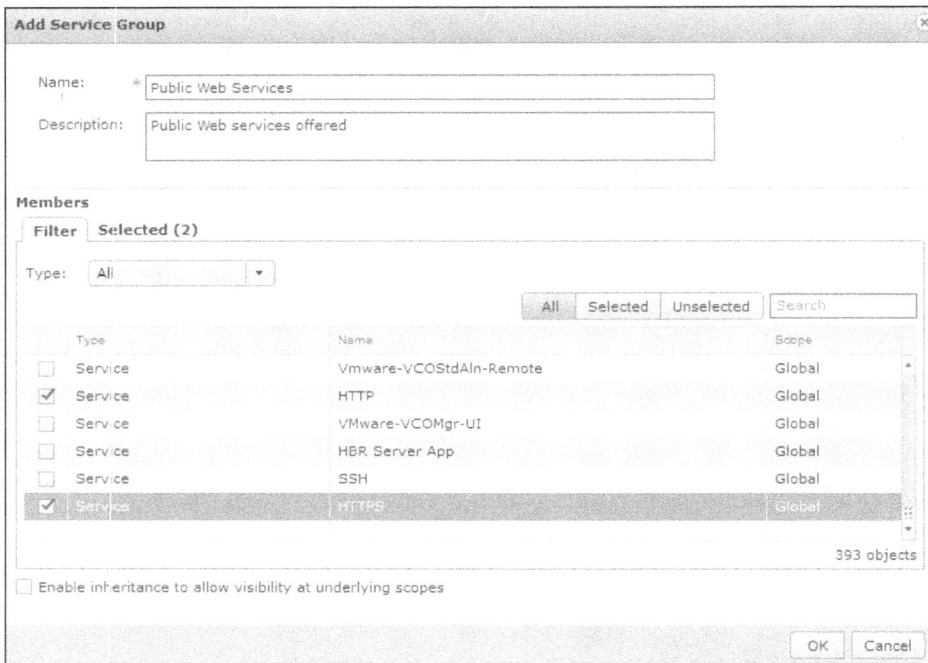

6. Click on **OK** to save the changes and close the window.

How it works...

Configuring security and service groups enables better isolation or compartmentalization of traffic and security controls based on the applications being used at different trust levels within the virtualized environment. Security groups, for example, are limited in scope to the resource level at which they were created. So, a security group created at the port group level will only be applied at the port group level, not at the cluster level.

In our example, we created a security group specifically for the web server traffic. Specifically, HTTP and HTTPS services were assigned to the **Public Web Services** group. This allows the compartmentalization of web service traffic to the public web server residing on the DMZ Network that resides on the Lab Cluster.

On the other hand, service groups are meant to bring together like or related services that applications require to function across the network. Common service groups found in vShield include Oracle, Active Directory, SharePoint, VMware View and vCenter.

8
Configuring vShield App

In this chapter, we will cover the following recipes:

- ▶ Installing vShield App
- ▶ Configuring vShield App using the Web Console
- ▶ Configuring vShield App Flow Monitoring
- ▶ Configuring vShield App Firewall
- ▶ Configuring vShield App SpoofGuard

Introduction

In most modern operating systems, there is an option to install a firewall on the host. The rules configured in a host-based firewall manage the traffic at the host level, and provide an additional layer of defense along with network firewalls and intrusion detection systems. Multiple layers of security provide a complete defense-in-depth architecture. As mentioned in *Chapter 1, Threat and Vulnerability Overview*, the concept of defense-in-depth builds layers of security providing protection, should another layer fail or be compromised.

The second component of the vShield family to be configured, which we'll discuss, is vShield App. vShield App is a host-based layer 2 firewall that is implemented at the vNIC level of the hypervisor. vShield App presents itself as a virtual appliance in the vCenter management tool. For each protected ESXi host, there is an associated vShield App virtual machine that runs on the said host. To protect the entire virtualization environment managed by vCenter, it is important to install vShield App on each ESXi host in the data center. Failure to protect each host will allow the opportunity for virtual machines to be moved to an unprotected host either by vMotion or manually. In the event where DRS is being used, it is very likely that virtual machines will be moved to an unprotected host, assuming that it has resources available and there is a high load on adjacent hosts.

Installing vShield App

The installation of vShield App is accomplished through the vShield web console as introduced in *Chapter 7, Configuring vShield Manager*. The vShield App is required to provide host-level security and firewall services to each individual ESXi host. This process must be completed on each ESXi host individually.

Getting ready

A **Core Infrastructure Suite** (**CIS**) or **vCloud Networking and Security** (**vCNS**) license must be installed prior to installing vShield App and vShield Edge.

vShield App is installed per ESXi host, and vShield Manager must have been previously installed as a prerequisite.

In order to proceed, we require access to vShield Web Console. The client can be run on any modern Windows or Mac desktop operating system or server operating system.

> vShield Web Console requires Adobe Flash, which is not supported on Linux operating systems at this time.

Ensure the account used for login has administrative rights to vShield Manager.

How to do it...

Perform the following steps:

1. We'll open the vShield Manager Web Console and log in with an administrative account.
2. Navigate to **Datacenter | Lab Cluster | esx5501.training.lab** within vShield Manager.

> Ensure the ESXi host targeted for installation is not hosting the VM running vCenter. A connection is required to vCenter and the installation of vShield App will disrupt the network connection to the ESXi host.

3. Locate **vShield App** from the **Summary** tab.

4. Click on **Install** next to **vShield App**.

5. Select **Datastore** to hold the vShield App service information. In our example, we'll use **datastore1**.

6. Select the available **Management Port Group** that can communicate with the vShield Manager installed previously. In our example, we'll use **Internal Network**.

7. Enter the **vShield App IP address**. In our example, we'll use **192.168.10.30**.

> The IP address of the vShield App must be unique and not previously assigned.

8. Enter the **Netmask**. In our example, we'll use **255.255.255.0**.

9. Enter the **Default Gateway**. In our example, we'll use **192.168.10.1**.

10. Ensure the **vShield Endpoint** checkbox is cleared.

11. Click on the **Install** button.

Summary	Endpoint

Select services to install/upgrade   Install   Cancel

☑ vShield App Installing latest version 5.5.0-1447281

Do not install on a host or cluster where the VC or vShield Manager reside. This can cause network disruptions.
The IP address below should be a unique IP address allotted to this vShield App appliance. Please do not use an IP address assigned to some other machine including VC, vShield Manager or any ESX host. Using an incorrect IP address will require you to uninstall and re-install vShield App on this host.

Please specify installation parameters for vShield App service:

Datastore:	datastore1 ▾
Management Port Group:	Internal Network ▾
vShield App IP address:	192.168.10.30
Netmask:	255.255.255.0
Default Gateway:	192.168.10.1

☐ vShield Endpoint Installing latest version 5.1.0-01255202

☐ vShield Data Security Not applicable until vShield Endpoint is installed.

12. The status will be shown during the installation, as shown in the following screenshot:

esx5501.training.lab

Summary	Endpoint

vShield Host Preparation Status for esx5501.training.lab

System is currently installing services on this host

Progress:

1. **Installing service modules**
2. Installing and configuring service virtual machines
3. Preparing guest virtual machines

13. Verify the completion of the setup with no errors.

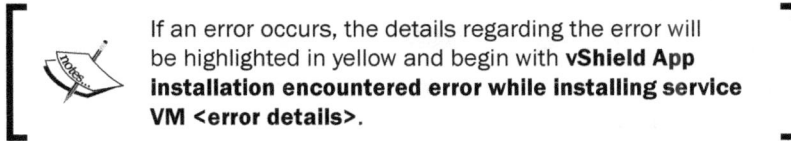

> If an error occurs, the details regarding the error will be highlighted in yellow and begin with **vShield App installation encountered error while installing service VM <error details>**.

esx5501.training.lab

Summary | Endpoint

vShield Host Preparation Status for esx5501.training.lab

Service	Installed	Available	
vShield App	5.5.0-1447281	-	Uninstall
vShield Endpoint	Not installed	5.1.0-01255202	Install
vShield Data Security	Not applicable until vShield Endpoint is installed.		

14. Repeat this process for additional ESXi hosts. If vCenter is running on an ESXi host, use vMotion to migrate that VM to another host prior to installation.

How it works...

vShield App provides firewall functionality to an ESXi host by installing a virtual appliance that is tied to the local host. The virtual appliance is stored on the local datastore to the host. Each firewall appliance is named with the host name included for clarity. In our example, we installed vShield App on the ESXi host named **esx5501.training.lab** and the corresponding firewall appliance is named **vShield-FW-esx5501.training.lab**.

One important point to consider is if the vShield App fails on a particular ESXi host and the default rule is set to deny, then all traffic will be denied to the host, which can make troubleshooting difficult.

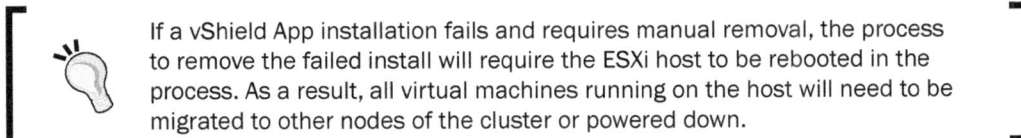

> If a vShield App installation fails and requires manual removal, the process to remove the failed install will require the ESXi host to be rebooted in the process. As a result, all virtual machines running on the host will need to be migrated to other nodes of the cluster or powered down.

Configuring vShield App using the Web Console

There are several important configurations to set in the vShield App management Web Console. Configuring **Fail Safe Mode** sets the actions that will be taken if the vShield App fails or is down. Fail Safe Mode can either be set to allow or block. Excluding virtual machines such as vCenter is key to allow proper functionality since it will exclude any virtual machine from firewall rules.

Getting ready

In order to proceed, we require access to vShield Web Console. The client can be run on any modern Windows or Mac desktop operating system or server operating system.

> vShield Web Console requires Adobe Flash, which is not supported on Linux operating systems at this time.

Ensure the account used to log in has administrative rights to vShield Manager.

How to do it...

Viewing the current status is the first step in assessing the state of the vShield App. Once the app is confirmed to be in a healthy state, additional configurations can be accomplished by performing the following steps:

1. Launch vSphere Client using an account with administrative rights.
2. Choose **Home | Inventory | Hosts and Clusters** from the menu bar.
3. Navigate to **Datacenter | Lab Cluster | esx5501.training.lab**.
4. Select the **vShield** tab.
5. Expand **vShield-FW-esx5501.training.lab (192.168.10.30)**.
6. Note the **Status: In Sync** status; there are two options to either **Force Sync** or **Restart**.

7. Current **Management Port Information** is displayed including the packet, byte, and error information.

8. **Syslog Servers** can be added by an **IP Address**.

esx5501.training.lab VMware ESXi, 5.5.0, 1331820

Getting Started | Summary | Virtual Machines | Performance | Configuration | Tasks & Events | Alarms | Permissions | Maps | Storage Views | Hardware Status | vShield

General   Endpoint

Name	Type
vShield Manager	vShield Manager
vShield-FW-esx5501.training.lab (192.168.10.30)	vShield App Download Support logs

Status: In Sync   Force Sync   Restart

Resource Utilization

CPU Usage (%):	0.000000	Base Software Storage (%):	70.309258
Memory Free (%):	93.040871	Configuration Storage (%):	97.564644

Management Port Information

Link Status:	UP	Admin Status:	UP				
MTU:	1500	Metric:	0	Collisions:	0	RX Multicast:	0

	RX	TX
Bytes	91745	114648
Packets	644	396
Compressed	0	0
Errors	0	0
Dropped	0	0
Overruns	0	0
Frame	0	N/A
Carrier	N/A	0

Syslog Servers

IP Address	Log Level
	Emergency ▾
	Emergency ▾
	Emergency ▾

Save   Cancel

Configuring the Fail Safe Policy allows traffic to flow or be blocked, should the vShield App Firewall be down or offline for any reason.

1. Navigate to **Settings & Reports | vShield App** within vShield Manager.

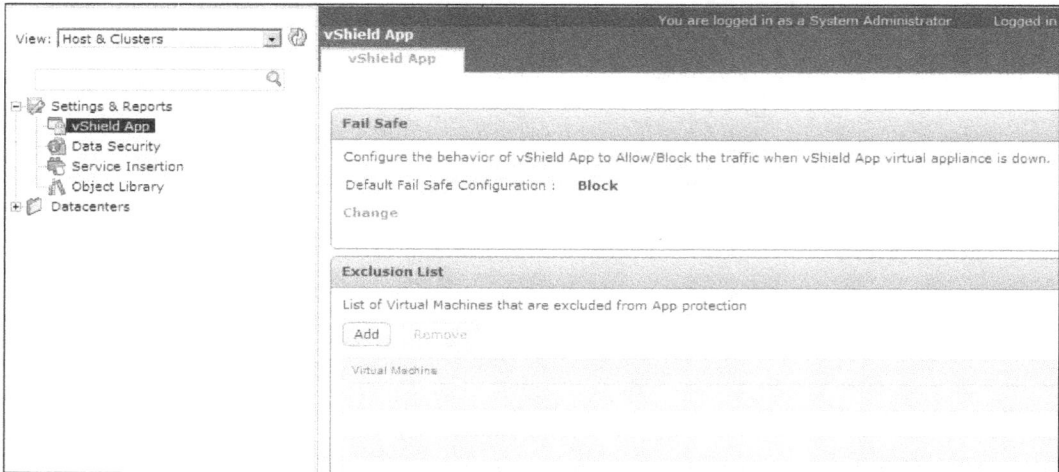

2. Click on **Change** under **Fail Safe.** This step will lead to the following screen:

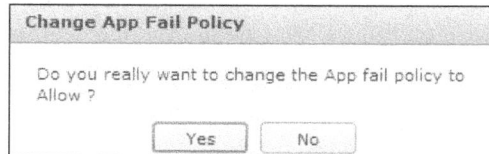

3. Click on **Yes**.

4. Note that **Default Fail Safe Configuration** set to **Block** has now been changed to **Allow**.

> In a production situation, there are few times when the fail safe setting will be changed to **Allow**. In a small test environment, should the vShield App be unavailable, all connectivity to the ESXi host will be blocked by default.

Configuring the **Exclusion List** allows certain virtual machines to function without host-based firewall rules being applied to them. This can be done by performing the following steps:

1. Navigate to **Settings & Reports | vShield App** within vShield Manager.

2. Click on **Add** under **Exclusion List**.
3. Select a virtual machine to exclude from vShield App (in our case, it is a **Linked vCenter** server). Click on **Add**.

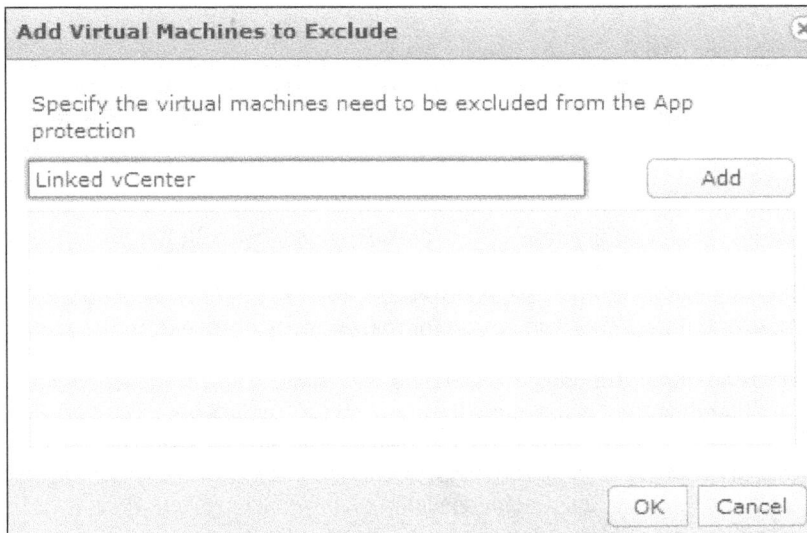

4. Click on **OK**.

5. Click on **OK** in the next dialog box to confirm.

6. The selected virtual machine is now excluded from protection.

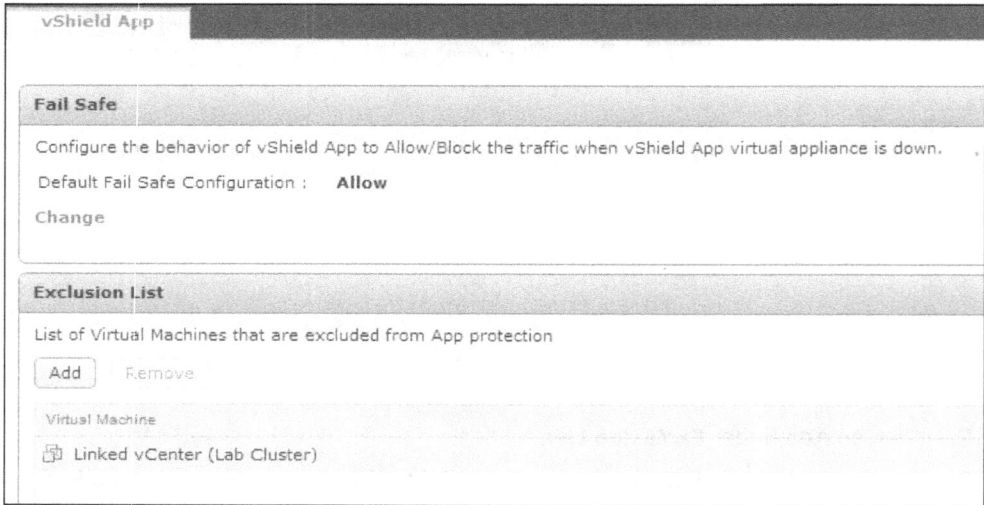

vShield App

Fail Safe

Configure the behavior of vShield App to Allow/Block the traffic when vShield App virtual appliance is down.

Default Fail Safe Configuration :   **Allow**

Change

Exclusion List

List of Virtual Machines that are excluded from App protection

Add   Remove

Virtual Machine

🔲 Linked vCenter (Lab Cluster)

How it works...

The vShield App host firewall is installed per ESXi host and automatically named by the installation program to include the name of the host. It is also important to note that when a host is put into maintenance mode, the vShield firewall must be shut down in order to let the host successfully achieve maintenance mode.

Current Status provides a single view of the firewall associated with the host including the traffic status displayed by packet count, link, and admin status. One important status check is whether the firewall is in sync with vShield Manager. Should the firewall fall out of sync, it can be forced to sync and if that fails, the option for restart is also present on the status page.

Fail Safe Policy is an important consideration should the vShield App virtual appliance fail for any reason. The default setting is to block all traffic and this might seem like a good idea at the outset. Careful consideration should be given to setting this flag, depending on what type of virtual machines are running on a specific host or cluster. In a situation where mission-critical applications are running on virtual machines within an internal cluster or host, it will make sense to allow traffic if the vShield App was down. The average time it will take to identify and remediate the failure could cause a significant impact on the amount of business lost.

Exclusion List, as the name implies, allows certain virtual machines to remain outside the protection of the vShield App firewall. Critical infrastructure such as DNS or Domain Controllers are good candidates to be added to the exclusion list. vCenter servers should *always* be added to the exclusion list.

Configuring vShield App Flow Monitoring

vShield App Flow Monitoring is a traffic analysis tool that provides statistics and graphs of the traffic on the virtual network as it passes through a host running vShield App. The information collected and displayed by Flow Monitoring is detailed to the protocol level and is very useful in spotting unwanted traffic flows.

Getting ready

In order to proceed, we require access to vShield App through the vSphere Client plugin. The plugin can be enabled through the **Plug-ins** menu in the vSphere Client. This client can run on any modern Windows desktop operating system or server operating system.

> The vShield vSphere Client plugin requires Adobe Flash, which is not supported on Linux operating systems at this time.

Ensure the vCenter account used for login has administrative rights to vShield Manager.

How to do it...

To view the current traffic flow, launch vSphere Client using an account with administrative rights.

1. Navigate to **Home | Inventory | Hosts and Clusters** from the menu bar.
2. Navigate to **Datacenter** and click on the **vShield** tab.
3. Select **Flow Monitoring**.

4. Note that the **Summary** information is displayed by default.

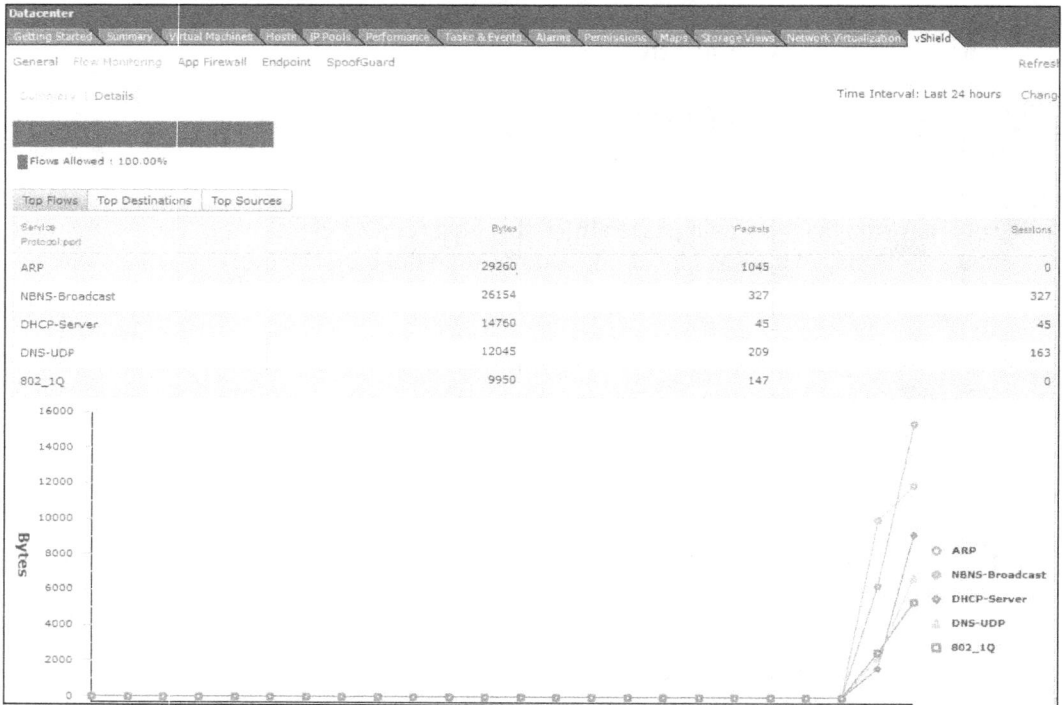

5. Click on **Details** to view detailed information.
6. **Allowed Flows** and **Blocked Flows** are available to view.

7. Select **DNS-UDP** to identify the host lookup traffic on port 53.

Rule Id	Time Stamp	Source	Destination	Packets	Sessions	Bytes	Actions	
1002	4/8/2014 8:55 PM	192.168.10.50	Web Server (192.168.10.101)	17	15	1024	Add R....	Edit R....
1002	4/8/2014 9:20 PM	Web Server (192.168.10.101)	192.168.10.50	19	15	1178	Add R....	Edit R....
1002	4/8/2014 9:30 PM	192.168.10.50	Web Server (192.168.10.101)	36	22	2044	Add R....	Edit R....
1002	4/8/2014 9:40 PM	192.168.10.50	Web Server (192.168.10.101)	28	22	1598	Add R....	Edit R....
1002	4/8/2014 9:45 PM	192.168.10.50	Web Server (192.168.10.101)	12	10	684	Add R....	Edit R....
1002	4/8/2014 9:50 PM	192.168.10.50	Web Server (192.168.10.101)	15	13	855	Add R....	Edit R....
1002	4/8/2014 9:55 PM	192.168.10.50	Web Server (192.168.10.101)	12	9	670	Add R....	Edit R....
1002	4/8/2014 10:00 PM	192.168.10.50	Web Server (192.168.10.101)	16	14	912	Add R....	Edit R....
1002	4/8/2014 10:05 PM	192.168.10.50	Web Server (192.168.10.101)	17	14	989	Add R....	Edit R....
1002	4/8/2014 10:10 PM	192.168.10.50	Web Server (192.168.10.101)	11	8	623	Add R....	Edit R....
1002	4/8/2014 10:15 PM	192.168.10.50	Web Server (192.168.10.101)	16	13	898	Add R....	Edit R....

8. Click on **Add Rule** for **Rule Id 1002**.
9. By changing **Action** from **Allow** to **Block**, a firewall rule can be modified to block the DNS traffic from the web server to the DNS Server.

10. Click on **Cancel**.

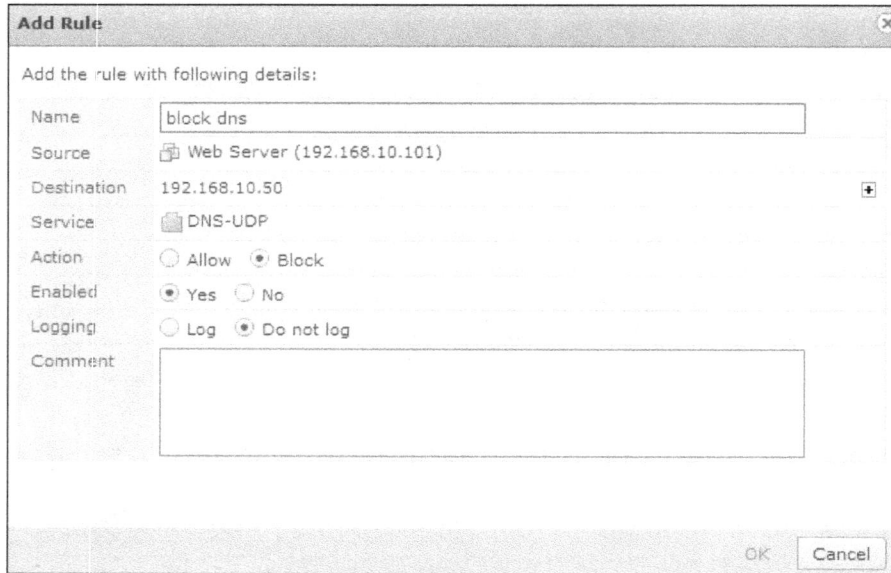

Add Rule	

Add the rule with following details:

Name	block dns
Source	🖥 Web Server (192.168.10.101)
Destination	192.168.10.50
Service	🗐 DNS-UDP
Action	○ Allow ⦿ Block
Enabled	⦿ Yes ○ No
Logging	○ Log ⦿ Do not log
Comment	

OK Cancel

How it works...

The Flow Monitoring component of vShield App, in addition to providing great detail, is able to create vShield App firewall rules on the fly. As shown in the preceding example, we were able to identify the DNS traffic from our web server accessing an internal DNS server. Due to our governance rules, servers accessed in the DMZ are not allowed to request DNS from internal servers. Implementing a firewall rule adds a control to this policy and gets easily implemented once the administrator notices the request.

The ability to view traffic by Top Flows, Top Destinations, and Top Sources is very valuable when troubleshooting a problem or tracking down a virus or trojan that is attempting to send valuable information outside the organization during a breach.

Configuring vShield App Firewall

The vShield App Firewall allows layer 2 and layer 3 firewall rules to be published, which affect virtual machines that reside on the ESXi hosts running vShield App. By default, the firewall is in passive mode, allowing all the traffic to and from the virtual machines that run on the specified ESXi host.

Getting ready

In order to proceed, we require access to vShield App through the vSphere Client plugin. The client can be run on any modern Windows desktop operating system or server operating system.

> The vShield vSphere Client plugin requires Adobe Flash, which is not supported on Linux operating systems at this time.

Ensure the vCenter account used for login has administrative rights to vShield Manager.

How to do it...

To add a firewall rule, perform the following steps:

1. Launch vSphere Client using an account with administrative rights.
2. Navigate to **Home | Inventory | Hosts and Clusters** from the menu bar.
3. Navigate to **Datacenter** and click on the **vShield** tab.
4. Select **App Firewall**, the **General** rules (layer 3) are shown by default, Note the **Default Rule** allows any traffic if no other rules apply.

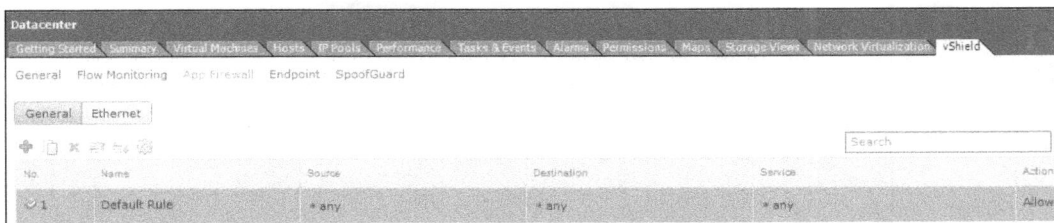

5. Click on the **+** icon to create a new rule.

6. In our scenario, we want to create a rule to block the ICMP traffic on the DMZ Network. Add **Block ICMP** to the **Name** field.

7. Click on **+** in **Source** and select **Public Web Server** from the **Available** column and move it to the **Selected** column.

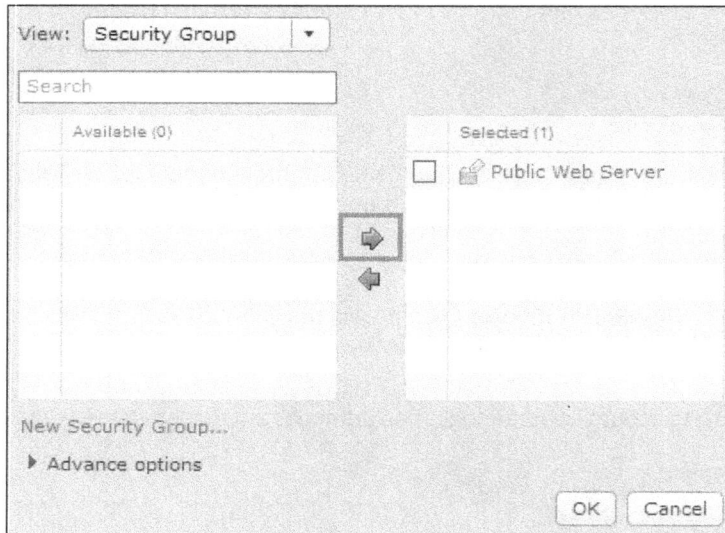

View:	Security Group ▼

Search

Available (0)   Selected (1)

☐ 🖼️ Public Web Server

➡️
⬅️

New Security Group...
▶ Advance options

OK   Cancel

8. Click on **OK**.

9. Click on **+** in **Destination** and change the **View:** option to **Network**.

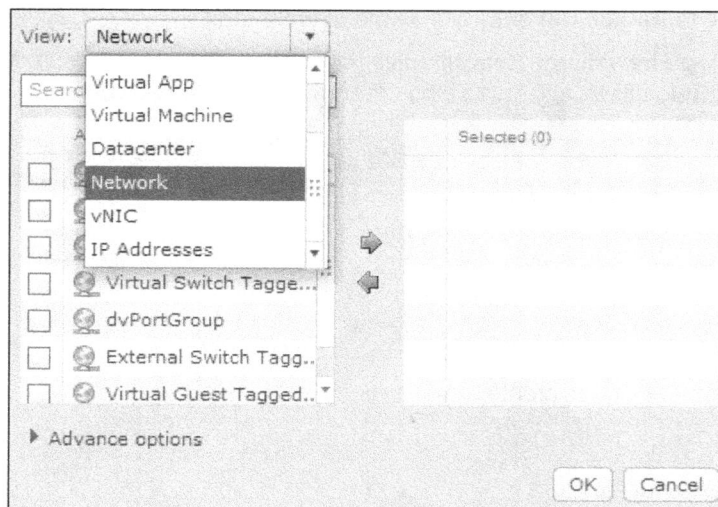

View:	Network ▼

Sear☐   Virtual App
Virtual Machine
Datacenter
Network
vNIC
IP Addresses

Selected (0)

☐   Virtual Switch Tagge...
☐   dvPortGroup
☐   External Switch Tagg..
☐   Virtual Guest Tagged..

➡️
⬅️

▶ Advance options

OK   Cancel

10. Select **DMZ Network** from the **Available** column and move it to the **Selected** column.

11. Click on **OK.**

12. Click on **+** in **Service** and type `icmp` in the search window.

13. Select **ICMP Echo** and **ICMP Echo Reply** from the **Available** column and move them to the **Selected** column.

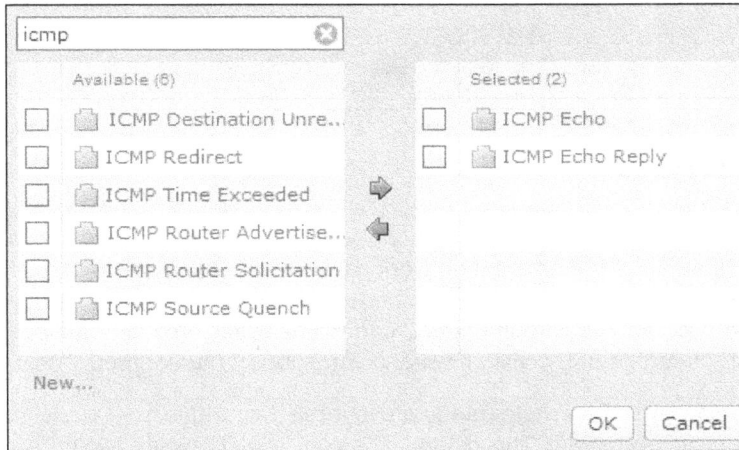

14. Click on **OK**.

15. In the **App Firewall** screen, click on **+** in the **Action** column.

16. Select the **Block** option for the **Action** field**.**

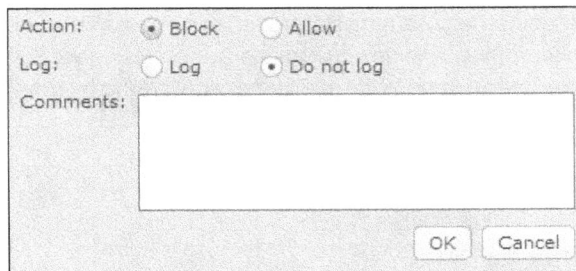

17. Click on **OK**.

18. Click **Publish Changes** to deploy the firewall changes and make them active; altered rules will not become active until published.

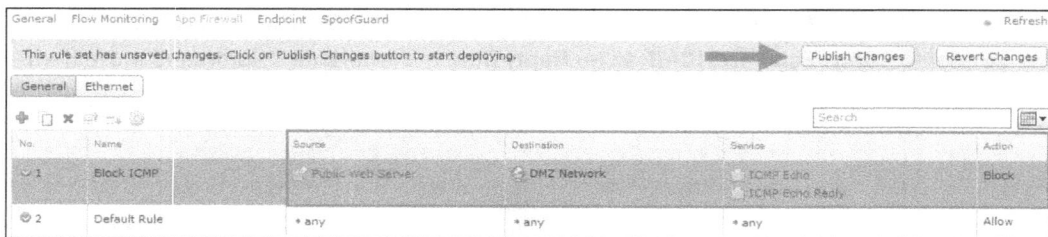

How it works...

Like many commercial firewalls, the vShield App firewall has *allow or deny rules* only at the hypervisor level instead of the physical network device level. Rules can be applied at the data center level, the virtual machine level, or the network level making vShield App very flexible in protecting the virtualization environment and controlling traffic on each ESXi host. vShield App Firewall rules are enforced at the vNIC level and can support multihomed VMs.

In our example, we created a simple rule to prevent the ping traffic from a specific virtual machine to a specific port group. This could just as easily be between two port groups or two virtual machines. It's important to note that unlike a traditional firewall, the default rule is *allow any* instead of the usual *deny any*.

Configuring vShield App SpoofGuard

SpoofGuard is another tool to help administrators limit unknown virtual machines from being spun-up in the environment. As new machines are provisioned, SpoofGuard can check whether a machine is trusted to send and receive network traffic by the vShield App Firewall.

SpoofGuard is disabled by default.

Getting ready

In order to proceed, we require access to vShield App through the vSphere Client plugin. This client can run on any modern Windows desktop operating system or server operating system.

> The vShield vSphere Client plugin requires Adobe Flash, which is not supported on Linux operating systems at this time.

Ensure the vCenter account used for login has administrative rights to vShield Manager.

How to do it...

To configure SpoofGuard at the data center level, perform the following steps:

1. Launch vSphere Client using an account with administrative rights.
2. Navigate to **Home | Inventory | Hosts and Clusters** from the menu bar.
3. Navigate to **Datacenter** and click on the **vShield** tab.
4. Select **SpoofGuard**.
5. The **Datacenter Status** is displayed (in our example, we have only one VM running).

6. Click on **Edit** in the upper-right corner to enable SpoofGuard.

7. Select the **Enabled** option for **SpoofGuard**.

8. Ensure that **Automatically trust IP assignments on their first use** is selected for **Operation Mode**.

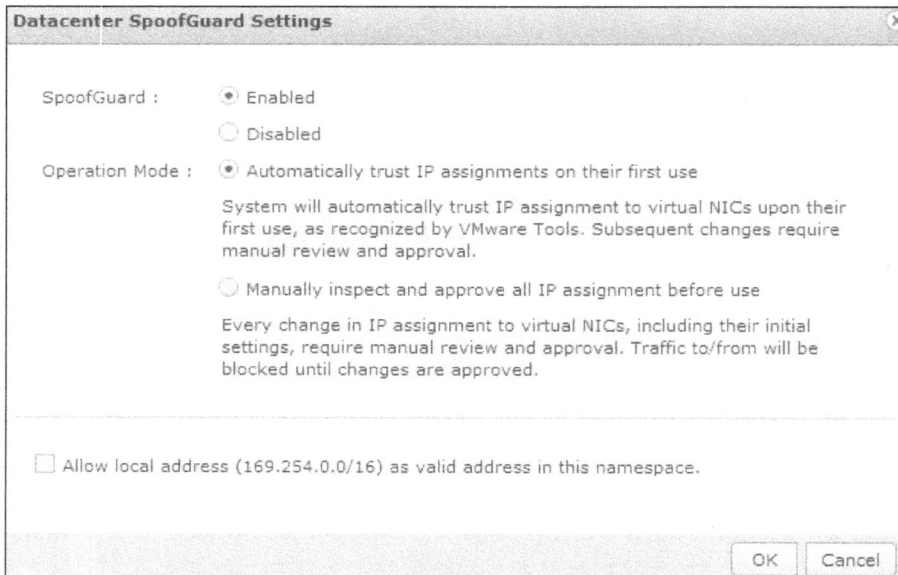

Datacenter SpoofGuard Settings   ⊗

SpoofGuard :   ⊙ Enabled

                      ○ Disabled

Operation Mode :   ⊙ Automatically trust IP assignments on their first use

                      System will automatically trust IP assignment to virtual NICs upon their
                      first use, as recognized by VMware Tools. Subsequent changes require
                      manual review and approval.

                      ○ Manually inspect and approve all IP assignment before use

                      Every change in IP assignment to virtual NICs, including their initial
                      settings, require manual review and approval. Traffic to/from will be
                      blocked until changes are approved.

───

☐ Allow local address (169.254.0.0/16) as valid address in this namespace.

                                                        OK   Cancel

---

9. Click on **OK**.

10. Click on **Publish Changes** to make settings effective on the prompted screen:

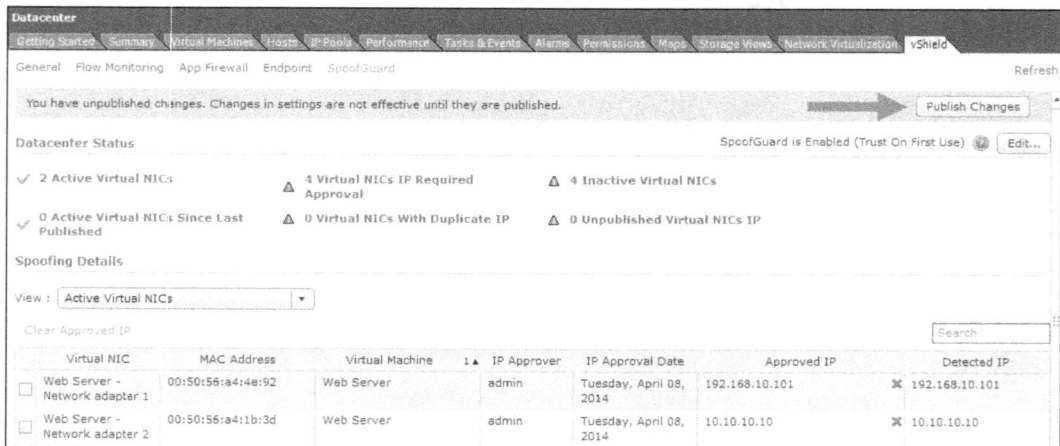

Datacenter

Getting Started | Summary | Virtual Machines | Hosts | IP Pools | Performance | Tasks & Events | Alarms | Permissions | Maps | Storage Views | Network Virtualization | **vShield**

General Flow Monitoring App Firewall Endpoint *SpoofGuard*   Refresh

You have unpublished changes. Changes in settings are not effective until they are published.   ⟶ [Publish Changes]

Datacenter Status   SpoofGuard is Enabled (Trust On First Use) ⓘ [Edit...]

✓ 2 Active Virtual NICs   ⚠ 4 Virtual NICs IP Required   ⚠ 4 Inactive Virtual NICs
                                    Approval

✓ 0 Active Virtual NICs Since Last ⚠ 0 Virtual NICs With Duplicate IP ⚠ 0 Unpublished Virtual NICs IP
  Published

Spoofing Details

View : | Active Virtual NICs   ▼ |

Clear Approved IP   [Search   ]

	Virtual NIC	MAC Address	Virtual Machine	IP Approver	IP Approval Date	Approved IP	Detected IP
☐	Web Server - Network adapter 1	00:50:56:a4:4e:92	Web Server	admin	Tuesday, April 08, 2014	192.168.10.101	✖ 192.168.10.101
☐	Web Server - Network adapter 2	00:50:56:a4:1b:3d	Web Server	admin	Tuesday, April 08, 2014	10.10.10.10	✖ 10.10.10.10

11. **Active Virtual NICs** are now approved.

How it works...

Essentially, SpoofGuard provides a mechanism to trust certain IP addresses based on a vNIC to IP mapping or a MAC to IP mapping. This allows administrators to rely on a valid VMware tool installation ensuring that the IP does in fact belong to a virtual machine and not some other device or probe.

In our example, we enabled SpoofGuard at the data center level with the default setting of **Automatically Trust IP Assignments On Their First Use**. This option allows all the traffic from machines with valid VMware tools installs and does not require manual intervention unless the IP address changes from its initial value. Should the IP address change, the administrator must manually approve the new IP address so it will be trusted by SpoofGuard.

The alternate option, **Manually Inspect and Approve All IP Assignments Before Use**, requires administrative intervention to approve IP addresses manually. This option pulls the MAC address from the virtual machine's VMX file and associates it with the IP address.

Both options allow DHCP requests by default, although the manual option still requires approval of that DHCP assigned address before traffic is allowed to flow to the virtual machine.

9
Configuring vShield Edge

In this chapter, we will cover the following recipes:

- ▶ Installing vShield Edge
- ▶ Managing appliances
- ▶ Managing interfaces
- ▶ Managing certificates and revocation lists
- ▶ Managing firewall rules
- ▶ Managing NAT Rules and static routes
- ▶ Managing the IPSec VPN service
- ▶ Managing SSL VPN-Plus
- ▶ Configuring the load-balancing service

Introduction

Networks have been protected and partitioned by physical or software-based firewalls for many years now. These devices are deployed in an attempt to protect resources and direct traffic in a safe and productive manner. In the past, a virtualization environment of any sort was totally reliant on physical firewalls for defense and advanced features, including **Network Address Translation** (**NAT**) and **Virtual Private Network** (**VPN**) services.

As the industry moves toward the era of **Software Defined Networking (SDN)** with protocols such as **OpenFlow**, the virtualization of traditional physical networking components becomes more prevalent. SDN enables the abstraction of network devices through a controller layer, which, in turn, communicates with the virtual services at the SDN layer. While still in its infancy at the time of writing this book, SDN promises to become the next evolution of networking and to offer further integration of virtual and physical network components. OpenFlow is an open standard protocol that provides network infrastructure abstraction through the implementation of user policies to control multi-vendor networks.

The vShield Edge component of the vShield suite is specifically designed to bring key security features to the virtualized data center based on virtual appliances that are based within the virtual environment, not external or physical. As mentioned in *Chapter 1, Threat and Vulnerability Overview*, defense-in-depth utilizes firewalls and VPNs as security control interfaces and defensive layers.

In this chapter, we will implement a classic hardware firewall functionality with vShield Edge. The scenario covers the classic *internal network – firewall – DMZ network* with both SSL and IPSEC VPN along with load balancing. We'll also configure firewall and NAT rules since we're using a private internal IP scheme.

Installing vShield Edge

vShield Edge provides physical firewall and VPN capabilities at the virtualization level. In this recipe, we will configure a vShield edge appliance to pass traffic from our internal network to the DMZ network in a classic firewall scenario. When the edge appliance is configured, it will look like the following figure:

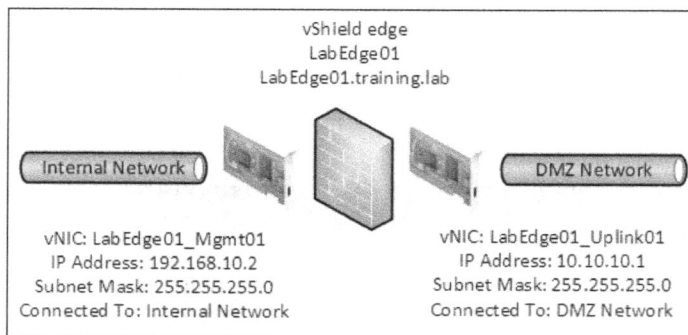

Getting ready

The installation of vShield Edge is accomplished through the vShield Web Console as introduced in *Chapter 7, Configuring vShield Manager*. A **Core Infrastructure Suite** (**CIS**) or **vCloud Networking and Security** (**vCNS**) license must be installed prior to installing vShield App and vShield Edge.

Multiple vShield Edge virtual appliances can be installed per data center within vCenter. Each vShield Edge can have as many as ten uplink ports, which allows for load balancing, NAT, and VPN services. vShield Manager must have been previously installed as a prerequisite.

In order to proceed, we require access to vShield App through the vSphere Client plugin. The client can be run on any modern Windows desktop operating system or server operating system.

> The vShield vSphere Client plugin requires Adobe Flash, which is not supported on Linux operating systems at this time.

Ensure the vCenter account used to log in has Enterprise administrator rights to vShield Manager.

How to do it...

Perform the following steps:

1. Launch vSphere Client using an account with administrative rights, if it is not already open.
2. Navigate to **Home** | **Inventory** | **Hosts and Clusters** from the menu bar.
3. Navigate to **Datacenter**.
4. Select the **Network Virtualization** tab.
5. Click on **+** to add an Edge gateway.

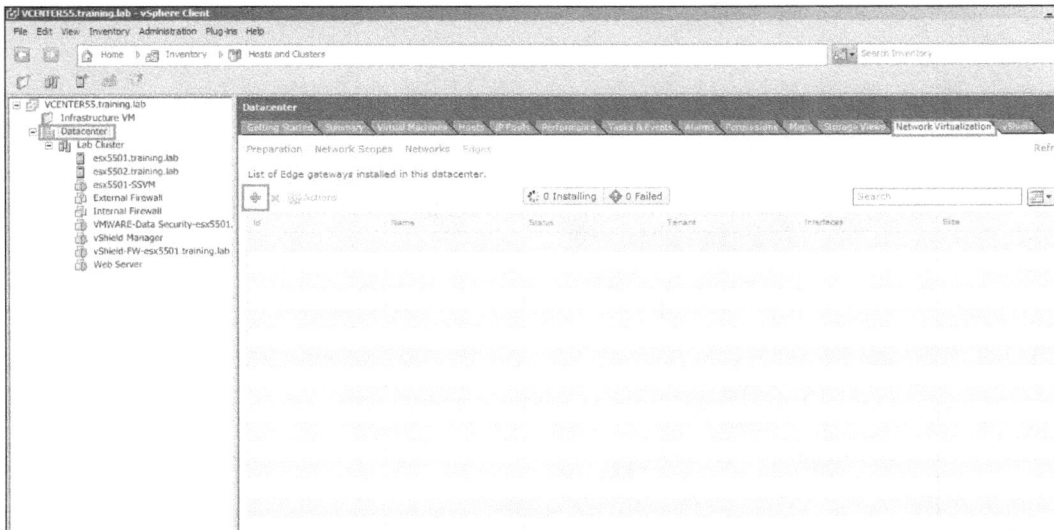

Installation of Edge gateways

6. Within the **Add Edge** dialog box, type the name of the virtual machine (in our example, **LabEdge01**).

7. Enter the value for the **Hostname** field (in our example, **LabEdge01.training.lab**).

8. Ensure that the **Enable HA** option is not checked. The High Availability option provides an active and standby configuration to ensure that a vShield Edge appliance is always available.

9. Click on **Next**.

10. Enter a **User Name** and **Password** for command-line access to the appliance.

> **User Name** will default to admin and **Password** will default to default. These are the default credentials for vShield Manager.

11. Ensure that the **Enable SSH access** option is not checked.

12. Click on **Next**.

13. Accept the default settings for **Appliance Size** as **Compact**. For information on appliance size, please refer to the *How it works...* section of this recipe.

14. Ensure that the **Enable auto rule generation** option is checked and confirm that **Rule Priority** is set to **High**.

Configuring the Edge appliance

The Edge gateway requires an edge appliance to become operational. The edge appliance can be added during the edge gateway creation or afterwards. To add an Edge appliance, perform the following steps:

1. Click on **+** to add/specify the location of the Edge appliance.
2. Select a valid **Cluster/Resource Pool** (in our example, **Lab Cluster**).
3. Select a valid **Datastore** (in our example, **Web Zone Data**).
4. Select a valid **Host** (in our example, **esx5501.training.lab**).
5. Select a valid **Folder** (in our example, **Edge Appliances**).

6. Click on **Add** to save the **Add Edge Appliance** information.

7. Click on **Next** to move to the interface configuration section.

Configuring Edge interfaces

Similar to Edge appliances, an operational Edge gateway requires interfaces. These interfaces can be added during the edge gateway creation or afterwards. To add an Edge interface, perform the following steps:

1. Click on the **+** sign to add **Interfaces** to the Edge gateway.

Add Edge						⊗
Name & Description	**Interfaces**					
CLI Credentials						
Edge Appliances	Configure interfaces of this Edge gateway.					
Interfaces	✦ ✎ ✕					📋 ▼
Default Gateway	vNIC#	Name	IP Address	Subnet Mask	Connected To	
Firewall & HA						
Summary						
				Previous	Next	Cancel

2. Within **Add Edge Interface**, select **Uplink** for **Type:**.

> 💡 The **Uplink** interface type is connecting to our external vNIC for Internet traffic. The **Internal** interface type is connected to our internal network by vNIC for private traffic.

3. Enter a name for the interface (in our example, **LabEdge01_Uplink01**).

4. For the **Connected To:** network, click on **Select**.

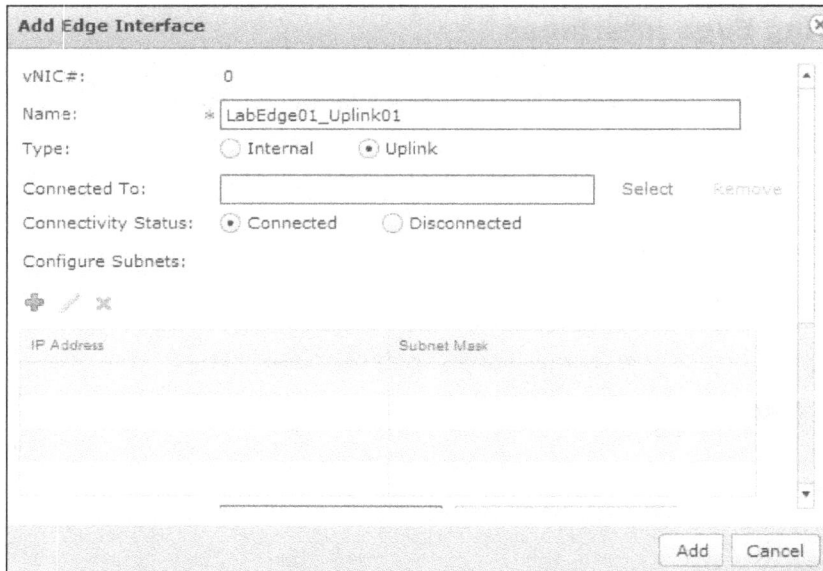

5. Within the **Connect Edge to a Network** dialog box, navigate to the **Standard Portgroup** tab.

6. Select a network (in our example, **DMZ Network**).

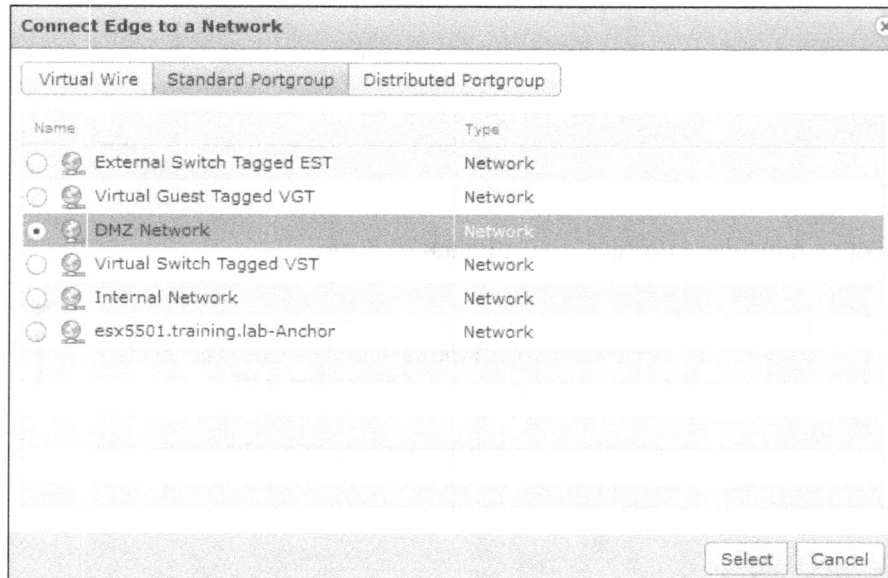

7. Click on **Select.**

8. Ensure that **Connectivity Status:** is set to **Connected** on the **Add Edge Interface** page.

9. Click on **+** to add a subnet.

10. Enter a valid **Subnet Mask** in the next pop up window (in our example, **255.255.255.0**).

11. Click on **+** to add a primary IP.

12. Click on **OK** to add the IP address.

13. Click on **Save** to add the subnet.

14. Click on **Add** in the **Add Edge Interface** window to add the interface.

15. Repeat these steps to add a management interface, as shown in the following screenshot:

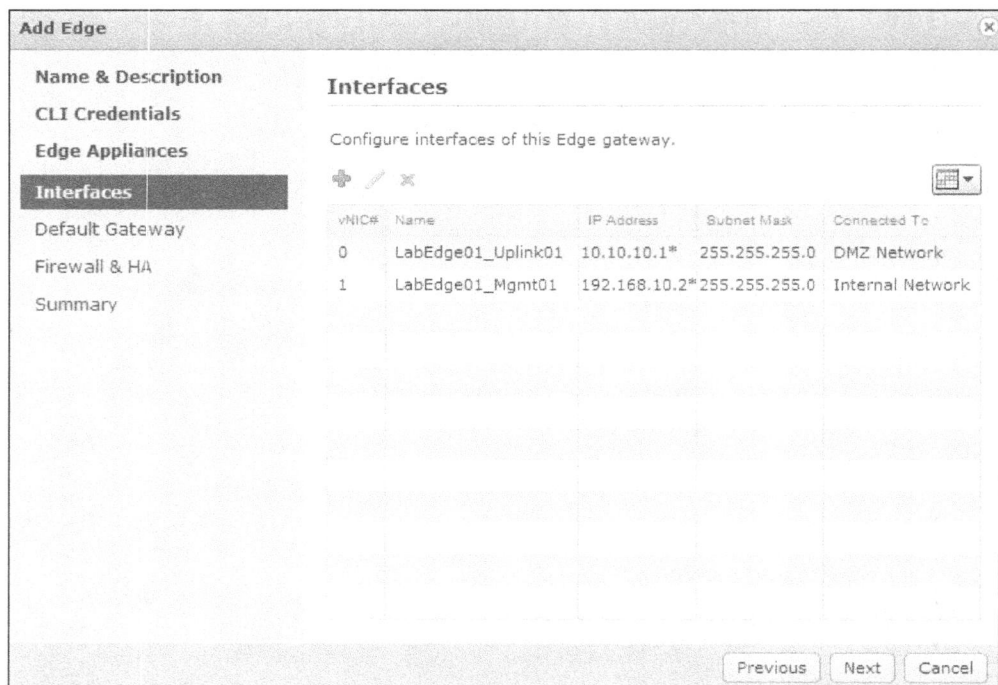

Add Edge					⊗
Name & Description	**Interfaces**				
CLI Credentials					
Edge Appliances	Configure interfaces of this Edge gateway.				
Interfaces	✚ / ✕				▦ ▾
Default Gateway	vNIC# Name		IP Address	Subnet Mask	Connected To
Firewall & HA	0 LabEdge01_Uplink01		10.10.10.1*	255.255.255.0	DMZ Network
Summary	1 LabEdge01_Mgmt01		192.168.10.2*	255.255.255.0	Internal Network

Previous | Next | Cancel

16. Click on **Next**.

At this point, we have configured our edge appliance and added two interfaces to it. One interface is our uplink that connects to our external or DMZ network. The second interface is for private management traffic and connects to our internal network.

In this section, we'll complete our vShield Edge setup by configuring the default gateway, firewall, and HA by performing the following steps:

1. Enter the **Default Gateway** information. In our example, we'll add a **Gateway IP** of **10.10.10.251** for the **LabEdge01_Uplink01** vNIC.

2. Click on **Next**.

3. Enable the **Configure Firewall default policy** option.

4. Set **Default Traffic Policy** to **Deny**.

5. Set **Logging** to **Disable**.

6. Click on **Next**.

Add Edge				⊗

Name & Description

CLI Credentials

Edge Appliances

Interfaces

Default Gateway

Firewall & HA

Summary

Summary

Name:	LabEdge01		Size:	Compact
Tenant:			HA:	Disabled

Auto rule generation: Enabled   Rule Priority: High

Description:

Edge Appliances:

Resource Pool	Host	Datastore	Folder
Lab Cluster	esx5501.training.l:	Web Zone Data	Edge Appliances

Interfaces:

vNIC#	Name	IP Address	Subnet Mask	Connected To
0	LabEdge01_Up	10.10.10.1*	255.255.255.0	DMZ Network
1	LabEdge01_Mc	192.168.10.2*	255.255.255.0	Internal Netwo

Previous   Next   Finish   Cancel

7. Click on **Finish**.

How it works...

vShield Edge provides network security and gateway services through isolating virtual machines in standalone or distributed port groups. The isolated networks, known as stub networks, are uplinked to other networks via a gateway. vShield Edge is commonly used for multitenant environments where several organizations share a common infrastructure such as cloud or hosting scenarios. Deployments of VPN extranets and DMZ infrastructures can also be implemented with virtual components, which reduces the cost of the networking and security hardware.

The installation of vShield Edge requires three main configuration tasks: creating a gateway instance, adding an appliance, and adding interfaces to communicate with uplink and protected networks.

The vShield Edge gateway is an instance that contains the appliance and interface components that make up the base implementation. In our example, we set up a single gateway with default CLI credentials. The internal subnets used are RFC 1918-compliant private addresses.

The vShield Edge appliance is the core of vShield Edge functionality and should be sized appropriately. In our example, we selected a compact size appliance that requires only 256MB of memory. For most production scenarios, a large size appliance should be sufficient. High Availability for the vShield Edge appliance is also recommended for fault tolerance. The details of the vShield Edge instances are as follows:

- ▸ **Compact**: 256 MB memory and 200 MB disk space
- ▸ **Large**: 1 GB memory and 256 MB disk space
- ▸ **Extra Large**: 8 GB memory and 256 MB disk space

> Note that an X-Large size appliance does not support SSL VPN.

At least one internal and one uplink interface must be added to the appliance in order to provide connectivity from the private network to the public or external network. In our example, a DMZ network and an internal network were added.

> Note that at least one internal interface must be present for HA to function.

Managing appliances

When at least one vShield Edge appliance has been configured and deployed, the status of the edge can be viewed from the data center network virtualization tab within vCenter. In addition to monitoring, the configuration settings for the appliance can be managed from the same interface within vSphere Client.

Getting ready

In order to proceed, we require access to vShield App through the vSphere Client plugin. The client can be run on any modern Windows desktop operating system or server operating system.

> The vShield vSphere Client plugin requires Adobe Flash, which is not supported on Linux operating systems at this time.

Ensure the vCenter account used to log in has administrative rights to vShield Manager.

How to do it...

Perform the following steps:

1. Launch vSphere Client using an account with administrative rights, if it is not already open.

2. Navigate to **Home | Inventory | Hosts and Clusters** from the menu bar.

3. Navigate to **Datacenter**.

4. Select the **Network Virtualization** tab.

5. Navigate to **Actions | Manage** to open a vShield Edge.

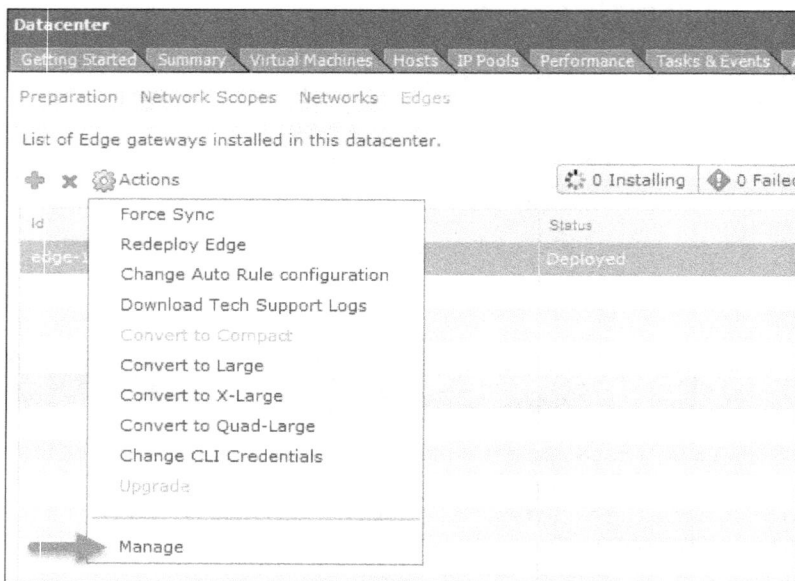

6. Click on the **Statistics** tab to display the current throughput and connection information.

7. Select the **Settings** tab to display the Edge settings.

8. Settings for **Syslog** servers, **HA**, and **DNS** configuration can be amended by clicking on **Change** in the appropriate content area.

9. Highlight the **LabEdge01-0** Edge appliance and click on the pencil icon to edit.

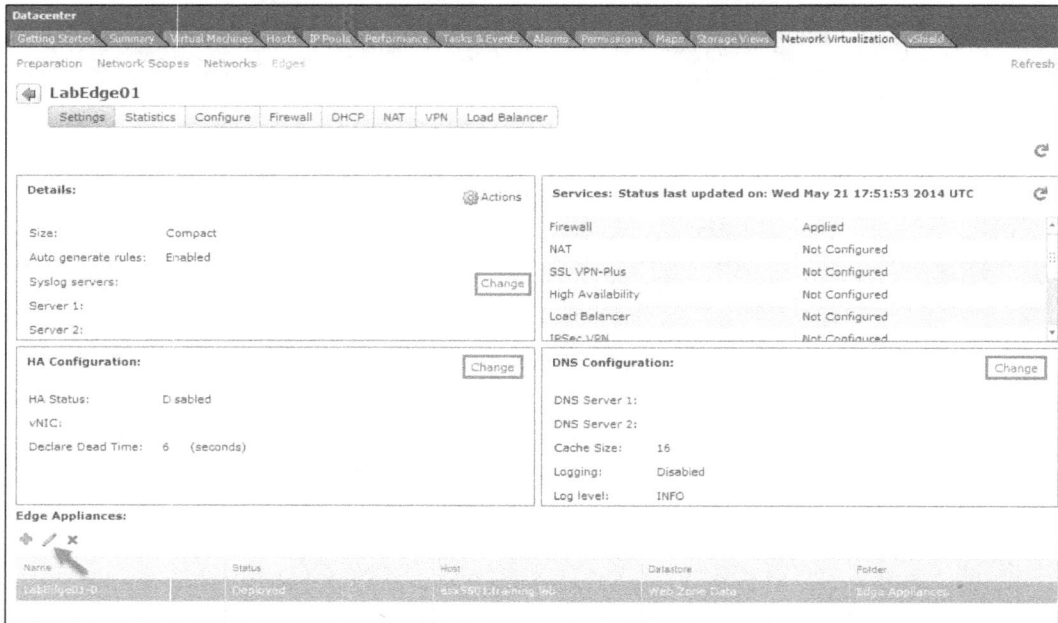

10. The **Edit Edge Appliance** dialog box allows the appliance to be moved within the vSphere environment. In our example, we can change the values for **Datastore, Host,** and **Folder.**

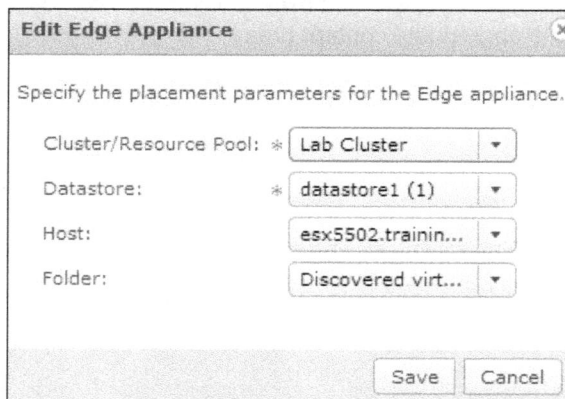

11. Click on **Cancel** to close without saving the changes.

How it works...

vShield Edge appliances can be modified to use an alternate cluster or resource pool, datastore, host, or folder. The appliance can be moved to a different datastore, for example, by selecting a new datastore while editing the appliance and saving the configuration. Normally, no further configuration is required, especially if HA is enabled for fault tolerance.

Managing interfaces

A vShield Edge gateway can have up to 10 **virtual network cards** (**vNIC**). These interfaces can be utilized as two types: Internal and Uplink. vShield Edge must have at least one internal interface defined before it can be deployed.

Getting ready

In order to proceed, we require access to vShield App through the vSphere Client plugin. The client can be run on any modern Windows desktop operating system or server operating system.

> The vShield vSphere Client plugin requires Adobe Flash, which is not supported on Linux operating systems at this time.

Ensure the vCenter account used to log in has administrative rights to vShield Manager.

How to do it...

Perform the following steps:

1. Launch vSphere Client using an account with administrative rights, if it is not already open.
2. Navigate to **Home** | **Inventory** | **Hosts and Clusters** from the menu bar.
3. Navigate to **Datacenter**.
4. Select the **Network Virtualization** tab.
5. Navigate to **Actions** | **Manage** to open vShield Edge.

6. Select the **Configure** tab, and then, click on the **Interfaces** link.

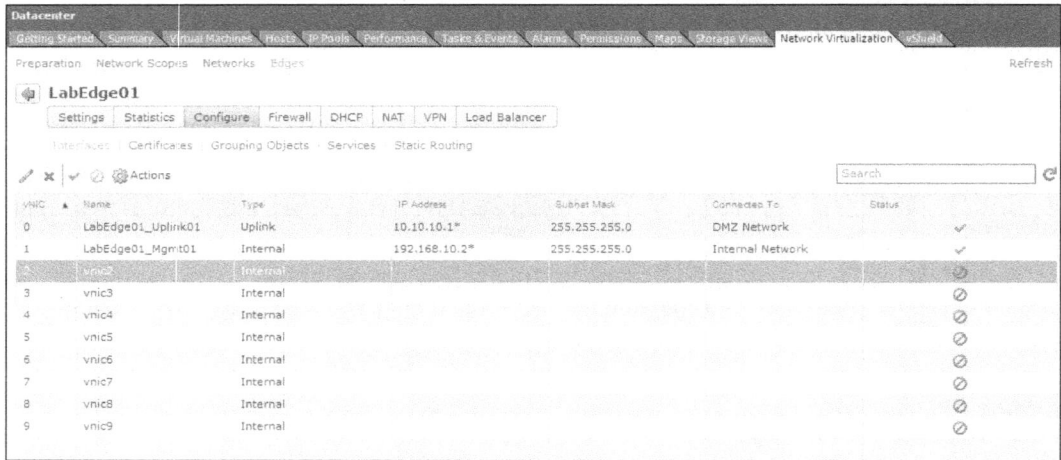

7. Highlight **vnic2** and then click on the pencil icon.

8. Edit the Edge interface to allow traffic to the **PII_dvPortGroup** distributed port group.

9. Set the type as **Internal** and **Name** to **LabEdge01_PII_Net01**.

10. Set **Connectivity Status** to **Connected**.

11. Add an IP address of **10.10.30.1** with a subnet mask of **255.255.255.0**.

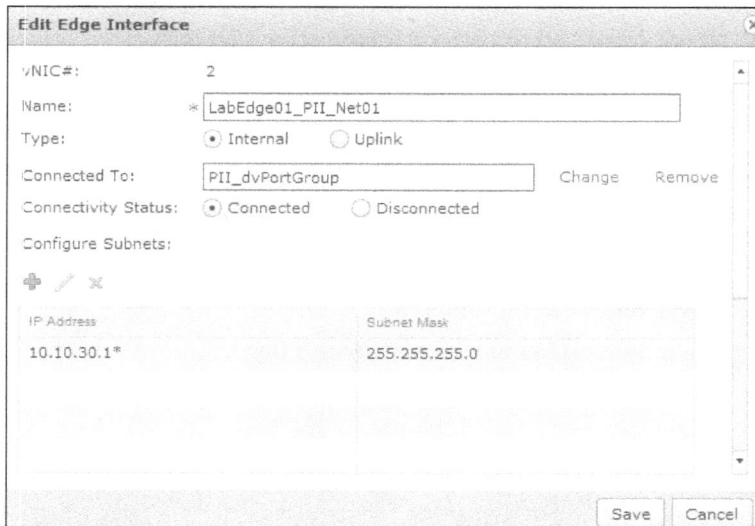

12. Click on **Save**.

13. Note that **vNIC 2** is now configured and connected.

vNIC	Name	Type	IP Address	Subnet Mask	Connected To	Status
0	LabEdge01_Uplink01	Uplink	10.10.10.1*	255.255.255.0	DMZ Network	✓
1	LabEdge01_Mgmt01	Internal	192.168.10.2*	255.255.255.0	Internal Network	✓
2	LabEdge01_P1_Net01	Internal	10.10.30.1*	255.255.255.0	P1_dvPortGroup	✓

How it works...

The interfaces on a vShield Edge instance are analogous to the interfaces on a physical firewall such as a Cisco ASA. Interfaces can be added, altered, or deleted through the **Configure interfaces** interface within vSphere Client. In our example, we added an additional interface to allow access to a private classified network through a distributed switch port group.

Managing certificates and revocation lists

Certificates can be assigned for use with VPN if required. A trusted certificate can be obtained by a private (internal) certificate authority, a public certificate authority such as Verisign, or a number of other providers. Revocation lists are checked periodically to ensure that a certificate that has been issued has not been revoked for any reason and is still valid.

Getting ready

In order to proceed, we require access to vShield App through the vSphere Client plugin. The client can be run on any modern Windows desktop operating system or server operating system.

> The vShield vSphere Client plugin requires Adobe Flash, which is not supported on Linux operating systems at this time.

Ensure the vCenter account used to log in has administrative rights to vShield Manager.

How to do it...

Perform the following steps:

1. Launch vSphere Client using an account with administrative rights, if it is not already open.

2. Navigate to **Home | Inventory | Hosts and Clusters** from the menu bar.

3. Navigate to **Datacenter**.

4. Select the **Network Virtualization** tab.

5. Navigate to **Actions | Manage** to open the **LabEdge01** vShield Edge.

6. Select the **Configure** tab, and then, click on the **Certificates** link.

7. Navigate to **Actions | Generate CSR**.

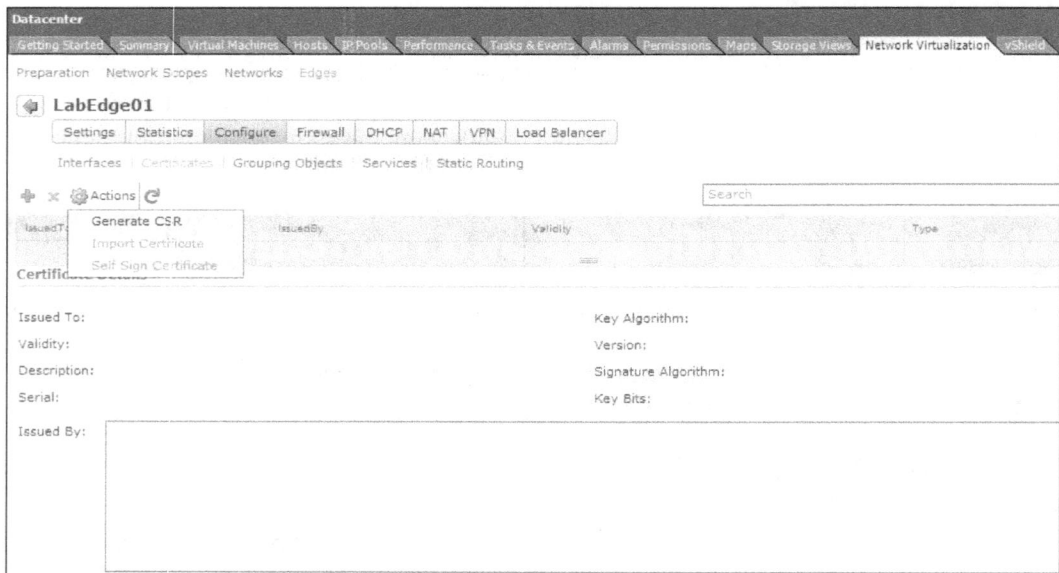

8. Enter a **Common Name** (in our example, **LabEdge01**).

9. Enter an **Organization Name** (in our example, **Training Lab**).

10. Verify that **Message Algorithm** is **RSA** and **Key Size** is **2048**.

Generate CSR   ⊗

Common Name:	∗ LabEdge01
Organization Name:	∗ Training Lab
Organization Unit:	
Locality:	
State:	
Country:	▾
Message Algorithm:	RSA ▾ Key Size: 2048 ▾
Description:	

                                                              Ok   Cancel

11. Click on **Ok** to generate a request.

12. Copy the **Pem Encoding** request, as shown in the following screenshot, and submit it to the appropriate CA for processing.

Datacenter

Getting Started | Summary | Virtual Machines | Hosts | IP Pools | Performance | Tasks & Events | Alarms | Permissions | Maps

Preparation   Network Scopes   Networks   Edges

⊕ **LabEdge01**

| Settings | Statistics | Configure | Firewall | DHCP | NAT | VPN | Load Balancer |

Interfaces | Certificates | Grouping Objects | Services | Static Routing

⊕ ✕ ⚙ Actions | ⟳   Search

IssuedTo	IssuedBy	Validity
LabEdge01		

Certificate Details

Algorithm:	RSA		Key Bits:	2048
Description:			Revision:	1
Name:	LabEdge01		Type:	CSR

Pem Encoding:

```
-----BEGIN CERTIFICATE REQUEST-----
MIICbjCCAVYCAQAwKzESMBAGA1UEAwwJTGFiRWRnZTAxMRUwEwYDVQQKDAxUcmFp
bmluZyBMYWIwggEiMA0GCSqGSIb3DQEBAQUAA4IBDwAwggEKAoIBAQC+1uVY65VR
eoS770PDMIv5+2C1Y65NACeeIlsIvhqZlbTJl/RhxSj9QbDIZXk9Ap+vGA1NWoW+
57rbwfchrIw5mj8nV9Jk15XeyzSSlD6jY1cVm41asNlVZN20T7+TvLG4rlQwzYtj
i0/LgXrCgINIaz+2AvHP88H+TBRftyP0eMd/KruIYAD4/P/3mZ/2LJu3SG6WlO+e
3QPu0tyfhrmEYvNO0q8IKLdFyKCaj8O+N1y4QsGSWaPIzzQ1ewYRF8Ba2X6/Dpb5
lRj7BZkos1Si6JEOXvgfzwHznOuY/TQNH6koV98Vd45GreVTSPxTEJP9TbCs3Vgn
i2TLIbOqnbcZAgMBAAEwDQYJKoZIhvcNAQELBQADggEBAJxCqnSFycnxJtlEd0AD
J0D4RIrYjGZBmvaiG9uVPkueHE5yT1agTgZmi5BNQgAZXvJnBmEwX2kgqERcI46j
hYIYJGVo0WQm3kteEGwRmwtuvepYSUEyzh4cjiQHrP+paJH8jPsEHyB/+qy2iE88
nSIR1ranTW0jV2Fk938dn33cuXO+a0oWvRi+5bl8gSaQnOkkjRE/bBk9GICHVdGb
8bJanXRWXr5YJjHO+oYDepeCmipJ/0KZn4h3cO8zuxrBIxBfa0hmIN7RpOhZGD5M
qIauc6WrarjXnb4R72hhuWXqFt+VwmQu4m6992/frkXGiy8iJvhmI60rCm5AdKVm
oXk=
-----END CERTIFICATE REQUEST-----
```

13. Once the certificate has been issued by the CA, open the certificate in a notepad and copy the contents.

14. Navigate to **Actions | Import Certificate**.

15. Paste the certificate into the **Import Certificate** dialog box.

16. Click on **Ok**.

17. Note that the certificate is now shown as valid.

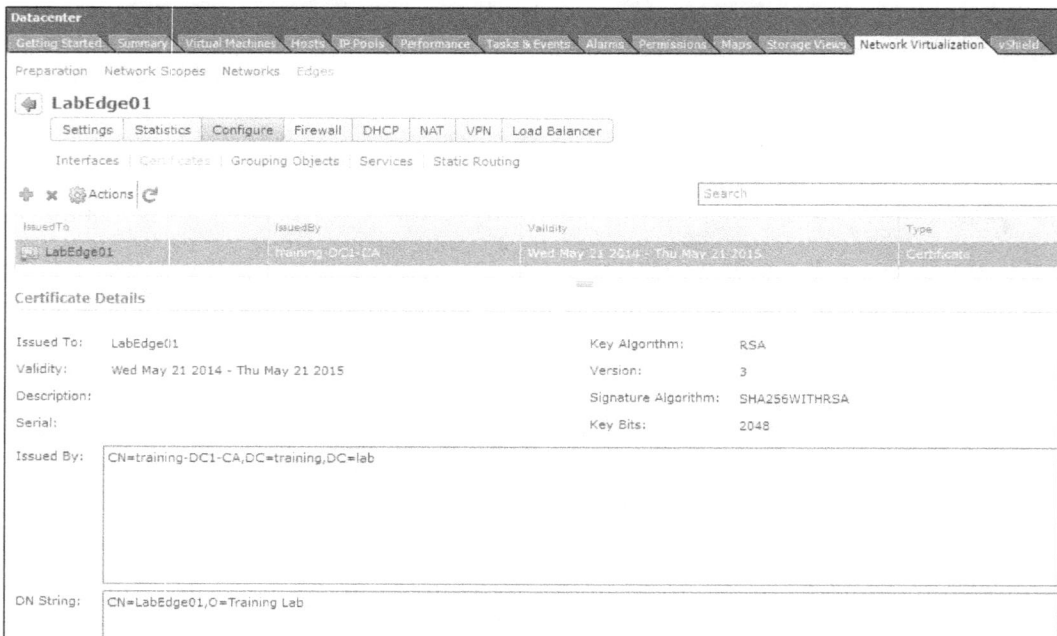

18. To add the associated certificate revocation list, click on **+** and **CRL**. The CRL lists revoked certificates with the reason for revocation, including expiration. The CRL ensures that the certificate is valid for use.

19. Open the `file.crl` file in a notepad and copy the entire contents.

20. Paste the CRL into the **Add CRL** dialog box and add a description.

21. Click on **Ok**.

22. Follow the same process to import the CA certificate.

23. Note the item type to confirm the **CA Certificate**, **Certificate,** and **CRL** are loaded and valid.

IssuedTo	IssuedBy	Validity	Type
LabEdge01	training-DC1-CA	Wed May 21 2014 - Thu May 21 2015	Certificate
training-DC1-CA	training-DC1-CA	Mon May 19 2014 - Sun May 19 2024	CA
training-DC1-CA	training-DC1-CA	Next Update: Tue May 27 2014	CRL

How it works...

Requesting and generating certificates is a laborious task that involves a number of steps with a number of different systems. For many, working with certificates can be a frustrating experience if a step is missed during the process.

In our example, we create a CSR and send it to our certificate authority for processing. Once the certificate is issued, this is installed to vShield Edge along with the certificate revocation list and the certificate authority root certificate. By installing a valid certificate IPsec, VPN, and SSL, VPN-Plus can now use a certificate as an alternative form of authentication to a pre-shared key.

See also

▶ For more information on IPsec, VPN, and SSL, refer to *Chapter 1, Threat and Vulnerability Overview*

▶ For more information on certificates, refer to *Chapter 12, Configuring vSphere Certificates*

Managing firewall rules

vShield Edge provides port-level firewall functionality to isolate and allow specific traffic between networks configured on a given vShield Edge gateway. Firewall rule management consists of the source, destination, and traffic type as categorized by predefined services.

Getting ready

In order to proceed, we require access to vShield App through the vSphere Client plugin. The client can be run on any modern Windows desktop operating system or server operating system.

> The vShield vSphere Client plugin requires Adobe Flash, which is not supported on Linux operating systems at this time.

Ensure the vCenter account used to log in has administrative rights to vShield Manager.

How to do it...

Perform the following steps:

1. Launch vSphere Client using an account with administrative rights, if it is not already open.
2. Navigate to **Home** | **Inventory** | **Hosts and Clusters** from the menu bar.
3. Navigate to **Datacenter**.
4. Select the **Network Virtualization** tab.
5. Navigate to **Actions** | **Manage** to open the **LabEdge01** vShield Edge.
6. Select the **Firewall** tab to view current rules.

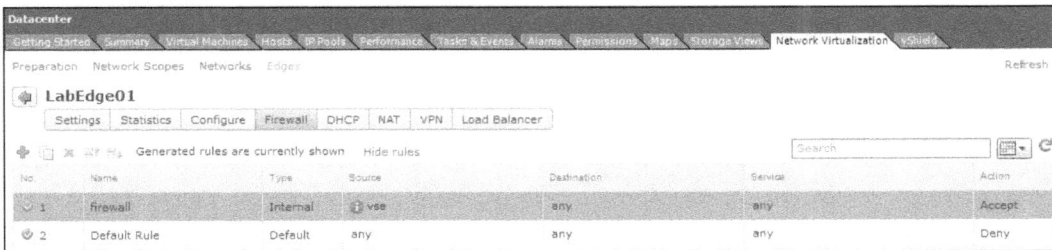

7. Click on **+** to add a rule.
8. Name the rule (in our example, **Allow SMTP**).

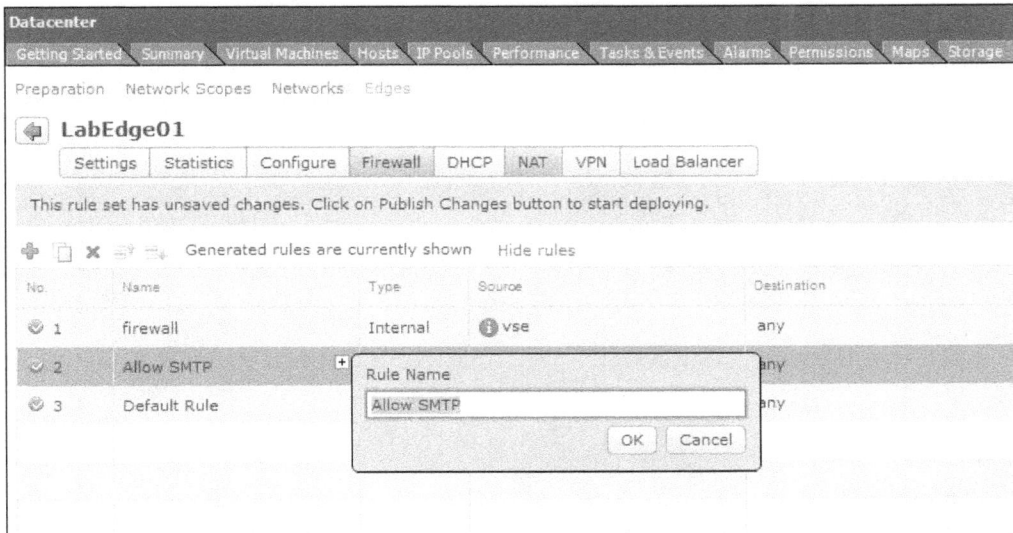

9. Click on **OK**.

10. Click on **+** in the **Service** column to add the traffic type to the rule.

11. Type smtp in the search box and select **SMTP_TLS** and **SMTP**.

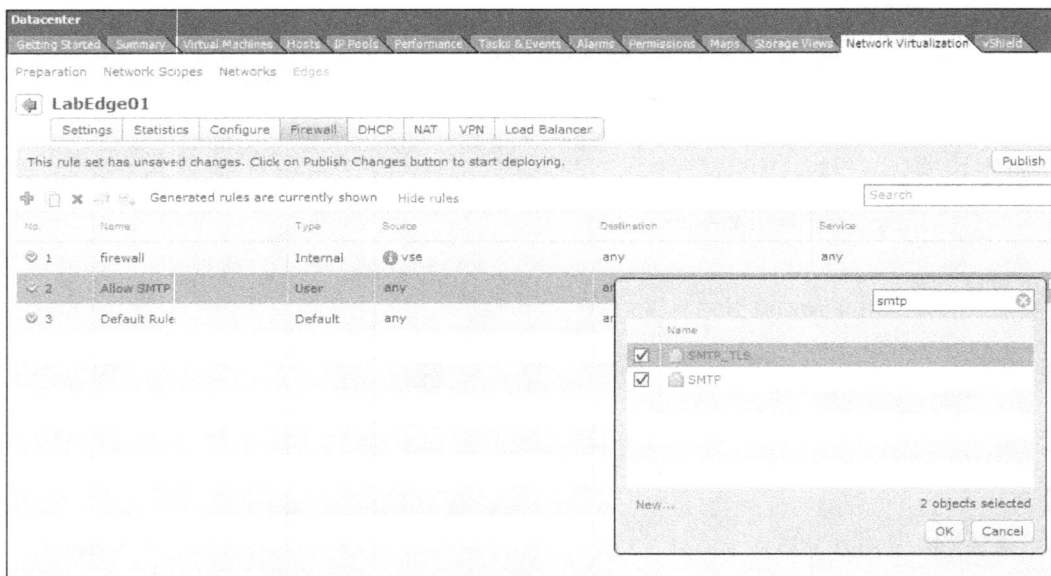

12. Click on **OK**.

13. Click on **+** in the **Destination** column to add the traffic destination.

14. Select **VnicGroup** from the drop-down box.

15. Select the **internal** VnicGroup.

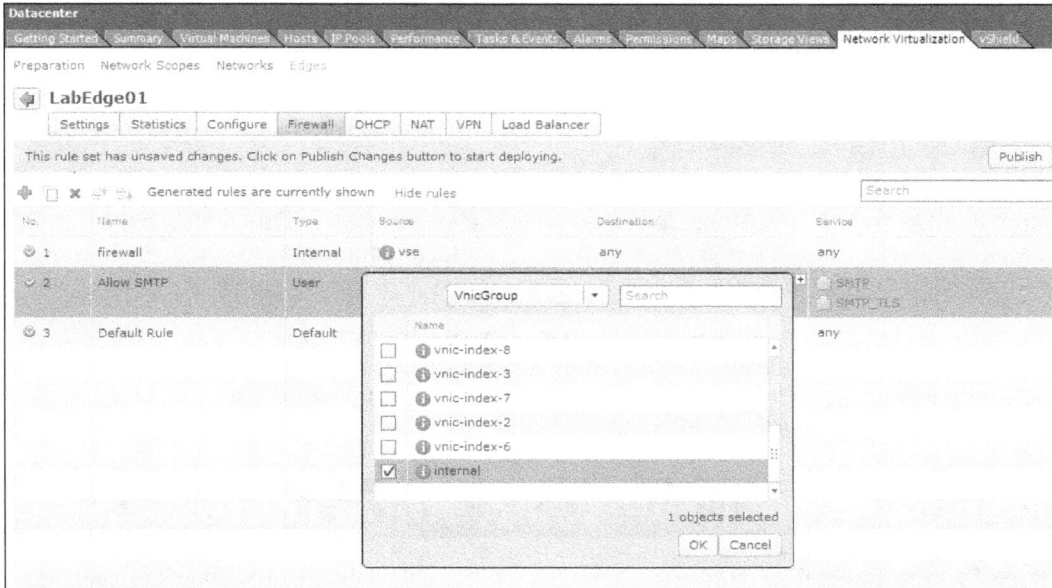

16. Click on **OK**.
17. Click on **+** in the **Source** column to add the traffic source.
18. Select **VnicGroup** from the drop-down box.
19. Select the **external** VnicGroup.

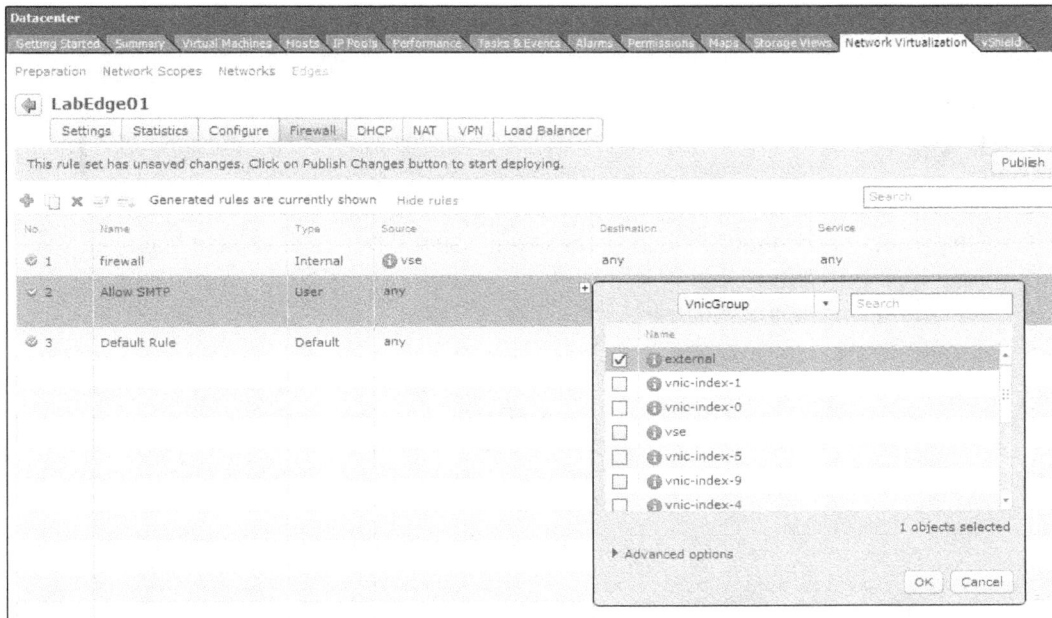

20. Click on **OK**.

21. Click on **Publish** to activate the rule.

How it works...

vShield Edge Firewall allows both source and destination rule definitions to be defined by either IP address(es) or VnicGroup. In our example, we selected a VnicGroup for the SMTP rule. The use of IP address is more granular between a range of addresses or even a single host IP address for allowed or denied traffic.

Alternatively, the VnicGroup allows definition of allowed or denied traffic at the virtual NIC group level. Using a VnicGroup, we can define a rule for any traffic moving from an interface in the external group to an interface in the internal group. Care should be taken when assigning rules within vShield Edge to ensure proper security and functionality.

Managing NAT rules and static routes

Name Address Translation (**NAT**) rules are often used to shield internal IP address ranges from those used in the public Internet. vShield Edge offers **Source NAT** (**SNAT**) and **Destination NAT** (**DNAT**) rule types. Static routes can also be defined when required to ensure that traffic reaches the correct subnet via a predetermined gateway.

Getting ready

In order to proceed, we require access to vShield App through the vSphere Client plugin. The client can be run on any modern Windows desktop operating system or server operating system.

> The vShield vSphere Client plugin requires Adobe Flash, which is not supported on Linux operating systems at this time.

Ensure the vCenter account used to log in has administrative rights to vShield Manager.

How to do it...

Perform the following steps:

1. Launch vSphere Client using an account with administrative rights, if it is not already open.

2. Navigate to **Home | Inventory | Hosts and Clusters** from the menu bar.

3. Navigate to **Datacenter**.

4. Select the **Network Virtualization** tab.

5. Navigate to **Actions | Manage** to open the **LabEdge01** vShield Edge.

6. Select the **NAT** tab. Source and Destination NAT are described in the *How it works...* section of this recipe.

7. Click on **+** and **Add DNAT Rule** to add a Destination NAT rule.

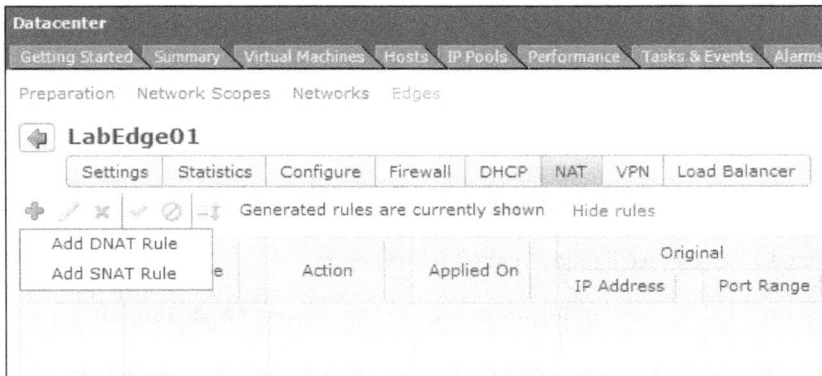

8. Within the **Add DNAT Rule** dialog box, verify that **Applied On** is set to **LabEdge01_Public**.

9. Enter a valid **Original IP/Range** (in our example, **67.154.180.244**).

10. Enter a valid **Protocol** (in our example, **tcp**).

11. Enter a valid **Translated IP/Range** (in our example, **10.10.10.10**).

12. Enter a valid **Translated Port/Range** (in our example, **80**).

13. Provide a brief description.

14. Check boxes for **Enabled** and **Enable logging**.

15. Click on **Add**.
16. Click on **Publish Changes** in the prompted window.

To add a Source NAT rule, we'll follow a similar procedure:

1. Click on **+** in the Datacenter window and click on **Add SNAT Rule** to add a Source NAT rule.
2. Within the **Add SNAT Rule** dialog box, verify that **Applied On** is set to **LabEdge01_Public**.
3. Enter a valid **Original Source IP/Range** (in our example, **67.154.180.243**).
4. Enter a valid **Translated Source IP/Range** (in our example, **10.10.10.1**).
5. Provide a brief description.
6. Check the boxes for **Enabled** and **Enable logging**.

Add SNAT Rule

Applied On:	LabEdge01_Public ▼
Original Source IP/Range: *	67.154.180.243
Translated Source IP/Range: *	10.10.10.1
Description:	inbound to gateway

☑ Enabled
☑ Enable logging

Add   Cancel

7. Click on **Add**.

8. Click on **Publish Changes**.

9. Confirm whether the rules are active.

Datacenter

Getting Started Summary Virtual Machines Hosts Networks IP Pools Performance Tasks & Events Alarms Permissions Maps Storage Views Network Virtualization vShield

Preparation   Network Scopes   Networks   Edges   Refresh

LabEdge01

Settings Statistics Configure Firewall DHCP NAT VPN Load Balancer

Generated rules are currently shown   Hide rules   Search

Order	Rule Type	Action	Applied On	Original IP Address	Original Port Range	Translated IP Address	Translated Port Range	Protocol	Status	Logging
1	USER	DNAT	LabEdge01_Pub	67.154.180.244	any	10.10.10.10	80	tcp	✓	✓
2	USER	SNAT	LabEdge01_Pub	67.154.180.243	any	10.10.10.1	any	any	✓	✓

Static Routes are set up through the Edge configuration menu by performing the following steps:

1. Launch vSphere Client using an account with administrative rights, if it is not already open.

2. Navigate to **Home | Inventory | Hosts and Clusters** from the menu bar.

3. Navigate to **Datacenter**.

4. Select the **Network Virtualization** tab.

5. Navigate to **Actions | Manage** to open the **LabEdge01** vShield Edge.

6. Select the **Configure** tab and the **Static Routing** link.

7. Click on **+** to add a static route statement.

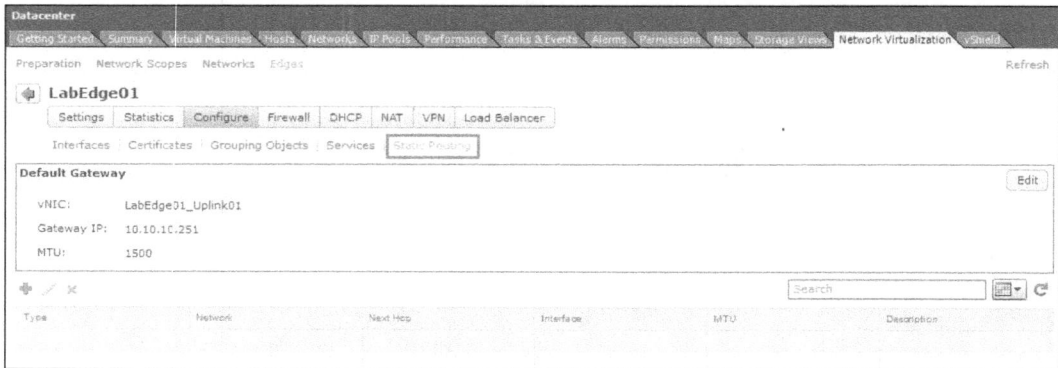

8. Within the **Edit Static Route** dialog box, enter a description.
9. Enter a valid **Interface** (in our example, **LabEdge01_Uplink01**).
10. Enter a valid **Network** (in our example, **30.30.30.0/24**).
11. Enter a valid **Next Hop** (in our example, **10.10.10.2**).
12. Enter a valid **MTU** (the default value is **1500**).

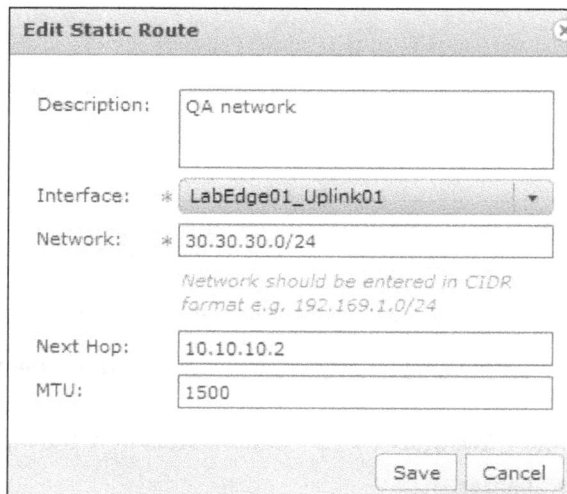

13. Click on **Save**.

14. Click on **Publish Changes**.

15. Confirm the new Static Route to the QA network.

How it works...

The concept of NAT has been around for quite a while and most, if not all, companies are implementing a NAT scheme in some form to keep a private IP range used internally segregated from the public Internet. vShield Edge offers similar NAT capabilities to those found in most firewalls today.

Destination NAT is used to expose or publish an internal IP address to the public Internet as a valid IP address. In our example, we published a web server with a private IP of **10.10.10.10** to a public IP address of **67.154.180.244**. This allows web traffic to be received on an Internet IP and its address translated to the private IP.

Source NAT provides a more generic rule for traffic typically from a private IP to a public IP. In our example, we are allowing all traffic destined for public IP **67.154.180.243** to be translated to **10.10.10.1**, which is part of the DMZ network.

Static routing allows traffic destined for a target network to find its way to that network by means of a defined gateway. Our example has another network that machines on the DMZ network need to access; however, they have no route to get there. Our new static route allows machines on the **10.10.10.0/24** network to utilize the **10.10.10.2** gateway to reach the **30.30.30.0/24** network.

Managing the IPSec VPN service

vShield Edge supports site-to-site IPSec VPN tunnels to remote sites. The remote site endpoint can be another vShield Edge instance or a number of other hardware-based endpoints such as a Cisco ASA. vShield Edge IPSec VPN supports pre-shared key and certificate authentication.

Getting ready

In order to proceed, we require access to vShield App through the vSphere Client plugin. The client can be run on any modern Windows desktop operating system or server operating system.

> The vShield vSphere Client plugin requires Adobe Flash, which is not supported on Linux operating systems at this time.

Ensure the vCenter account used to log in has administrative rights to vShield Manager.

How to do it...

Perform the following steps:

1. Launch vSphere Client using an account with administrative rights, if it is not already open.
2. Navigate to **Home | Inventory | Hosts and Clusters** from the menu bar.
3. Navigate to **Datacenter**.
4. Select the **Network Virtualization** tab.
5. Navigate to **Actions | Manage** to open the **LabEdge01** vShield Edge.
6. Select the **VPN** tab and **IPSec VPN** link.
7. Click on **+** to add a VPN.

8. Within the **Edit IPSec VPN** dialog box, ensure that **Enabled** is checked.

9. Enter the **Name** (in our example, **Remote Office**).

10. Enter a valid **Local Id** (in our example, a public IP of **67.154.180.242**).

11. Enter a valid **Local Endpoint** (in our example, **10.10.10.1**).

12. Enter valid **Local Subnets** (in our example, **192.168.10.0/24**).

13. Enter a valid **Peer Id** (in our example, **98.102.255.101**).

14. Enter a valid **Peer Endpoint** (in our example, **10.20.10.3**).

15. Enter valid **Peer Subnets** (in our example, **192.168.20.0/24**).

16. Select an **Encryption Algorithm** (in our example, **AES**).

17. Confirm that the value of **Authentication** is at the default of **PSK**. Note that the **Certificate** option is not available. The **Pre-Shared Key** is simply a secret string that allows two or more endpoints to communicate securely.

18. Enter a **Pre-Shared Key**.

19. Accept the default values for **Diffle-Hellman Group**, **MTU**, and **PFS**.

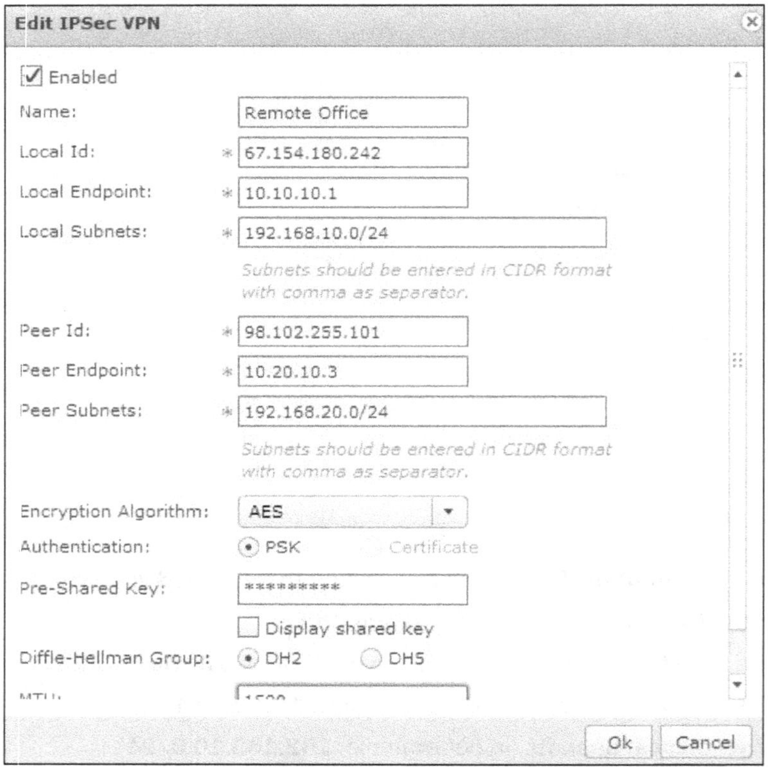

Edit IPSec VPN

☑ Enabled

Name:	Remote Office
Local Id:	✳ 67.154.180.242
Local Endpoint:	✳ 10.10.10.1
Local Subnets:	✳ 192.168.10.0/24

Subnets should be entered in CIDR format with comma as separator.

Peer Id:	✳ 98.102.255.101
Peer Endpoint:	✳ 10.20.10.3
Peer Subnets:	✳ 192.168.20.0/24

Subnets should be entered in CIDR format with comma as separator.

Encryption Algorithm:	AES ▾
Authentication:	⦿ PSK Certificate
Pre-Shared Key:	✳✳✳✳✳✳✳✳
	☐ Display shared key
Diffle-Hellman Group:	⦿ DH2 ◯ DH5
MTU:	1500

Ok   Cancel

20. Click on **Ok** to save and close the dialog box.

21. Click on **Enable** to enable the VPN.

22. Click on **Publish Changes** to activate the VPN service.

23. Once active, the VPN status will show **Enabled**.

A certificate can be used instead of a pre-shared key. To allow the use of a certificate, the global configuration must be completed. To apply a global configuration, perform the following steps:

1. Click on the **Change** link next to **Global Configuration status**.
2. Within the **Global Configuration** dialog box, check **Enable Certificate Authentication**.
3. Select a valid service certificate (in our example, **LabEdge01**).

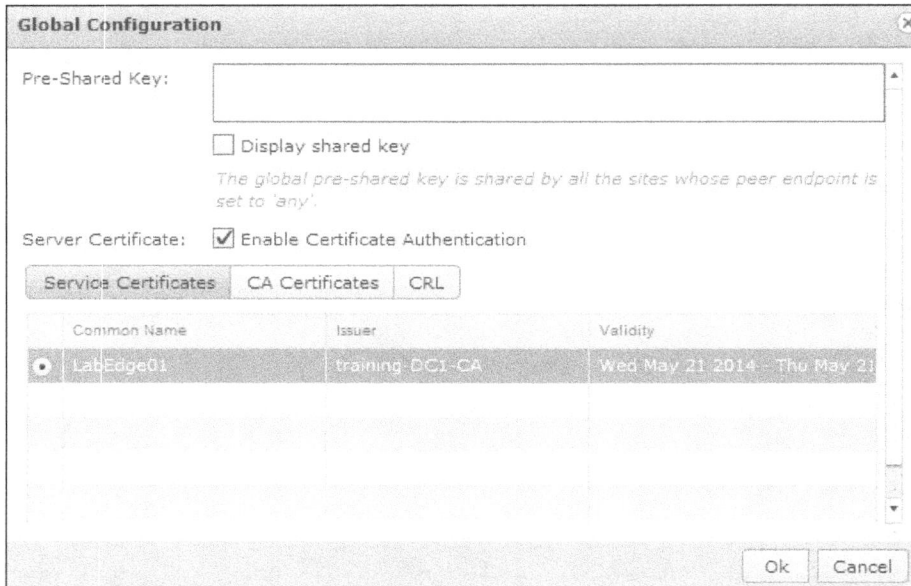

4. Click on **Ok**.
5. Edit the **Remote Office** VPN configuration.
6. Note that **Certificate** is now a valid option for **Authentication**.

Edit IPSec VPN ⊗

☑ Enabled

Name: | Remote Office

Local Id: | ＊ 67.154.180.242

Local Endpoint: | ＊ 10.10.10.1

Local Subnets: | ＊ 192.168.10.0/24

Subnets should be entered in CIDR format with comma as separator.

Peer Id: | ＊ 98.102.255.101

Peer Endpoint: | ＊ 10.20.10.3

Peer Subnets: | ＊ 192.168.20.0/24

Subnets should be entered in CIDR format with comma as separator.

Encryption Algorithm: | AES ▾

Authentication: | ◯ PSK   ⦿ Certificate

Pre-Shared Key: | ∗∗∗∗∗∗∗∗∗∗∗∗∗

☐ Display shared key

Diffle-Hellman Group: | ⦿ DH2   ◯ DH5

MTU: | 1500

Ok | Cancel

7. Click on **Cancel**.

How it works...

The vShield Edge IPSec VPN tunnel capability is on a par with that of a Cisco ASA or a CheckPoint Firewall in terms of creating a site-to-site tunnel. In our example, we've created a remote office IPSec VPN endpoint to allow another site to connect and exchange network traffic encrypted by IPSec. The encryption algorithm of AES, authentication type, and Diffle-Hellman Group type must all match the remote endpoint for the tunnel to be brought up. For more on IPSEC, please refer to *Chapter 1, Threat and Vulnerability Overview*.

Once a certificate is configured, the option to use a certificate for authentication is enabled for the tunnel configuration. While the use of a certificate is seen as a potentially more secure method of authentication, it also requires more maintenance such as certificate renewal. As a result, many production tunnels are configured with pre-shared keys.

Managing SSL VPN-Plus

The vShield Edge SSL VPN-Plus functionality provides a mechanism for remote-end users to access corporate assets over a secure connection. As with all SSL VPN solutions, a client is required to be downloaded prior to use of the SSL VPN-Plus service.

Getting ready

In order to proceed, we require access to the vShield App through the vSphere Client plugin. The client can be run on any modern Windows desktop operating system or server operating system.

> The vShield vSphere Client plugin requires Adobe Flash, which is not supported on Linux operating systems at this time.

Ensure the vCenter account used to log in has administrative rights to vShield Manager.

How to do it...

Perform the following steps:

1. Launch vSphere Client using an account with administrative rights, if it is not already open.
2. Navigate to **Home | Inventory | Hosts and Clusters** from the menu bar.
3. Navigate to **Datacenter**.
4. Select the **Network Virtualization** tab.
5. Navigate to **Actions | Manage** to open the **LabEdge01** vShield Edge.
6. Select the **VPN** tab and the **SSL VPN-Plus** link.
7. Under the **Configure** list, click on the **Server Settings** link.

8. Click on **Change** in the upper-right corner.

> The **Configure** list will be referenced after each configuration step to configure the next component.

9. Within the **Change Server Settings** dialog box, select an **IP address** (in our example, **67.154.180.244**).

10. Accept the default value (**443**) of **Port**.

11. Select **AES128-SHA** from the **Cipher List**. Ciphers listed are known as symmetric key algorithms, meaning that they use the same cryptographic keys for encryption and decryption. For more information on encryption, refer to *Chapter 1, Threat and Vulnerability Overview*.

12. Verify that **Use Default Certificate** is checked.

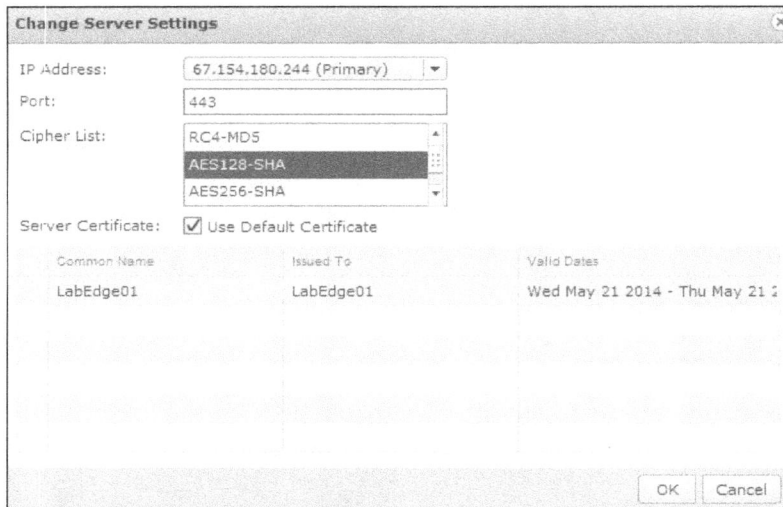

13. Click on **OK** to save the settings.

Configuring the IP pool

To configure an IP Pool for SSL VPN-Plus users, perform the following steps:

1. Under the **Configure** list, click on the **IP Pool** link.

2. Click on **+** to create a new IP pool.

3. Within the **Add IP Pool** dialog box, enter the following information.

    ❑ Valid **IP Range** (in our example, **192.168.100.10** to **192.168.100.200**).

    ❑ Valid **Netmask** (in our example, **255.255.255.0**).

    ❑ Valid **Gateway** (in our example, **192.168.100.1**).

4. Enter a brief description.

5. Enter the **Primary** and **Secondary DNS** if known (in our example, the former is **192.168.100.5**).

6. Enter the **DNS Suffix** (in our example, **training.lab**).

Add IP Pool   (x)

IP Range: * [192.168.100.10]   To [192.168.100.200]

Netmask: * [255.255.255.0]

Gateway: * [192.168.100.1]   (?)

Description: [Remote User Range   ]

Status: (•) Enabled ( ) Disabled

Advanced

Primary DNS: [192.168.100.5]

Secondary DNS: [   ]

DNS Suffix: [training.lab]

                 Example.eng.vmware.com

WINS Server: [   ]

                                                           [OK] [Cancel]

7. Click on **OK** to save the settings.

Configuring private networks

To configure private networks for SSL VPN-Plus users, perform the following steps:

1. Under the **Configure** list in **Datacenter**, click on the **Private Networks** link.
2. Click on **+** to create a new private network.
3. Within the **Add Private Network** dialog box, we'll add access to **Windows Terminal Services**.
4. Enter the target internal **Network** (in our example, **10.10.30.0**).
5. Enter a valid **Netmask** (in our example, **255.255.255.0**).
6. Enter a description.
7. Set **Send Traffic** to **Over Tunnel**.
8. Tick the checkbox for **Enable TCP Optimization**. Under the typical SSL VPN tunnel, the application data is encapsulated twice over two separate TCP streams. TCP optimization eliminates this double encapsulation for optimal performance.

9. Specify a specific port if needed; in our example, **3389** is the remote desktop port.

10. Set **Status** to **Enabled**.

> **Add Private Network**
>
> Network: * 10.10.30.0
>
> Netmask: * 255.255.255.0
>
> Description: Remote Desktop Access
>
> Send Traffic: (•) Over Tunnel ( ) Bypass Tunnel
>
>   ☑ Enable TCP Optimization
>
> Ports: 3389
>
> Status: (•) Enabled ( ) Disabled
>
>   OK   Cancel

11. Click on **Ok** to save the settings.

Configuring authentication

To configure authentication for SSL VPN-Plus users, perform the following steps:

1. Under the **Configure** list, click on the **Authentication** link.

2. Click on **+** to add an authentication server.

3. Within the **Add Server** dialog box, select the **Type** of server as **AD**.

> The search base for AD uses **Lightweight Directory Access Protocol** (**LDAP**) as a query language. Query syntax examples can be found at http://technet.microsoft.com/en-us/library/aa996205(v=EXCHG.65).aspx.

4. Enter the **IP Address** for a Domain Controller (in our example, **192.168.10.50**).

5. Accept the default value (**389**) of **Port**.

6. Accept the default **Timeout** value of **10** seconds.

7. Set **Status** to **Enabled**.

8. Enter a valid **Search base** (in our example, **OU=users,DC=training,DC=lab**).

9. Enter a valid **Bind DN** (in our case, **OU=auth,OU=users,DC=training,DC=lab**).

10. Enter the **Bind** password twice.

11. Accept the default values for **Login Attribute Name** and **Search Filter**.

Add Server			⊗
Type	AD ▾		▲
IP Address:	＊ 192.168.10.50		
Port:	＊ 389		Enable SSL: ☐
Timeout:	10	Sec(s)	
Status:	⦿ Enabled ◯ Disabled		
Advanced:			
Search base:	＊ DC=training,DC=lab		
Bind DN:	＊ DC=training,DC=lab		
Bind Password:	＊＊＊＊＊＊＊＊		
Retype Bind Password:	＊＊＊＊＊＊＊＊		
Login Attribute Name:	＊ sAMAccountName		
Search Filter:	＊ objectClass=＊		▼
		OK	Cancel

12. Click on **Ok**.

Configuring an installation package

To configure an installation package for SSL VPN-Plus users, perform the following steps:

1. Under the **Configure** list, click on the **Installation Package** link.

2. Click on **+** to create a new client installation package.

3. Within the **Add Installation Package** dialog box, enter a **Profile Name** (in our example, **Remote Clients**).

4. Enter the **Gateway** (in our example, **67.154.180.244**).

5. Accept the default port of **443** and click on **OK**.

6. Confirm **Status** is set to **Enabled**.

7. Ensure **Create desktop icon** is selected under **Installation Parameters for Windows**.

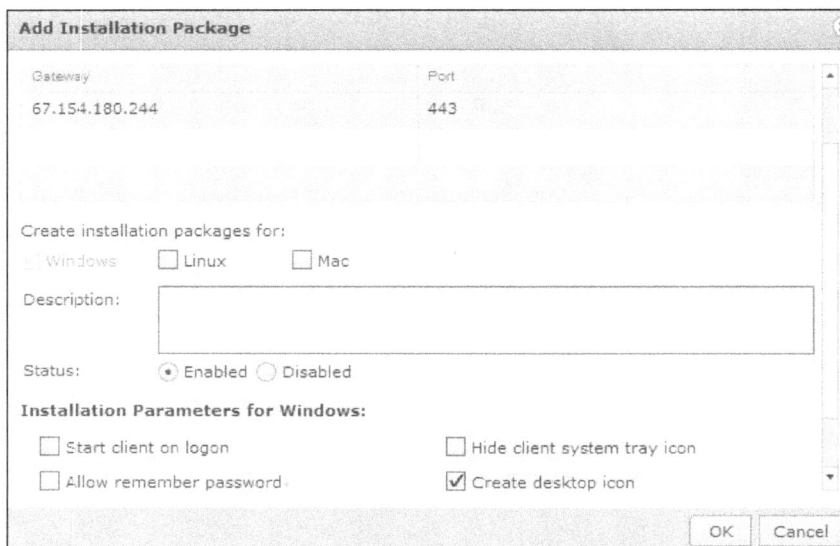

Add Installation Package

Gateway	Port
67.154.180.244	443

Create installation packages for:

☐ Windows   ☐ Linux   ☐ Mac

Description:

Status: ⦿ Enabled ○ Disabled

Installation Parameters for Windows:

☐ Start client on logon   ☐ Hide client system tray icon

☐ Allow remember password   ☑ Create desktop icon

OK   Cancel

8. Click on **OK**.

9. Review **Client Configuration** to ensure that settings such as **Auto reconnect** and **Tunneling mode** are set appropriately.

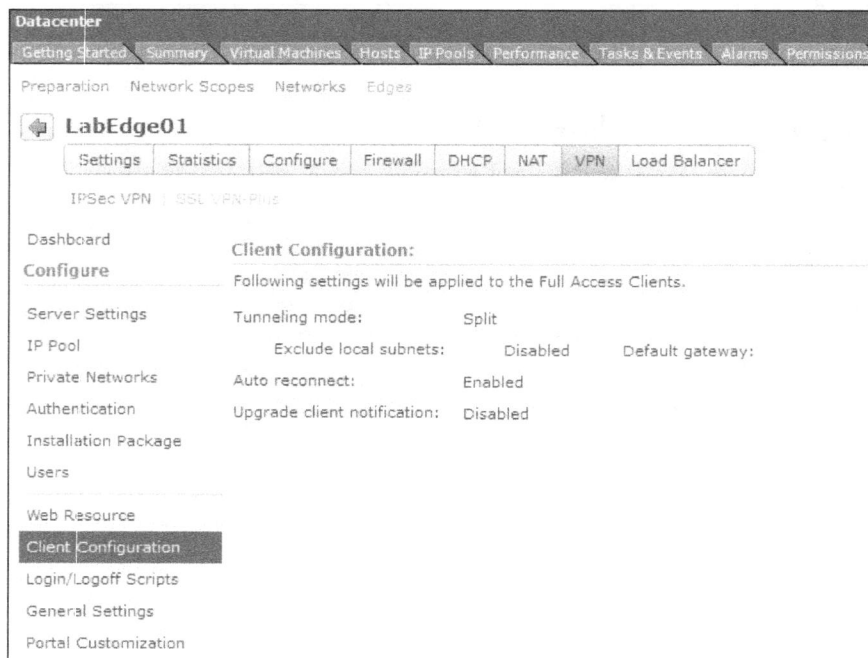

Datacenter

Getting Started | Summary | Virtual Machines | Hosts | IP Pools | Performance | Tasks & Events | Alarms | Permissions

Preparation   Network Scopes   Networks   Edges

◀ **LabEdge01**

Settings | Statistics | Configure | Firewall | DHCP | NAT | VPN | Load Balancer

IPSec VPN | SSL VPN-Plus

Dashboard

Configure

Server Settings

IP Pool

Private Networks

Authentication

Installation Package

Users

Web Resource

Client Configuration

Login/Logoff Scripts

General Settings

Portal Customization

Client Configuration:

Following settings will be applied to the Full Access Clients.

Tunneling mode:	Split	
Exclude local subnets:	Disabled	Default gateway:
Auto reconnect:	Enabled	
Upgrade client notification:	Disabled	

10. Return to **Dashboard** and click on **Enable**.

11. Click **Yes** within the **Enable SSL VPN-Plus Service** dialog box.

12. The **Service enabled successfully!** message is displayed

How it works...

vShield Edge SSL VPN-Plus requires a great deal of configuration for the service to start and receive client connections. Port 443 is required for the service to function correctly and this port must be on a public IP address available to vShield Edge.

▶ **Server Settings**: Set a valid public IP, an IP routable on the Internet. A certificate signed by a public certificate authority is highly recommended; the client device will trust the certificate by default. The minimum cipher strength recommended is AES128-SHA to ensure secure transmission.

▶ **IP Pool**: The IP pool, in most cases, should be set to a private range that is available within the organization. This pool of IP addresses will be handed out to clients that connect via a SSL VPN. Typically, a primary and secondary DNS server and DNS suffix are set. WINS should not be used or set unless absolutely necessary.

▶ **Private Networks**: Private networks should not be confused with IP pools. Private networks are networks that the clients will have access to after they establish a secure VPN connection. In our example, we're allowing Microsoft Remote Desktop Protocol traffic (TCP 3389) to our 10.10.30.0 network.

▶ **Authentication**: Simple local user authentication can be configured under the **Users** option; however, in an enterprise deployment, an existing authentication server might be utilized. In our example, we are using our internal Active Directory as the authentication source for remote users and their passwords. The **Lightweight Directory Access Protocol** (**LDAP**) syntax can be confusing; ensure that the Search base and Bind DN are correct in your particular environment.

Other valid authentication sources include LDAP, Radius, RSA-ACE, and local.

▶ **Installation Package**: The installation package must be configured so that the remote clients can download it in order to create a secure connection. The client installation package is available for Windows, Linux, and Mac. A member of the desktop support team should be consulted to ensure that the installation parameters are in line with the current desktop standards.

▶ **Client Configuration**: The most important setting in the client configuration is the option for split tunneling. Split tunneling, when enabled, allows certain corporate traffic to pass through the SSL VPN tunnel while allowing other Internet traffic to bypass the tunnel. Ensure that this setting is configured in accordance with corporate security policies and guidelines for remote users.

Configuring the load-balancing service

Load balancers are common in High Availability scenarios, particularly those involving web and database transactions. The vShield Edge load-balancing service allows traffic to be spread across the available IP addresses, reducing the load on a single host and improving performance during heavy traffic periods. The supported protocols are HTTP, HTTPS, and TCP.

Getting ready

In order to proceed, we require access to vShield App through the vSphere Client plugin. The client can be run on any modern Windows desktop operating system or server operating system.

> The vShield vSphere Client plugin requires Adobe Flash, which is not supported on Linux operating systems at this time.

Ensure the vCenter account used to log in has administrative rights to vShield Manager.

How to do it...

Perform the following steps:

1. Launch vSphere Client using an account with administrative rights, if it is not already open.

2. Choose **Home | Inventory | Hosts and Clusters** from the menu bar.

3. Navigate to **Datacenter**.

4. Select the **Network Virtualization** tab.

5. Navigate to **Actions | Manage** to open the **LabEdge01** vShield Edge.

6. Select the **Load Balancer** tab.

7. Click on **+** to add a load balancing pool.

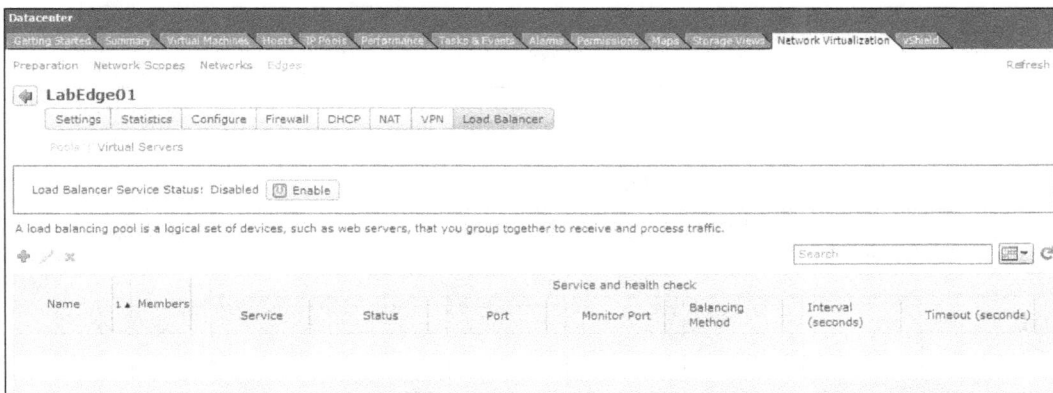

8. Within the **Add Pool** dialog box, add a value for **Name** (in our example, **Web-Pool-1**).

9. Enter a **Description** (in our example, **Web frontend load balancer**).

10. Click on **Next**.

11. Set the **HTTP** service to **Enabled**.

12. Set the **Balancing Method** to **ROUND_ROBIN**. For explanations of balancing methods, see the *How it works...* section.

13. Click on **Next**.

14. Confirm **Health Check Enabled** for the **HTTP** service. This setting checks that all servers in the pool are active and answering queries.

15. Accept the default value for **URI for HTTP service**.

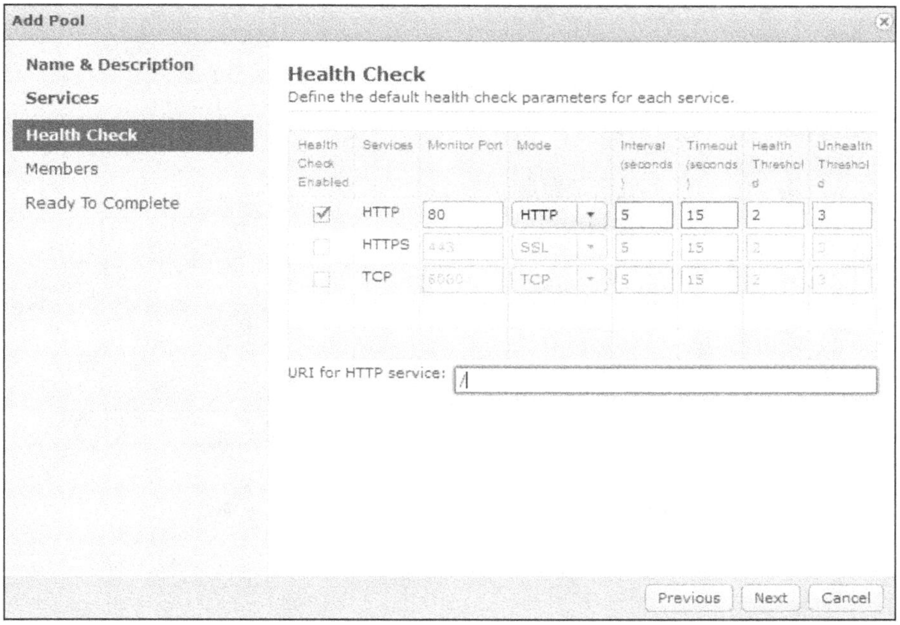

Add Pool								(x)

Name & Description
Services
Health Check
Members
Ready To Complete

Health Check
Define the default health check parameters for each service.

Health Check Enabled	Services	Monitor Port	Mode		Interval (seconds)	Timeout (seconds)	Health Threshold	Unhealth Threshold
✓	HTTP	80	HTTP	▼	5	15	2	3
☐	HTTPS	443	SSL	▼	5	15	2	3
☐	TCP	8080	TCP	▼	5	15	2	3

URI for HTTP service: [/]

Previous | Next | Cancel

16. Click on **Next**.

17. Click on **+** to add servers.

18. In the **Add Member** dialog box, set the server **IP Address** to **10.10.10.10.**

19. Click on **Add**.

20. Repeat **Add Member** with the **IP Address 10.10.10.11** server.

21. Click on **Next**

22. Click on **Finish** in **Ready to Complete** after validating the settings.

23. Click on **Enable** to start the load balancer service.

24. Click on **Publish Changes** to activate the load balancer service.

How it works...

In our example, we load-balanced two web servers to process web transactions over port 80, HTTP. The pool was created and servers added to the pool; round-robin was selected as the balancing method. Round robin uses each server in turn according to the weight assigned; in our example, an equal weight of 1 is assigned to both servers. Alternate load balancing methods include IP_HASH, LEAST_CONN, and URI.

▸ IP_HASH: This balances based on a hash of the source and destination IP address for each packet.

▸ LEAST_CONN: This balances requests to multiple servers based on the number of existing connections to that server. New connections are sent to the server with the fewest connections at that time.

> ► URI: This balances based on the left part of the Uniform Resource Identifier, which is hashed and divided by the total weight of running servers. The result determines the server that will receive the request.

The vShield Edge load balancing service also has the ability to continually check the health of servers participating in the pool, specified by the HTTP, HTTPS, or TCP services. Should a server reach the unhealthy threshold, it will be considered dead, and no further requests will be sent to it until it is marked operational by satisfying the Health Threshold.

10
Configuring vShield Endpoint

In this chapter, we will cover the following recipes:

- ► Installing vShield Endpoint
- ► Configuring vShield Endpoint using an antivirus

Introduction

The vShield Endpoint component of the vShield suite is specifically designed to enable efficient scanning of virtual machines by interfacing with third-party endpoint vendors. By allowing a security appliance to scan many virtual machines, the computing resource requirements are offloaded to a single security appliance instead of 30 virtual machines, for example. Ordinary antivirus scans take place within the OS of each VM. The vShield Endpoint scanning takes place at the hypervisor level, which minimizes compute resources and has a positive effect on virtual machine performance, including the underlying ESXi host.

Antivirus scanning is key to detecting and mitigating new threats. Endpoint protection provides another layer in the defense-in-depth methodology. As mentioned in *Chapter 1, Threat and Vulnerability Overview*, defense-in-depth utilizes endpoint protection as a monitoring and control defensive layer.

The vShield endpoint installation and configuration involves vSphere, vShield, and a third-party endpoint security product. These products provide an optimized method for antivirus scanning of a large number of virtual machines. It's important to note that an endpoint solution must already be in place to be extended to vSphere using vShield Endpoint.

vShield Endpoint provides optimized scanning by consuming resources at the hypervisor level instead of the resources of each individual virtual machine. For example, if scans were set to be run at 2 A.M., each VM will take the resources required to complete these scans. This scheduled scan can potentially cripple the host by consuming resources. Utilizing the vShield Endpoint reduces this risk by offloading the scan to minimize a potential antivirus storm.

> The VMware vShield Endpoint is not a standalone antivirus scanning engine.

VMware-approved endpoint protection solutions can be found at `http://www.vmware.com/products/vsphere/features/endpoint.html`.

Installing vShield Endpoint

The installation of vShield Endpoint requires a previously installed and running vShield Manager Version 5.5. The vShield Manager installation steps are covered in *Chapter 7, Configuring vShield Manager*. The installation of the vShield Endpoint service must be completed prior to the deployment of the third-party endpoint security appliance.

Getting started

In order to proceed, we require access to the vShield App through the vSphere Client plugin. The plugin can be enabled through the **Plug-ins** menu in vSphere Client. The client can be run on any modern Windows desktop operating system or server operating system.

> The vShield vSphere Client plugin requires Adobe Flash, which is not supported on Linux operating systems at this time.

vShield Manager must be installed and the vCenter account used for login has Enterprise Administrator rights to vShield Manager.

How to do it...

Perform the following steps to install vShield Endpoint:

1. Launch vSphere Client using an account with administrative rights, if it is not already open.

2. Navigate to **Home | Inventory | Hosts and Clusters** from the menu bar.

3. Navigate to **Datacenter | Lab Cluster | esx5501.training.lab**.

4. Select the **vShield** tab.

5. Click on the **General** option, locate vShield Endpoint, and click on **Install**.

6. Select **vShield Endpoint Installing latest version 5.1.0-01255202,** and then, click on **Install**.

7. Verify that the **vShield Endpoint** service is installed and repeat the installation for any additional hosts.

How it works...

The vShield Endpoint service is required to be running on each ESXi host that will interact with a third-party endpoint virtual appliance. Each vShield Endpoint service is installed only at the ESXi host level, not the data center, virtual machine, or network level.

The vShield Endpoint service provides an interface or hook for the third-party endpoint virtual appliance to interface and communicate with vSphere and vShield Manger.

Configuring vShield Endpoint using an antivirus

Configuring vShield Endpoint requires two main components: the third-party endpoint product and a custom installation of VMware Tools. For our examples, we'll be using Sophos Anti-Virus for VMware vShield and Sophos Enterprise Console for management of antivirus settings.

vShield Endpoint provides the structure or plumbing for third-party endpoint products to utilize. Sophos, McAfee, Trend Micro, and Symantec are just a few of the vendors that support vShield Endpoint. The vShield Endpoint component provides the mechanism to allow the third-party antivirus software to gain access to the VM through VMware Tools.

> This is not intended to be a step-by-step installation of the Sophos product. It is given out only as a reference to the relevant portions as they relate to vShield Endpoint.

Getting started

The Sophos software must be registered and a trial version downloaded from `https://www.sophos.com/en-us/products/virtualization-security/free-trial/download.aspx`.

We'll also require access to vShield App through the vSphere Client plugin. The plugin can be enabled through the **Plug-ins** menu in vSphere Client. The client can be run on any modern Windows desktop operating system or server operating system.

> The vShield vSphere Client plugin requires Adobe Flash, which is not supported on Linux operating systems at this time.

vShield Manager must be installed and the vCenter account used for login has Enterprise Administrator rights to vShield Manager.

How to do it...

Perform the following steps:

1. Install the Sophos Enterprise Console if not already available by running `sec_521r2_sfx.exe`.
2. Once the installation is complete, verify that the vShield protection platform has been installed by navigating to **View | Bootstrap Locations**.

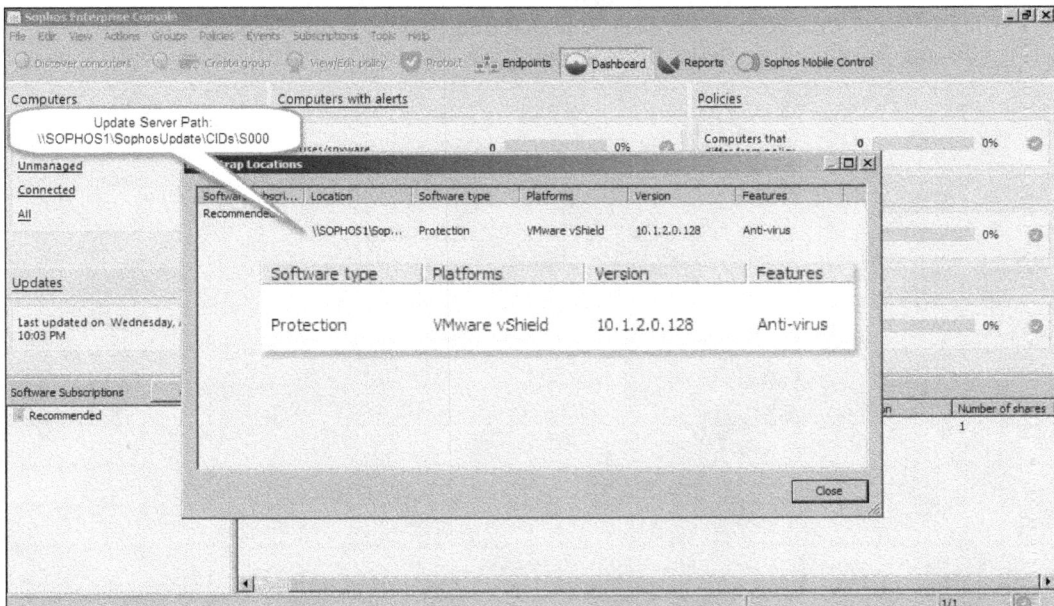

3. Install Sophos Anti-Virus for VMware vShield by running `ssvm_sfx_1_1_4.exe`.

4. Once the installation is complete, configure the ESXi hosts for deployment, as shown in the following screenshot:

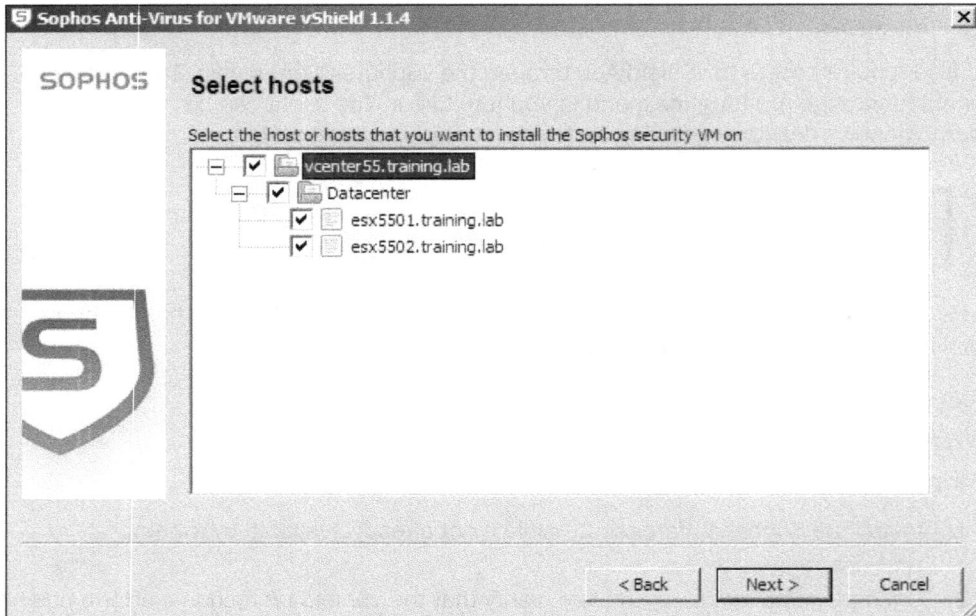

5. Once the ESXi hosts are selected, the Sophos Anti-Virus Endpoint virtual appliances will be provisioned on each host. The **esx5501-SSVM** host, for example, is the appliance bound to the **esx5501.training.lab** ESXi host.

esx5501-SSVM

Getting Started | Summary | Resource Allocation | Performance | Tasks & Events | Alarms | Console | Permissions | Maps | Storage Views | vShield

General

Product:	Sophos Anti-Virus for VMware vShield
Version:	1.1.4 (1.1.4.22)
Vendor:	Sophos Limited
Guest OS:	Other Linux (64-bit)
VM Version:	7
CPU:	2 vCPU
Memory:	2048 MB
Memory Overhead:	34.52 MB
VMware Tools:	⑦ Running (3rd-party/Independent)
IP Addresses:	192.168.10.41 View all
DNS Name:	esx5501-SSVM.training.lab
EVC Mode:	N/A
State:	Powered On
Host:	esx5501.training.lab
Active Tasks:	
vSphere HA Protection:	⑦ N/A ⬚

Resources

Consumed Host CPU:	182 MHz
Consumed Host Memory:	967.00 MB
Active Guest Memory:	81.00 MB
	Refresh Storage Usage
Provisioned Storage:	20.23 GB
Not-shared Storage:	20.23 GB
Used Storage:	20.23 GB

Storage	Status	Drive Type
🗄 Web Zone Data	⊘ Normal	Non-SSD

Network	Type	Sta
🖳 Internal Network	Standard port group	⊛
🖳 esx5501.training.l...	Standard port group	⊛
🖳 vmservice-vshield...	Standard port group	⊛

VM Storage Profiles

Refresh

VM Storage Profiles:
Profiles Compliance:

Commands

- 🖳 Shut Down Guest
- ⏸ Suspend
- 🔄 Restart Guest
- 🖆 Edit Settings
- 🖳 Open Console
- 🖳 Migrate
- 🖳 Clone to New Virtual Machine

Annotations

✎ Edit

Notes: The Sophos Anti-Virus for VMware vShield
Appliance, part of the Sophos Endpoint

> Each virtual appliance will have a network dedicated to the host, the vShield service, and the communications network (in our example, we use **Internal Network**).

Installing VMware Tools with the vShield driver is required for the third-party endpoint protection to interact with the virtual machine. To do so, please perform the following steps:

1. Launch vSphere Client using an account with administrative rights, if it is not already open.

2. Navigate to **Home | Inventory | Hosts and Clusters** from the menu bar.

3. Navigate to **Datacenter** and expand **Lab Cluster**.

4. First select a virtual machine to modify from the current inventory (in our example, we'll use **Web Server**).

5. Right-click on **Web Server** and navigate to **Guest | Install/Upgrade VMware Tools**.

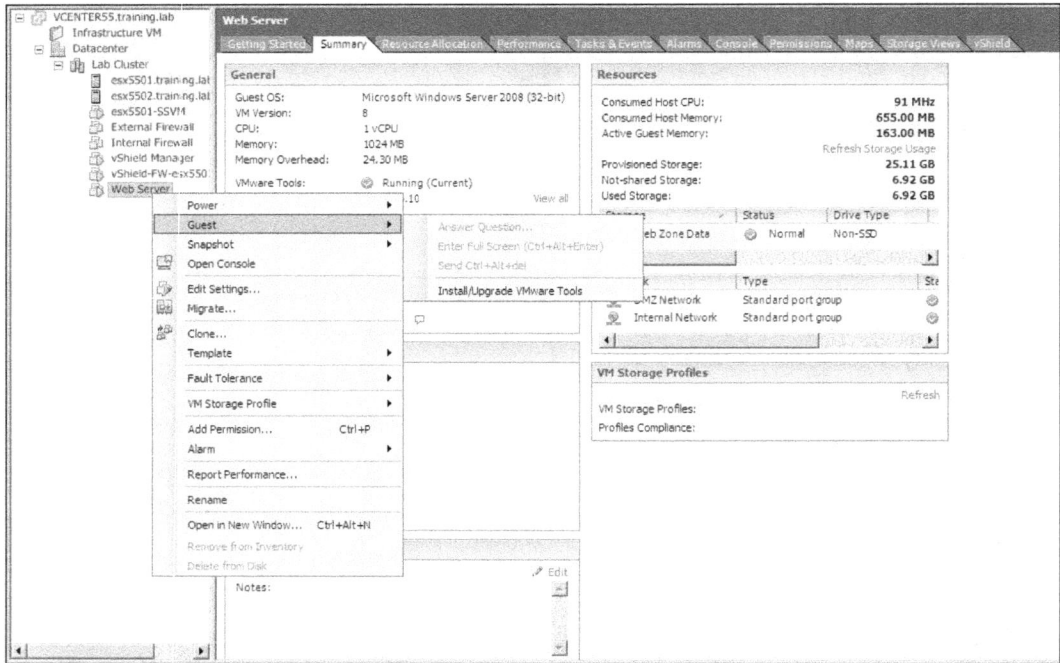

6. A dialog box will present two options: **Interactive Tools Upgrade** and **Automatic Tools Upgrade**; we'll select **Interactive Tools Upgrade** in our example.

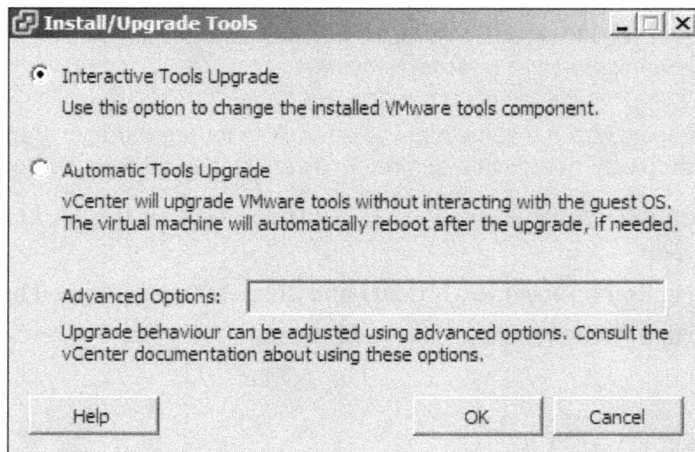

7. Click on **OK** to confirm the setting.

8. Right-click **Web Server** and click **Open Console**, this will allow interaction with the tools installer within the guest operating system.

9. With the tools installer running, select **Custom Setup**.

10. Expand the **VMCI Driver** option.

11. Select **vShield Driver** and click on **Will be installed on local hard drive**.

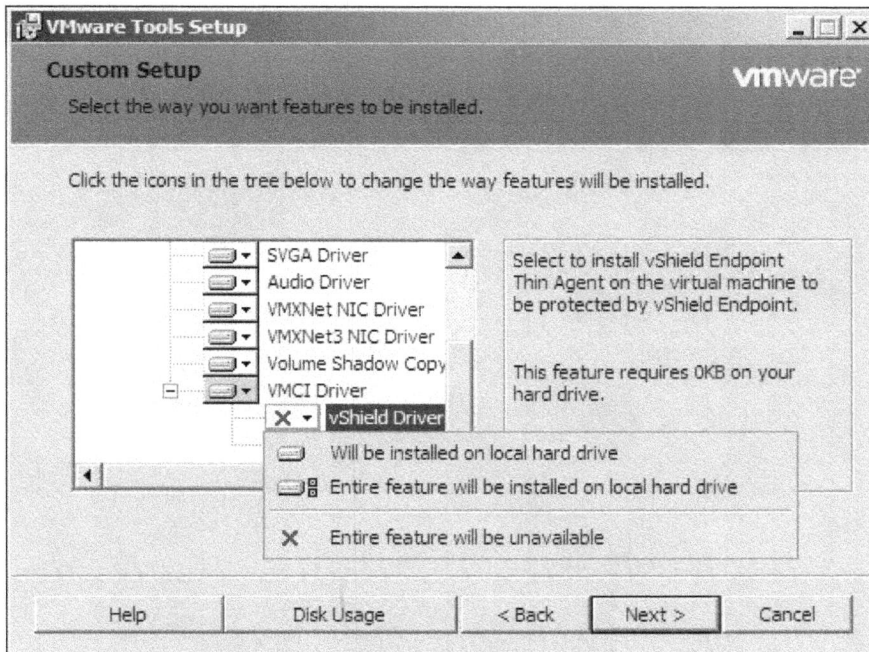

12. Click **Next>** to finish the installation; a reboot of the virtual machine might be required.

Now that all the components have been configured, we need to check the status of the endpoint protection. To do so, perform the following steps:

1. Launch vSphere Client using an account with administrative rights, if it is not already open.

2. Navigate to **Home | Inventory | Hosts and Clusters** from the menu bar.

3. Navigate to **Datacenter | Lab Cluster | esx5501.training.lab**.

4. Select the **vShield** tab.

5. Click on the **Endpoint** option to view the status, and note the normal event log entries.

Now that we've confirmed the endpoint protection is functioning properly from a VMware perspective, the third-party endpoint management console can be viewed for the state of the monitored virtual machines.

> Note that the security appliance is configured correctly and the status is green.

In our Sophos example, we must run another utility to display the actual virtual machines being scanned by the endpoint security appliance (note that our web server is listed):

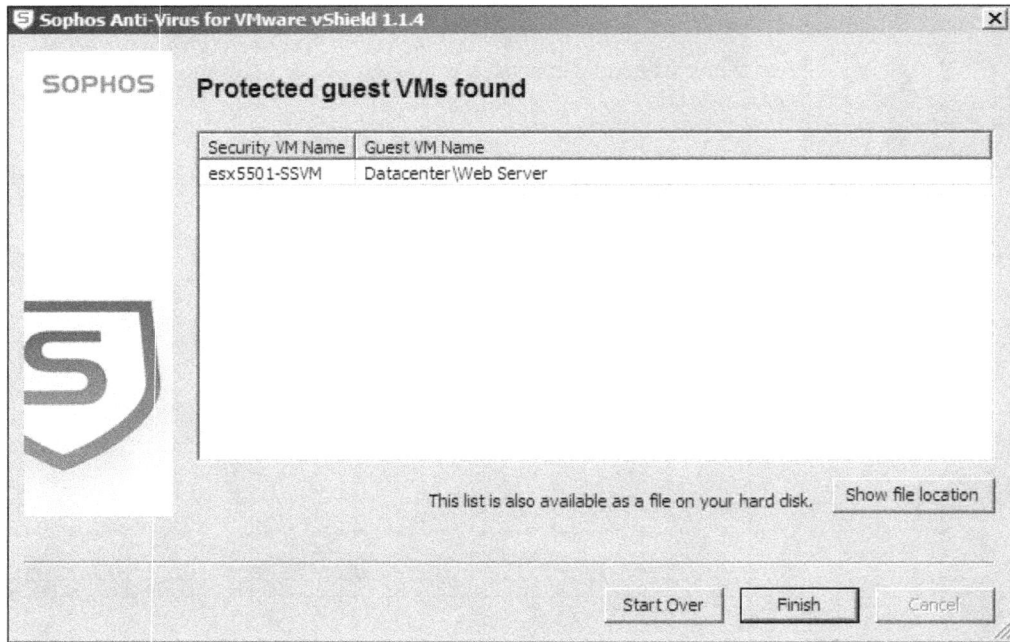

Sophos Anti-Virus for VMware vShield 1.1.4

SOPHOS

Protected guest VMs found

Security VM Name	Guest VM Name
esx5501-SSVM	Datacenter\Web Server

This list is also available as a file on your hard disk. | Show file location

Start Over | Finish | Cancel

How it works...

The vShield Endpoint configuration is one of the more complex configurations simply because there are several points of interaction between vSphere, vShield, and the third-party endpoint virtual appliance as well as the third-party endpoint management console.

In this example, we protected a VM called **Web Server** through the Sophos Anti-Virus appliance called **esx5501-SSVM** that resides on an ESXi host called **esx5501.training.lab**. If we were to add six additional VMs for a total of seven VMs, we will have a scenario like the one shown in the following figure:

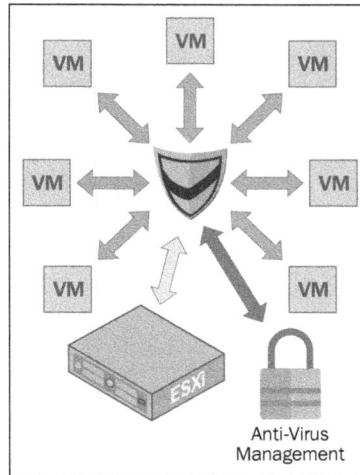

This diagram highlights the scalability of the vShield Endpoint solution and the ease of management afforded by the architecture. Additionally, the power of a single hypervisor and endpoint appliance has replaced seven individual virus scanning engines as well as the resources each engine will normally consume during a scan.

Once the installation has been completed for all the components involved in the scenario, the management and configuration is done on the third-party endpoint management console.

11
Configuring vShield Data Security

In this chapter, we will cover the following recipes:

- ▶ Installing vShield Data Security
- ▶ Configuring the vShield Data Security policies
- ▶ Managing vShield Data Security reports

Introduction

The vShield Data Security component of the vShield suite is specifically designed to scan virtual machines for governance and compliance violations. vShield Data Security runs at the hypervisor level and provides **Data Loss Prevention** (**DLP**) functionality. Specific to each organization's regulatory requirements, over 80 predefined templates are included, covering compliance regulations from around the world. These predefined templates enable the discovery and reporting of sensitive data in unstructured files.

The importance of data regulation is an increasing requirement of internal and external systems. As more mission-critical applications and their associated data move out into the cloud, it is imperative to monitor data integrity and confidentiality. In a pure virtualization environment, all of the data is presumably owned by the same company with virtualization hardware stored in their datacenter. The public cloud, on the other hand, puts forth the concern of data commingling where multiple companies have data and virtual machines running on the same physical host. The ability to segment and control data and communication is key in providing a compliant environment.

Governance and compliance data are required to satisfy requirements such as **Payment Card Industry Data Security Standard** (**PCI-DSS**) (`https://www.pcisecuritystandards.org`) and **Health Insurance Portability and Accountability Act** (**HIPAA**) (`http://www.hhs.gov/ocr/privacy/index.html`) regulations. vShield Data Security provides a control framework that allows the scanning of virtual machines from a central point. While vShield Data Security doesn't provide an active defense mechanism, it does provide a robust set of predefined regulations and standards-based reports. These reports can be used by the compliance team to evaluate the virtual machines being monitored, or as a proof of compliance to auditors.

vShield Data Security installation and configuration requires vSphere, vShield Manager, and vShield Endpoint. The vShield driver option in VMware Tools is also required, much like vShield Endpoint Protection, in order to gain access to the data within the virtual machine.

Installing vShield Data Security

vShield Data Security provides the ability to identify and monitor sensitive data stored in the virtualization environment. In this recipe, we will install the vShield Data Security module using vShield Manager.

Getting ready

The installation of vShield Data Security requires a previously installed and running vShield Manager (Version 5.5). The vShield Manager installation steps are covered in *Chapter 7, Configuring vShield Manager*.

In order to proceed, we require access to vShield App through the vSphere Client plugin. The plugin can be enabled through the **Plug-ins** menu in vSphere Client. The client can be run on any modern Windows desktop operating system or server operating system.

> The vShield vSphere Client plugin requires Adobe Flash, which is not supported on Linux operating systems at this time.

vShield Manager must be installed and the vCenter account used for login must have Enterprise Administrator rights to vShield Manager. vShield Endpoint must be installed in order to install vShield Data Security.

How to do it...

Perform the following steps:

1. Launch vSphere Client using an account with administrative rights, if it is not already open.

2. Navigate to **Home | Inventory | Hosts and Clusters** from the menu bar.

3. Navigate to **Datacenter | Lab Cluster | esx5501.training.lab**.

4. Select the **vShield** tab.

5. Click on the **General** option and locate **vShield Data Security,** and click on **Install**.

6. Select **vShield Endpoint Installing latest version 5.1.0-01255202** and click on **Install**.

7. Select a **Datastore** local to the host if possible (in our example, we'll use **datastore1**).

8. Select a management port group that will allow vShield Data Security to communicate with vShield Manager (in our example, we'll use **Internal Network**).

9. Enter the proper IP information for the Data Security appliance.

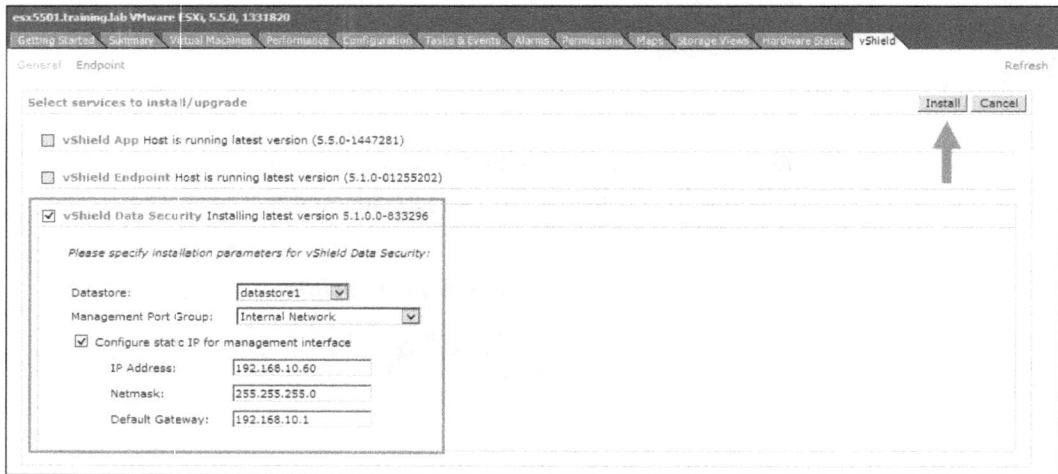

10. Verify that the **vShield Endpoint** service is installed by ensuring the version number is displayed as shown in the following screenshot; repeat installation for any additional hosts.

How it works...

The completed installation procedure creates a vShield Data Security appliance that is dedicated to a specific host. In our example, we installed to the `esx5501.training.lab` ESXi host. The resulting vShield Data Security appliance is named **VMWARE-Data Security-esx5501.training.lab**. A vShield Data Security appliance must be installed on each ESXi host in order to access the virtual machines hosted on that particular host.

The vShield Data Security scan uses the vShield driver that was installed with VMware Tools in *Chapter 10, Configuring vShield Endpoint*. Each virtual machine must have the vShield driver installed to be successfully scanned and cataloged by vShield Data Security.

Configuring the vShield Data Security policies

Configuring the vShield Data Security policies requires some knowledge of current regulations that are applicable to the organization. The governance or compliance group within the organization should be able to provide guidance on which regulatory policies are required. Configuring an incorrect policy will likely cause false positives and confusion as to the secure state of the virtual machines being scanned.

Permissions are often given to the internal audit group to view policy and violation reports. For example, the auditing Active Directory group can be added to the vShield role of **Auditor** to accomplish this task.

The vShield Data Security policies consist of three components:

▸ **Regulations and standards to detect**: These predefined content blades are available for standard regulations, including PCI. Custom detection strings can also be used for detection.

▸ **Areas to exclude**: These components can be excluded from detection by the datacenter, cluster, or resource pool.

▸ **Files to scan**: The files to scan can be filtered by size, date, and file extension type.

In this recipe, we'll be adding a file to a file server that contains numbers in the **Social Security Number** (**SSN**) format. We'll then add a regulation to our scan policy for *US Social Security Numbers* and observe the results.

Getting ready

To proceed, we'll require access to vShield App through the vSphere Client plugin. The plugin can be enabled through the **Plug-ins** menu in vSphere Client. The client can be run on any modern Windows desktop operating system or server operating system.

> The vShield vSphere Client plugin requires Adobe Flash, which is not supported on Linux operating systems at this time.

vShield Manager must be installed and the vCenter account used for login should have Enterprise Administrator rights to vShield Manager. Refer to *Chapter 7, Configuring vShield Manager*, for additional information.

How to do it...

Perform the following steps:

1. Launch vSphere Client using an account with administrative rights, if it is not already open.

2. Navigate to **Home** | **Inventory** | **Hosts and Clusters** from the menu bar.

3. Navigate to **Datacenter** and select the **vShield** tab.

4. Select **Policy**.

5. Click on the triangle next to **Regulations and standards to detect**.

6. Click on **Edit**.

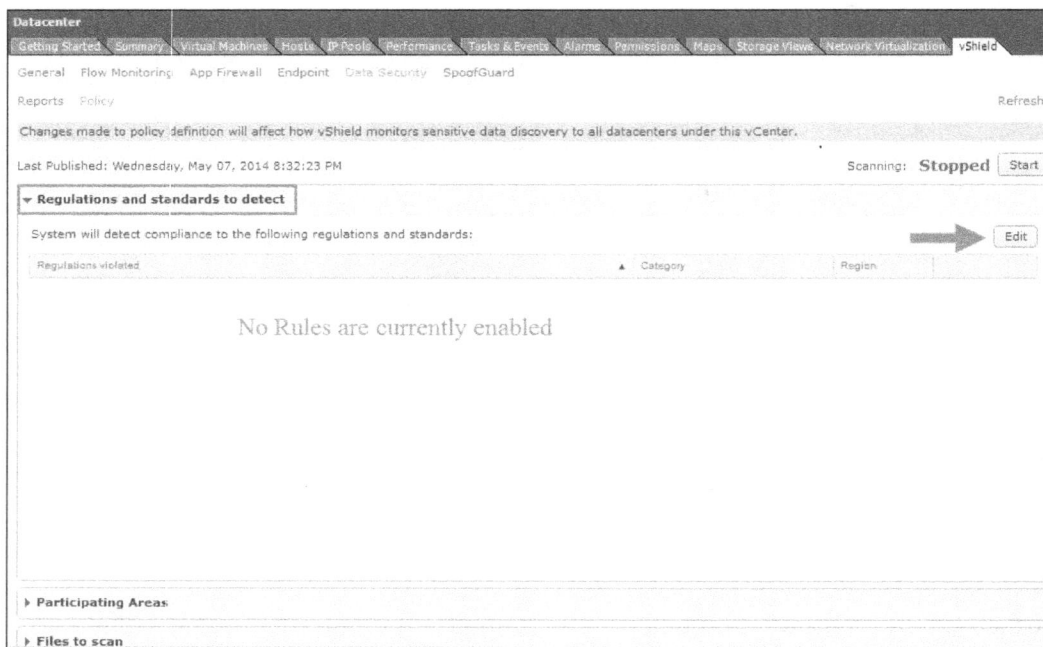

7. Click on **All** for a listing of all regulations.

8. Select **US Social Security Numbers**.

9. Click on **Next**.

Select regulations and standards   ⊗

Select Regulations   **Select Regulations**

Set Data Pattern   Selected   All

Regulations violated ▲	Category	Region	
☐ UK Tax Identification Numbers	PII	EU	Details
☐ UK VAT Numbers	PII	EU	Details
☐ US Drivers License Numbers	PII	NA	Details
☐ US ITIN Numbers	PII	NA	Details
☐ US National Provider Identifiers (NPI)	PHI,PII	NA	Details
☐ US Passport Numbers	PII	NA	Details
☑ US Social Security Numbers	PHI,PII	NA	Details

                                    Previous   [Next]   [Cancel]

> Note that this regulation *does not* have any options for **Set Data Pattern**. Some regulations such as *California AB-1298* have additional data patterns that can be defined.

10. Click on **Finish** to complete the rule creation. For additional rules, repeat the steps to add each additional rule.

Select regulations and standards   ⊗

Select Regulations   **Set Data Pattern**

Set Data Pattern   Pattern for recognizing sensitive data in user's files.

                                The selected regulations and standards do not require you to
                                specify a pattern for recognizing sensitive data.

                                Click Finish to complete the change.

                        [Previous]   Next   [Finish]   [Cancel]

11. Click on **Publish Changes** to publish the detection criteria we just added.

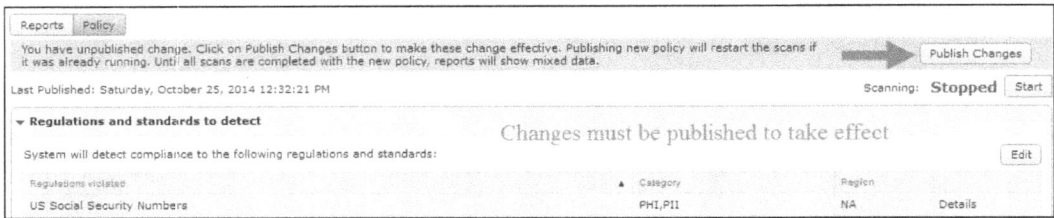

12. Click on **Start** to start the regulations scan.

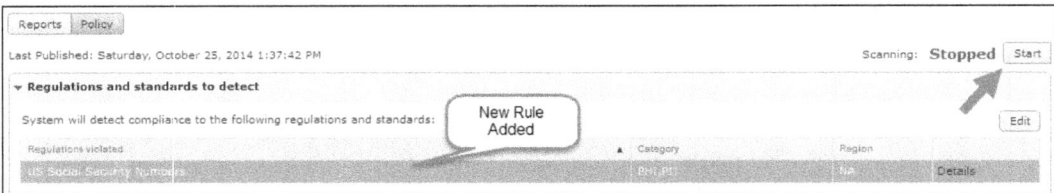

13. Note the options for **Participating Areas** and **Files to scan**.

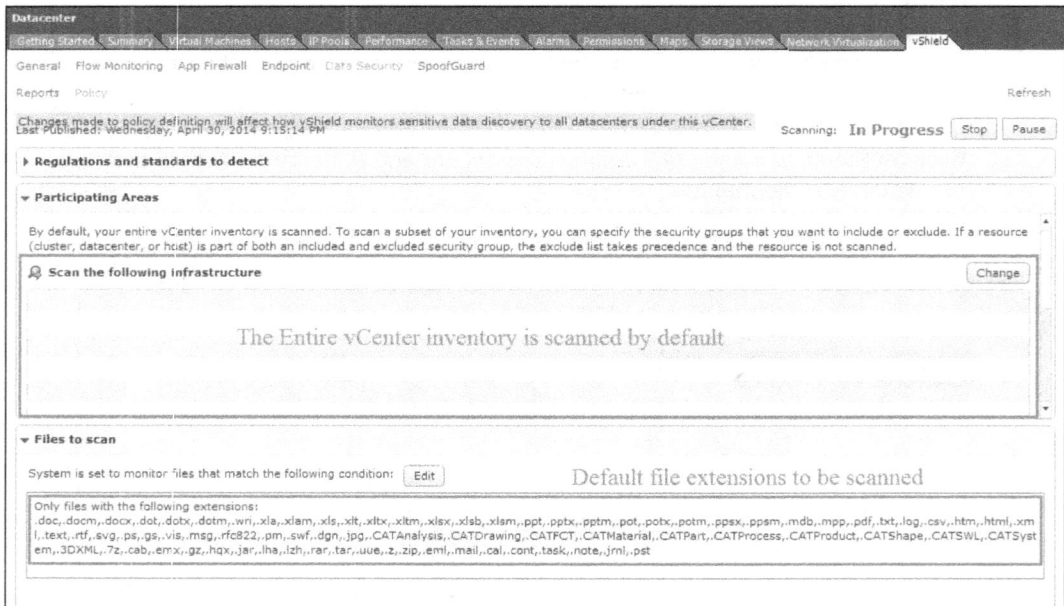

How it works...

Once the regulations and standards are added to vShield Data Security and published, a scan can be run to detect any violations present within the protected virtual machines. Multiple regulations can also be added to run concurrently. Applicable regulations to your organization should be added during this step to ensure compliance.

The participating area option allows different areas or groups of objects to be excluded from the scan. Currently, the tool does not support enabling different regulations and standards on a per group basis. In other words, a scan for HIPAA on a selected group of virtual machines and a PCI-DSS scan on an alternate group of virtual machines cannot take place simultaneously without reconfiguration after each scan.

The default listing in **Files to scan** covers the most common file extensions. Specifying files to monitor provides options for the conditional monitoring of files based on the size, last date modified, and file extension type. The default setting is the file extension type and is populated with common file extensions used by current enterprise applications.

Some regulations have an option to specify additional file characteristics through custom expressions. For example, selecting the *California AB-1298* regulation will result in the following **Set Data Pattern** screen. This allows custom expressions to find the data formatted in a certain pattern.

Certain regulations offer the option to search for certain pattern strings through the use of expressions. Custom expressions can be created by visiting http://userguide.icu-project.org/strings/regexp.

Managing vShield Data Security reports

Following the configuration of a vShield Data Security policy, a scan can be initiated. Once a scan is in progress or has completed, the statistics and reporting can be viewed, utilizing the vShield Data Security reports option within vCenter.

Getting ready

To proceed, we'll require access to vShield App through the vSphere Client plugin. The plugin can be enabled through the **Plug-ins** menu in vSphere Client. The client can be run on any modern Windows desktop operating system or server operating system.

> The vShield vSphere Client plugin requires Adobe Flash, which is not supported on Linux operating systems at this time.

vShield Manager must be installed and the vCenter account used for login should have Enterprise Administrator rights to vShield Manager.

How to do it...

Perform the following steps:

1. Launch vSphere Client using an account with administrative rights, if it is not already open.
2. Navigate to **Home | Inventory | Hosts and Clusters** from the menu bar.
3. Navigate to **Datacenter** and select the **vShield** tab.
4. Select **Reports**. We see the current **Scan Statistics** option along with violations reported. In this example, the SSN information in a text file on the VM **File Server** has been detected by the **US Social Security Numbers** policy.

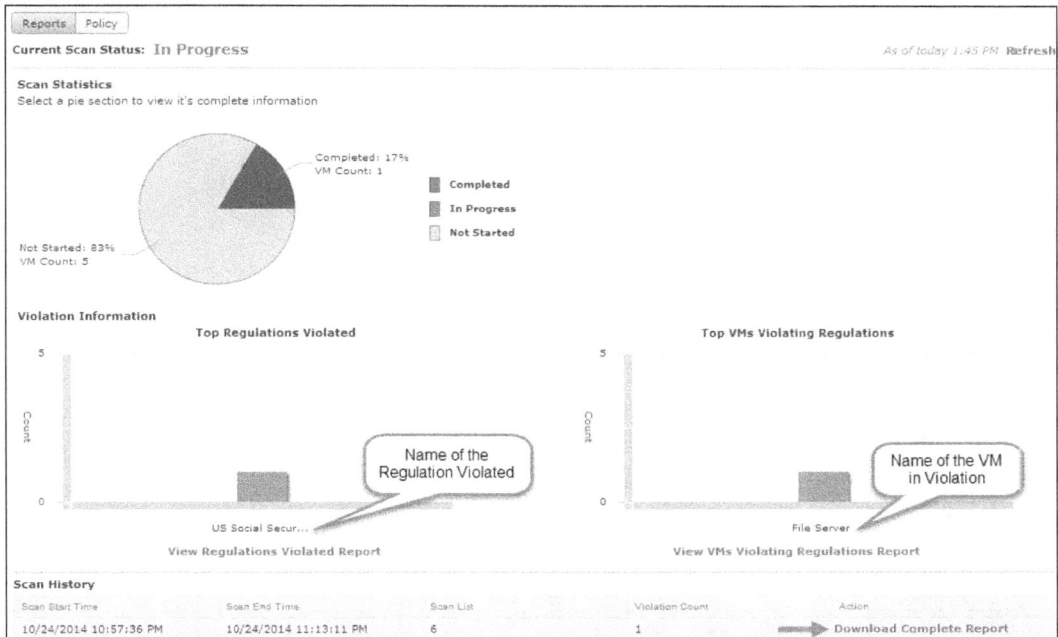

Scan reports can also be downloaded in their native format of CSV for the list of violations and list of scanned VMs. Scan policies can be downloaded in the XML format.

5. From the **vShield Reports** screen, select **Download Complete Report,** as noted in the preceding image.

6. Click on **Initiate Download** for each report.

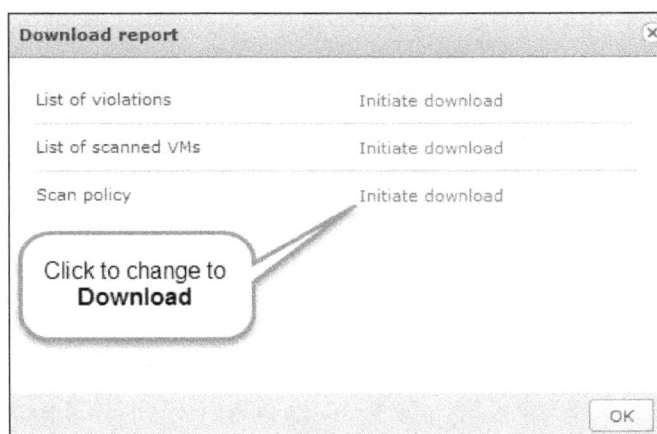

7. Click on **Download** to open the save file dialog box and save each file.

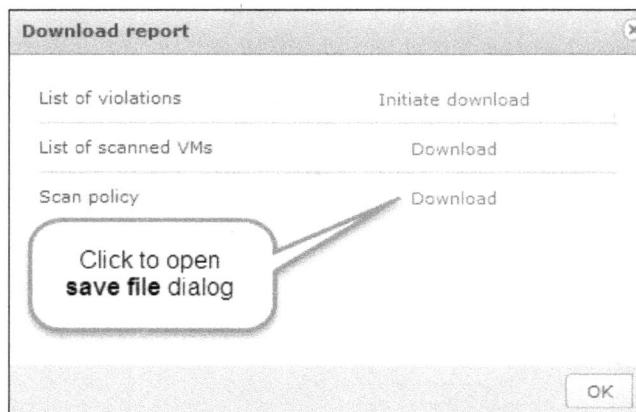

8. Click on **OK** to close.

9. The `ScannedVMs.csv` downloaded file can be viewed in Excel.

	A	B	C	D	E	F	G	H	I
1	VM Id	VM Name	Host	Datacenter	Cluster	Scan Status	Scan Start	Scan End	Violation Count
2	vm-209	esx5501-SSVM	esx5501.training.lab	Datacenter	Lab Cluster	not started			0
3	vm-213	Web Server 2	esx5501.training.lab	Datacenter	Lab Cluster	not started			0
4	vm-214	Internal Firewall	esx5501.training.lab	Datacenter	Lab Cluster	not started			0
5	vm-215	SQL DataWarehouse 1	esx5501.training.lab	Datacenter	Lab Cluster	not started			0
6	vm-218	Web Server	esx5501.training.lab	Datacenter	Lab Cluster	not started			0
7	vm-225	File Server	esx5502.training.lab	Datacenter	Lab Cluster	completed	21:44.0	22:24.0	1

10. The violations file shows the name and location of the file in violation.

	A	B	C	D	F
1	Cluster	Data Center	Virtual Machine	File	Regulations Violated
2	Lab Cluster	Datacenter	File Server	C:\Users\Administrator\Documents\ssn.txt	US Social Security Numbers
3					

How it works...

vShield Data Security reporting is straightforward in its implementation and design. As we've seen in our example environment, the status can be easily seen graphically in the vShield reports view with the option to see a more detailed status with a single mouse click. Basic reports in the CSV format can be downloaded and saved to a file share for periodic review.

The file used to test the US Social Security Numbers policy was simply a text file with several fictitious numbers in the format of xxx-xx-xxx. During the testing phase, both the PCI and HIPAA rules were used. However, due to the lack of detail of a valid record, a violation cannot be generated.

12
Configuring vSphere Certificates

In this chapter, we will cover the following recipes:

- Configuring a Windows CA template
- Requesting certificates from a Windows CA
- Using SSL Certificate Automation Tool 5.5
- Process certificate requests
- Registering the Single Sign-On certificate
- Registering the Inventory Service certificate
- Registering the vCenter certificate
- Registering the Web Client certificate
- Registering the Log Browser certificate
- Registering the Update Manager certificate
- Installing an ESXi host certificate

Introduction

Certificates provide digital identification and a mechanism to establish trust. We can think of a certificate as a driver's license or a government-issued ID card. The trusted root authority can be thought of as the government in this example. The license or ID can be thought of as the certificate. When someone checks our ID to verify our identity, they trust the authority that issued that ID. Likewise, when a certificate is issued from a trusted authority, we can be assured that the identity represented by the certificate is genuine.

The default installations of both an ESXi host and vSphere are configured to use self-signed certificates. A self-signed certificate, as the name implies, is signed by the host machine on which the software is installed. Subsequently, there is no inherent trust between each machine since the certificate signature differs from machine to machine. A self-signed certificate is akin to a fake ID using our analogy.

More information on PKI can be found at `http://en.wikipedia.org/wiki/Public_key_infrastructure`.

Certificates that are signed by a common root or trusted authority provide each host and vSphere component the ability to verify the identity of each component. To establish trust within a closed or local environment, a private **Certificate Authority** (**CA**) is adequate as long as every machine that will communicate has a common trusted root. Users and machines in a corporate **Active Directory** (**AD**) are an example of where a private or internal CA is extremely valuable considering its inexpensive cost.

When endpoints include devices outside the local AD or corporate environment, a public certificate issued by a public CA is required. This allows machines in different environments to trust each other when using a commonly trusted root such as Verisign, Entrust, and Thawte, to name a few.

Before the release of VMware SSL Certificate Automation Tool, it was very difficult to install and configure all the services associated with vSphere to use a certificate from either a private or public CA.

Configuring a Windows CA template

The web server template included in a Windows Server CA is not sufficient for use with vSphere and must be altered to meet the certificate requirements. The Windows Server CA is a role installed to a standalone or enterprise Windows 2008 server or higher.

Getting started

In order to proceed, we require access to the Server Manager Management console with administrative access to the Windows CA.

Windows 2008 must be installed along with the following prerequisites:

- ▸ Administrative privileges on the Windows CA server(s) on which you are running the tool

- ▸ Prior installation of a Windows CA, including the web request option

- ▸ Administrative privileges to the certificate authority and certification templates container

> This configuration is intended to be performed in a development or lab environment. Do not reconfigure a root or issue a CA in your production environment without first knowing the impact.

How to do it...

The following steps require administrative access to either a standalone CA or an enterprise CA:

1. Open Server Manager.

2. From the pane on the left-hand side, navigate to **Roles | Active Directory Certificate Services**.

3. Highlight **Certificate Templates** and select **Web Server** from the template list.

	Certificate Templates (DC1.training.lab)		
Server Manager (DC1)	Template Display Name ▾	Minimum Supported CAs	Version
Roles	Workstation Authentication	Windows Server 2003 Ent...	101.0
Active Directory Certificate	Web Server	Windows 2000	4.1
Enterprise PKI	VMware Certificate	Windows Server 2003 Ent...	100.2
training-DC1-CA (V(	User Signature Only	Windows 2000	4.1
Certificate Templates (I	User	Windows 2000	3.1
training-DC1-CA	Trust List Signing	Windows 2000	3.1
Revoked Certificate	Subordinate Certification Authority	Windows 2000	5.1
Issued Certificates	Smartcard User	Windows 2000	11.1
Pending Requests			
Failed Requests			

4. Right-click on **Web Server** and click on **Duplicate Certificate**.

5. Select **Windows Server 2003 Enterprise**.

6. Click on **OK**.

7. Set **Template display name** to **VMware Certificate**.

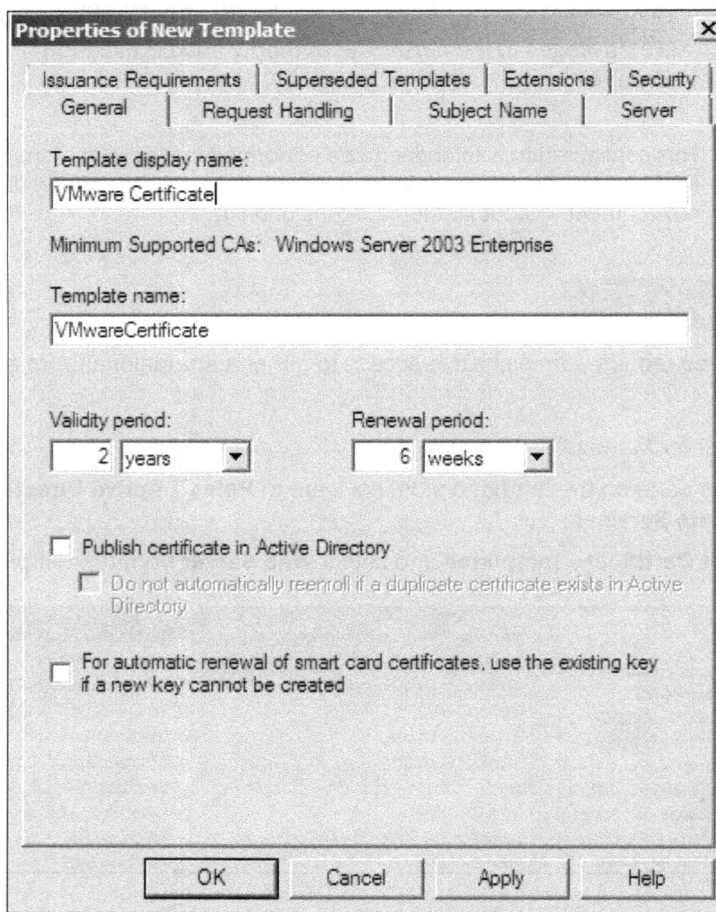

8. Select the **Extensions** tab.

9. Highlight **Key Usage** and click on **Edit....**.

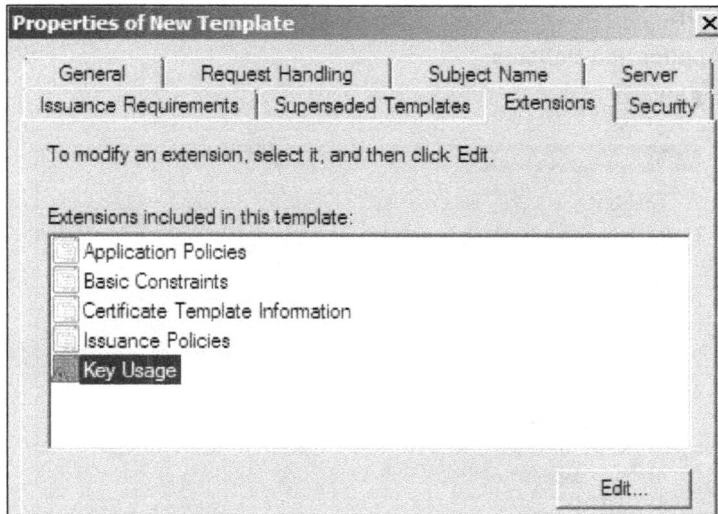

10. Check the **Signature is proof of origin (nonrepudiation)** option. This option ensures that the data signed can be traced back to the signature, safeguarding the integrity of the original data.

11. Check the **Allow encryption of user data** option.

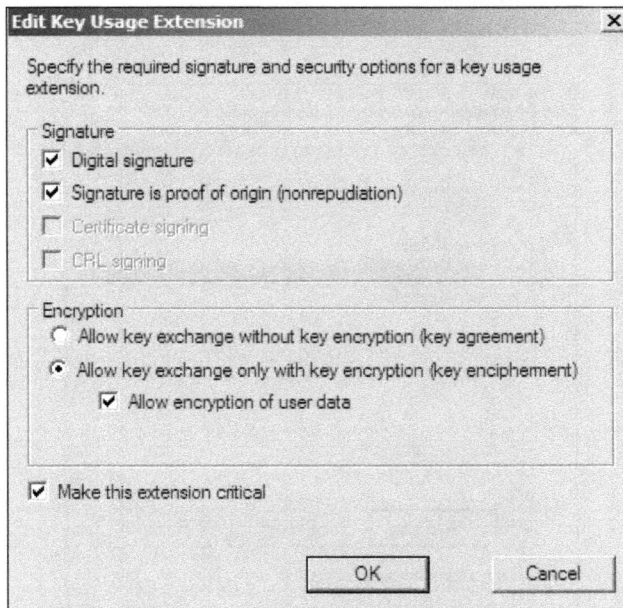

12. Click on **OK**.

13. Select **Application Policies**.

14. Click on **Edit...**.

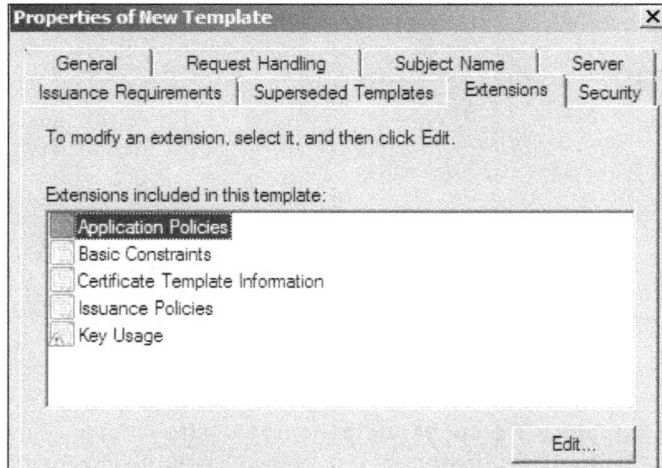

15. Click on **Add...**.

16. Select **Client Authentication** from the list.

17. Click on **OK**.

18. Click on **OK** to close the **Edit Application Policies Extension** dialog box.

19. Select the **Subject Name** tab.

Properties of New Template ☒

| Issuance Requirements | Superseded Templates | Extensions | Security |
| General | Request Handling | Subject Name | Server |

◉ Supply in the request

☐ Use subject information from existing certificates for autoenrollment
renewal requests.

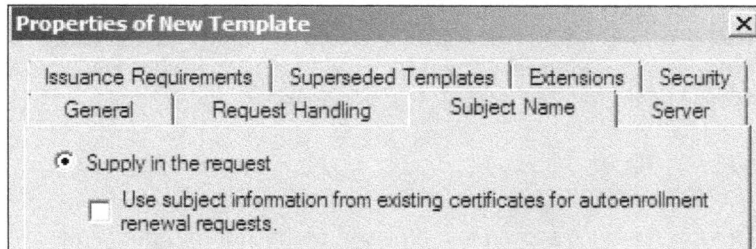

20. Ensure that **Supply in the request** is selected. This option allows you to create a request with multiple names such as `servername.domain.com` and `servername`.

21. Click on **OK**.

How it works...

vSphere requires specific options that are not present in the default web server certificate template that is included in the Windows 2008 CA. vSphere 5.5 requires the following options, which are not included by default:

▶ **Data Encipherment**: This ensures the encryption of the data

▶ **Nonrepudiation**: This protects the integrity and origin of the information

▶ **Client Authentication**: This allows mutual authentication of the client as well as the server

A copy is made of the existing web server certificate template with the proper settings configured and permissioned so that it can be requested through the certificate console or the web service request.

See also

▶ Refer to the VMware Knowledge Base article at `http://kb.vmware.com/selfservice/microsites/search.do?language=en_US&cmd=displayKC&externalId=2062108` for more information.

Requesting certificates from a Windows CA

Once a certificate request is generated, it must be submitted to a certificate authority and processed to receive a valid X.509 certificate. In cases where the virtualization environment will require internal trust, an internal CA can be used. One of the more common CAs that will most likely already exist in the environment is a Windows CA.

Getting started

In order to proceed, we require access to a browser, preferably Internet Explorer Version 9 or higher to connect to the Windows CA.

Ensure that the account used for login has rights to request a certificate from the Windows CA. In our example, the user is a member of the domain admins group for simplicity; however, any authenticated user can request a certificate by default.

To proceed further, a certificate request must have been previously generated from the automation tool or an open SSL tool.

How to do it...

Let's perform the following steps to request certificates from a Windows CA:

1. Launch Internet Explorer using an account with the permission to request a certificate.
2. Navigate to the certificate server website (in our example, `https://dc1/certsrv/`).
3. Choose **Request a certificate** from the task list.

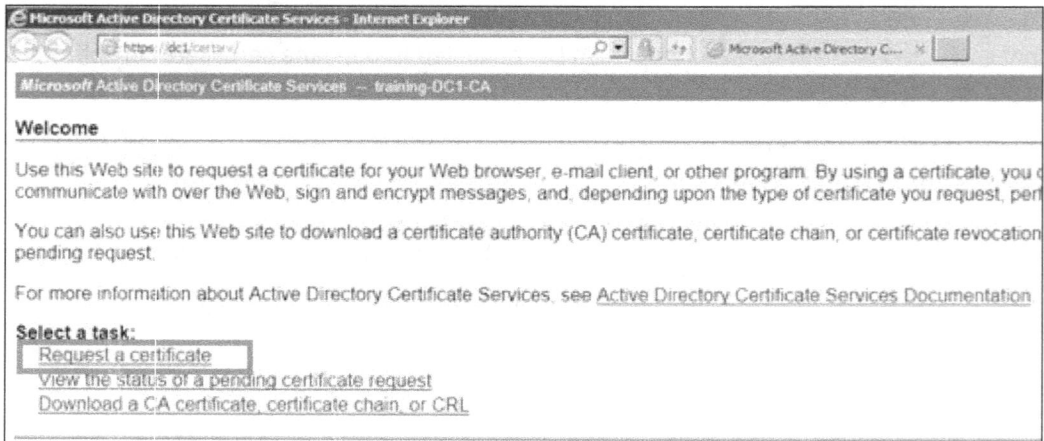

Selecting the **Request a certificate** option

4. Select **submit an advanced certificate request**.

5. Paste the certificate request information into the request box.

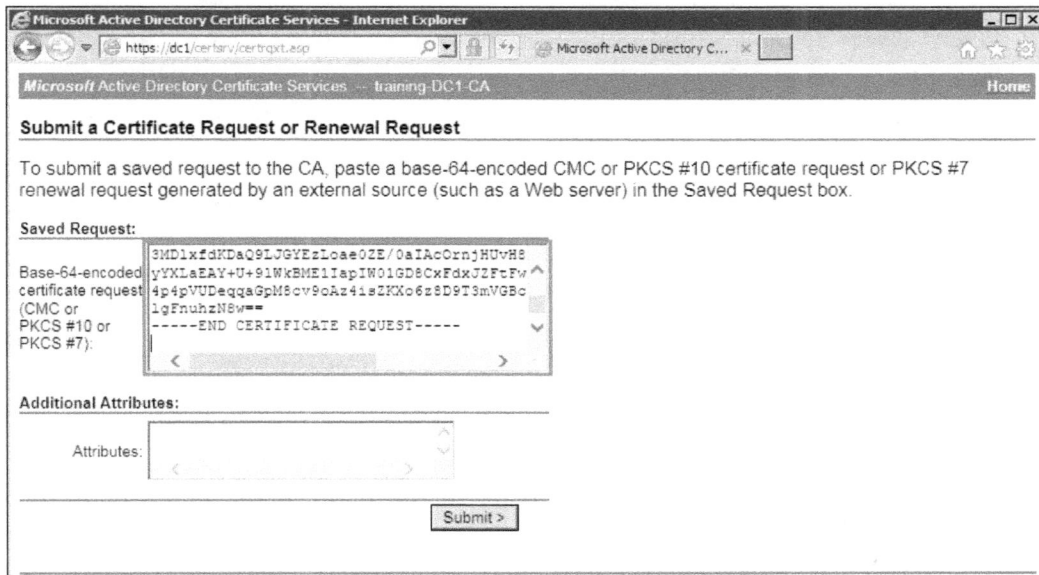

Pasting the request

6. Click on **Submit**.

7. Once the certificate has been processed by the CA, it will be available for download; ensure that the **Base 64 encoded** option is selected.

8. Select **Download certificate**.

9. Save the file in the proper folder as `rui.crt` (in our example, this is a certificate for Single Sign-On).

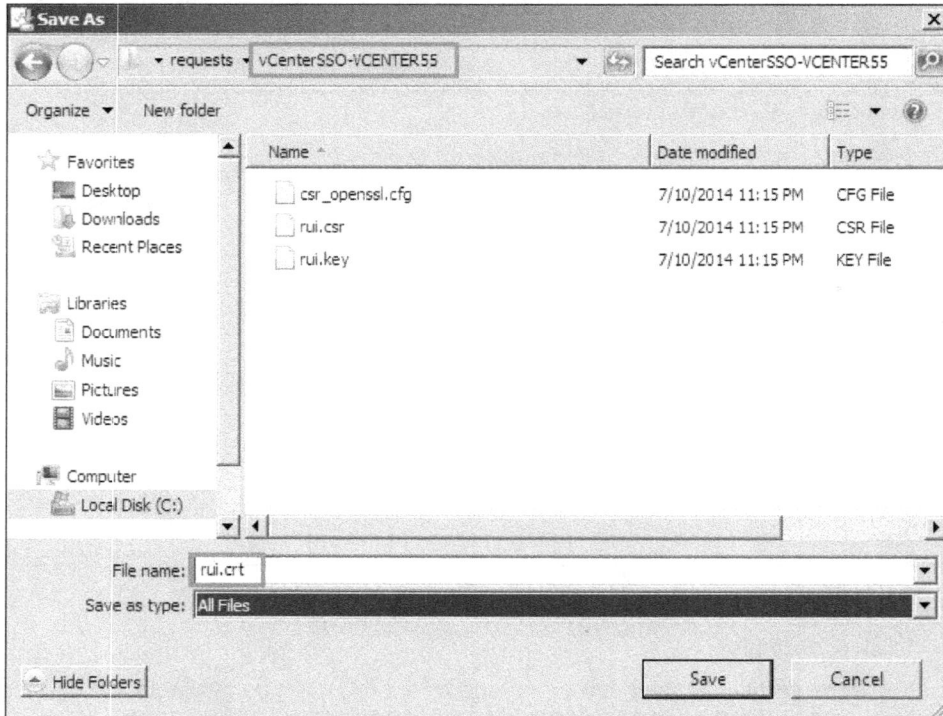

10. Click on **Save**.

Install the certificate authority root certificate to ensure that any certificate issued is trusted, by performing the following steps:

1. Navigate to the certificate server website (in our example, `https://dc1/certsrv/`).

2. Select the **Download a CA certificate, certificate chain, or CRL** task.

3. Select **Download CA certificate**.

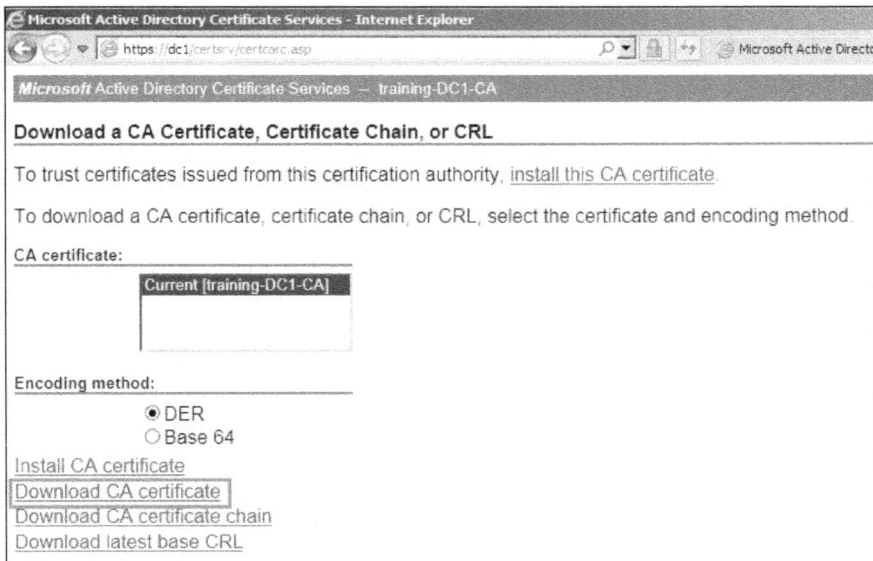

4. Save the file; the default filename is `certnew.cer`.

> Note that the `.cer` extension typically identifies a DER-based encoding method, which is the default for Windows; Base64 encoding is used for VMware and is typically identified with a `.p7b` extension.

5. Right-click on the file and select **Install Certificate**.

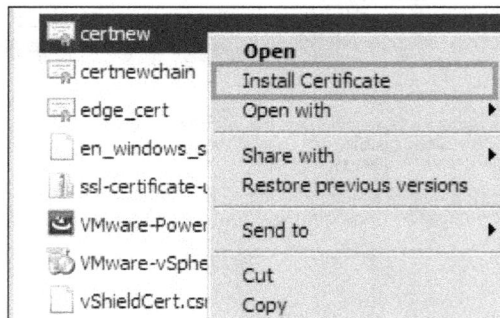

certnew	**Open**	
certnewchain	Install Certificate	
edge_cert	Open with	▶
en_windows_s		
ssl-certificate-ı	Share with	▶
	Restore previous versions	
VMware-Power	Send to	▶
VMware-vSphe		
vShieldCert.csı	Cut	
	Copy	

6. Click on **Next** in **Certificate Import Wizard**.

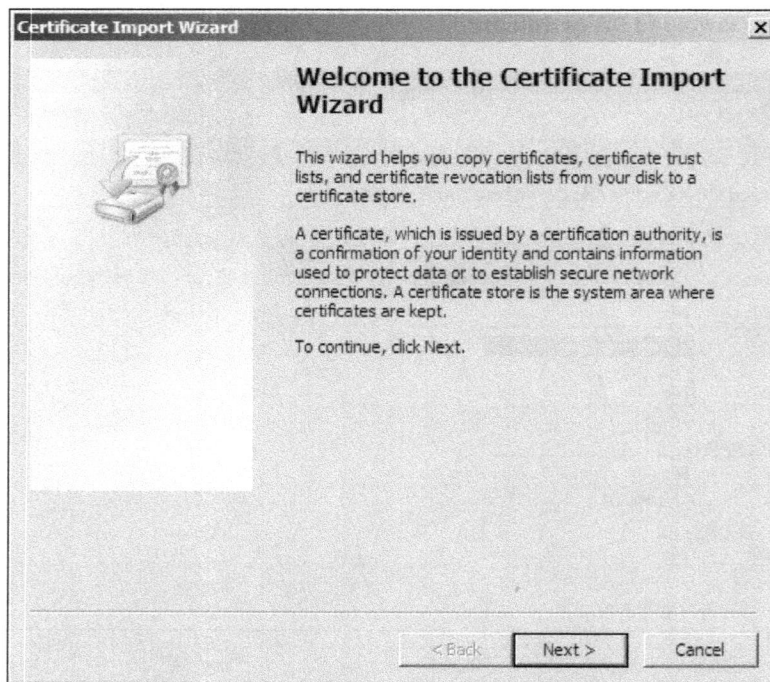

Certificate Import Wizard

Welcome to the Certificate Import Wizard

This wizard helps you copy certificates, certificate trust lists, and certificate revocation lists from your disk to a certificate store.

A certificate, which is issued by a certification authority, is a confirmation of your identity and contains information used to protect data or to establish secure network connections. A certificate store is the system area where certificates are kept.

To continue, click Next.

< Back   Next >   Cancel

7. Click on **Next** to store the certificate in the default `Trusted Root Authority` folder.

8. Ensure that the **Automatically select the certificate store based on the type of certificate** option is selected and click on **Next**.

9. Click on **Finish** to close the wizard.

10. Verify that the file is in the certificate management console.

How it works...

vSphere requires specific options that are not present in the default web server certificate template that is included in the Windows 2008 CA. vSphere 5.5 requires the following options that are not present in the default web server certificate template: Data Encipherment, Nonrepudiation, and Client Authentication. If the CA is not configured to issue a certificate with these options, the application of the certificate will fail. It is also important to note that VMware uses Base64 encoding in general, which is different from the DER encoding used by Windows operating systems as the default.

Using SSL Certificate Automation Tool 5.5

SSL Certificate Automation Tool Version 5.5 must be used with vSphere 5.5 as it is the only supported version for vSphere 5.5. This tool is essentially a collection of scripts that simplify the process of requesting and assigning certificates to VMware services within the vSphere infrastructure.

Getting started

In order to proceed, we require access to a command prompt run with administrator privileges. SSL Certificate Automation Tool must be downloaded from `www.vmware.com` and extracted from the `.zip` file.

> SSL Certificate Automation Tool Version 5.5 is downloaded in the `ssl-certificate-updater-tool-1308332.zip` file.

If the vCenter server is a virtual machine, it is recommended that you take a snapshot to enable easy recovery, should it be necessary. If a certificate assignment fails, it will usually fail gracefully; however, there are instances when rolling back to a snapshot is the most expedient recovery strategy. In addition, the following prerequisites apply:

- Each server on which a vSphere component resides that requires updating must have SSL Certificate Automation Tool deployed to it
- You must have administrative privileges on the server(s) on which you are running the tool
- All vCenter server components for which the certificates are to be updated are already installed and running

How to do it...

Install SSL Certificate Automation Tool by performing the following steps:

1. Download SSL Certificate Automation Tool from the vSphere drivers and tools section download pages or directly at `https://my.vmware.com/web/vmware/details?downloadGroup=SSLTOOL550&productId=353`.
2. Unzip the folder to a machine that requires certificate deployment.
3. Open the destination folder and locate the `ssl-environment` batch file, and click on **Edit**.

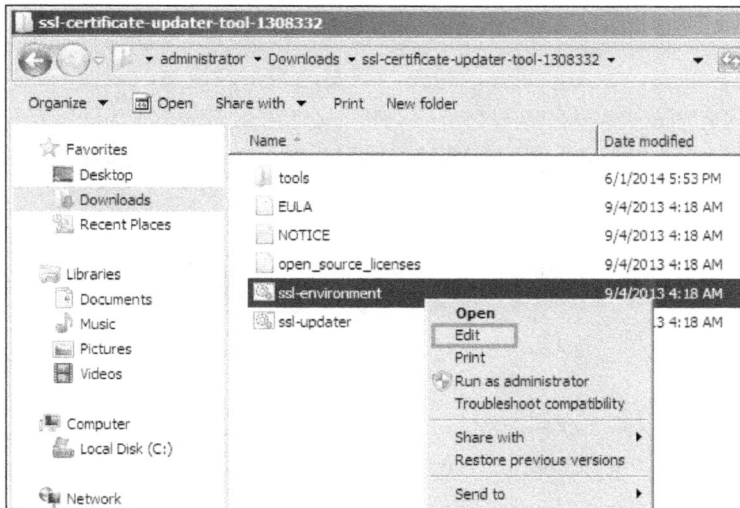

This file contains guidance information as well as the ability to enter variables that will be read by the update utility.

4. Navigate to **File** | **Exit** to close the file.

How it works...

SSL Certificate Automation Tool provides checks and complex scripting to update the SSL certificates for the vSphere services. There is no installation program that must be run after the ZIP file has been expanded, but the files must be deployed to each machine that will require a certificate update.

Normally, the **ssl-environment** settings will be used to simplify and speed up the update; in our example, we fill in the information at the prompts to demonstrate the process.

There's more...

There are a number of different issues that can be encountered during the setup of certificates in the vSphere environment. Most of these issues have resolution steps provided by VMware in the form of the **Knowledge Base** (**KB**) article on their website.

For example, it might be necessary to register a variable within the Server System Properties for JAVA in order for the SSL tool to assign a certificate in certain cases.

Inserting a new `JAVA_HOME` system variable pointed to `C:\Program Files\VMware\Infrastructure\jre` can alleviate some issues with certificate processing.

In addition, the logfiles found in the `SSLTool` log directory can be very useful in troubleshooting problems. In our example, these were located at `C:\Certificates\SSLTool\logs`.

Process certificate requests

SSL Certificate Automation Tool not only simplifies the process of applying certificates to the vSphere components, but it also simplifies the request of certificates from either the private or public CA. Key values can be defined in the `ssl-environment.bat` file for simplicity.

Getting started

In order to request certificates from the CA (a private CA in our example), the account must have rights to request a certificate using the VMware certificate template defined earlier in this chapter.

How to do it...

On a machine with SSL Certificate Automation Tool deployed, perform the following steps:

1. Launch the command prompt with administrative privileges.

2. Navigate to the SSL tool location and run `ssl-updater.bat`.

3. Type 2 to generate certificate requests.

```
C:\Certificates\SSLTool>ssl-updater.bat

===============================================================================
Main menu

Enter the action you want to run
    1. Plan your steps to update SSL certificates(Update Steps Planner)
    2. Generate Certificate Signing Requests
    3. Update Single Sign-On
    4. Update Inventory Service
    5. Update vCenter Server
    6. Update vCenter Orchestrator(vCO)
    7. Update vSphere Web Client and Log Browser
    8. Update vSphere Update Manager(VUM)
    9. End the update process and exit

The chosen action is: _
```

4. Type 1 to generate a request for **Single Sign-On**.

```
===============================================================================
  2. Generate Certificate Signing Request for:

    1. Single Sign-On
    2. Inventory Service
    3. vCenter Server
    4. vCenter Orchestrator
    5. vSphere Web Client
    6. Log Browser
    7. vSphere Update Manager
    8. Other service
    9. Return to the main menu

The chosen service is: 1_
```

5. Verify or enter the information requested by the certificate request: **Fully Qualified Domain Name**, **IP Address**, **short hostname**, **country code**, **state**, **city**, and **organization**. Then, save the location.

```
Enter the Fully Qualified Domain Name of the server (default value is: UCENTER55
.training.lab):
---IP addresses assigned to this server:
192.168.10.20
172.21.7.155
fe80::f4be:6bb1:5d0f:806f
Enter the IP Address of the server (default value is: 192.168.10.20):
Enter the short hostname of the server (default value is: UCENTER55):
Enter the 2 letter code of the country: US
Enter the name of the state or province: Ohio
Enter the name of the city, locality name: Columbus
Enter the name of the organization: Training Lab
Organizational Unit name will be DN of the certificate and has to be unique!
Enter the name of the organizational unit (default value is: vCenterSSO-UCENTER5
5):
Enter the location where the generated CSR will be saved (default value is: "C:\
Certificates\SSLTool\requests\vCenterSSO-UCENTER55"):

[Thu 07/10/2014 - 23:15:04.58]: Last operation generate CSR for Single Sign-On c
ompleted successfully.

[Thu 07/10/2014 - 23:15:04.58]: CSR is located here: C:\Certificates\SSLTool\req
uests\vCenterSSO-UCENTER55
```

6. The resulting files are a CFG file, a CSR file, or a KEY file.

Name	Date modified	Type	Size
csr_openssl.cfg	7/10/2014 11:15 PM	CFG File	1 KB
rui.csr	7/10/2014 11:15 PM	CSR File	2 KB
rui.key	7/10/2014 11:15 PM	KEY File	2 KB

7. Open the `rui.csr` file in Notepad.

8. Select all the text.

9. Copy the request and paste it into the certificate request form for the private or public CA.

10. Select **Base 64 encoded**.

11. Select **Download certificate**.

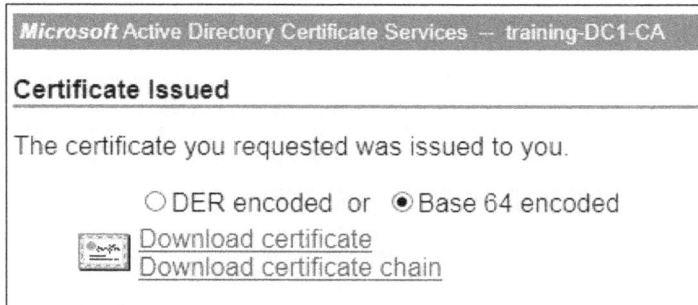

Microsoft Active Directory Certificate Services -- training-DC1-CA

Certificate Issued

The certificate you requested was issued to you.

    ○ DER encoded or ◉ Base 64 encoded

Download certificate
Download certificate chain

12. Save the issued certificate as `rui.crt` in the appropriate folder.

13. Repeat the process for the remaining services.

Download the CA chain and then perform the following steps:

1. Navigate to the certificate server website (in our example, `https://dc1/certsrv/`).

2. Select **Download a CA certificate, certificate chain, or CRL**.

3. Select **Base 64** as the encoding method.

4. Select **Download CA certificate chain**.

Microsoft Active Directory Certificate Services -- training-DC1-CA

Download a CA Certificate, Certificate Chain, or CRL

To trust certificates issued from this certification authority,

To download a CA certificate, certificate chain, or CRL, se

CA certificate:

    Current [training-DC1-CA]

Encoding method:

    ○ DER
    ◉ Base 64

Install CA certificate
Download CA certificate
Download CA certificate chain
Download latest base CRL

5. Save this as `cachain.p7b`.

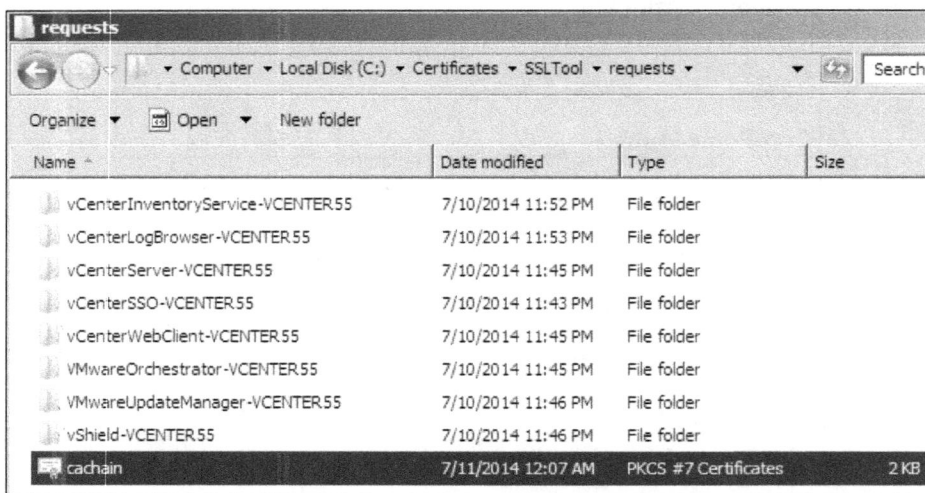

6. Double-click on the `cachain.p7b` file.

7. Navigate to the certificate, right-click on it, and click on **Export...**.

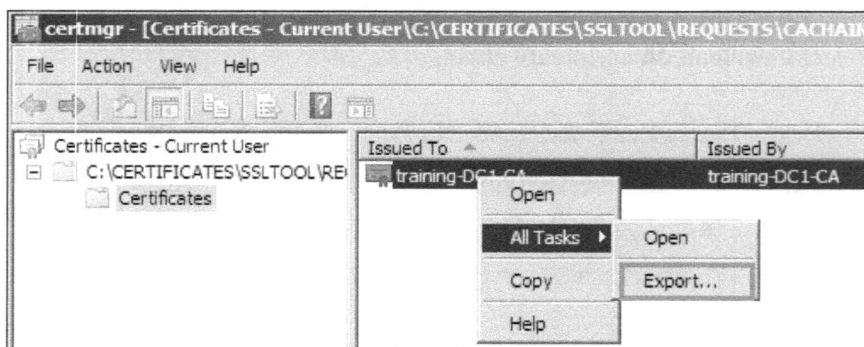

8. Click on **Next**.

9. Select **Base-64 encoded X.509**, and then click on **Next**.

10. Save this as `Root64.cer`, and click on **Next**.

How it works...

The certificate request is generated by entering or confirming the appropriate information set in SSL Certificate Automation Tool. Once the required information is provided for the request, a **Certificate Signing Request (CSR)** file is generated. This file is a **Public Key Cryptography Standard (PKCS)** #10 format.

Once the CSR file is submitted to the CA for processing, it might take some time to receive a certificate based on the CSR file, depending on the approval workflow in place for the selected CA. Once the certificate is issued, it is downloaded to the designated service folder structure until it is processed by SSL Certificate Automation Tool for the specific service.

Registering the Single Sign-On certificate

The Single Sign-On certificate needs to be bound to the corresponding service in order for the neighboring services to trust the service and not prompt for verification. The default certificate is self-signed and not trusted by any remote machine.

Getting started

In order to proceed, we require access to the directory that holds the certificate and private key that were generated as a result of the certificate request completed earlier. In our example, the certificates are located in the `C:\Certificates\SSLTool\requests\<service name>` folder.

Ensure that the command prompt account has administrative access to the vCenter and local servers.

How to do it...

Perform the following steps:

1. Open a command prompt on the local vCenter server as an administrator.
2. Navigate to the location where VMware SSL Certificate Automation Tool has been installed (in our example, `C:\Certificates\SSLTool`).
3. Run `ssl-updater.bat`.
4. From the main menu, enter 3 to update Single Sign-On.

5. Next, enter 1 to update the Single Sign-On SSL certificate.

```
==============+==============================================================
  Main menu  |
             |
  Enter the  action you want to run
      1. Plan your steps to update SSL certificates(Update Steps Planner)
      2. Generate Certificate Signing Requests
      3. Update Single Sign-On
      4. Update Inventory Service
      5. Update vCenter Server
      6. Update vCenter Orchestrator(vCO)
      7. Update vSphere Web Client and Log Browser
      8. Update vSphere Update Manager(VUM)
      9. End the update process and exit
  The chosen action is: 3
==============+==============================================================
  3. Update  the Single Sign-On SSL Certificate
             |
      1. Update the Single Sign-On SSL Certificate
      2. Rollback to the previous Single Sign-On SSL Certificate
      3. Return to the main menu to update other services
  The chosen service is: 1
```

6. Ensure that the SSL chain is set to the location of the Single Sign-On certificate (in our example, `C:\Certificates\SSLTool\requests\vCenterSSO-VCENTER55\rui.crt`).

7. Ensure that the private key is set to the location of the Single Sign-On private key (in our example, `C:\Certificates\SSLTool\requests\vCenterSSO-VCENTER55\rui.key`).

8. Enter the username and password for the Single Sign-On administrative account.

9. Check whether a load balancer is present or not.

```
Enter location to the new Single Sign-On SSL chain (default value is: C:\Certifi
cates\SSLTool\requests\vCenterSSO-VCENTER55): C:\Certificates\SSLTool\requests\v
CenterSSO-VCENTER55\rui.crt
Enter location to the new Single Sign-On private key (default value is: C:\Certi
ficates\SSLTool\requests\vCenterSSO-VCENTER55): C:\Certificates\SSLTool\requests
\vCenterSSO-VCENTER55\rui.key
Enter Single Sign-On Administrator user (default value is: administrator@vsphere
.local):
Enter Single Sign-On Administrator password (will not be echoed):
Do you have a load balancer installed? (yes/no) (default value is: no): no
```

10. The process will stop, restart the related services, and indicate that the update was completed successfully.

```
[.] Beginning certificate replacement procedure for Single Sign-On.
[.] The existing configuration will be backed up to C:\Certificates\SSLTool\back
up\sso-ssl-updater.backup
[.] Checking the password of administrator user administrator@vsphere.local.
[.] The vCenter Single Sign-On service is currently running but it must be stopp
ed in order to perform a portion of the SSL certificate update operation.
[.] Waiting for service VMwareSTS to stop, 15 seconds.
[.] Service did stop successfully.
[.] Updating service container configuration
[.] The vCenter Single Sign-On service is not currently running but it must be s
tarted in order to perform a portion of the SSL certificate update operation.
[.] Waiting for service VMwareSTS to start, 15 seconds.
[.] Service did start successfully.
[.] Updating the SSO endpoints in the Lookup Service.
[.] This is Single Sign-On single-node install. All Single Sign-On endpoints are
 served from this node.
[.] Lookup Service records updated successfully.

[Wed 08/06/2014 - 15:30:56.48]: Last operation update Single Sign-On SSL certifi
cate completed successfully.
[Wed 08/06/2014 - 15:30:56.49]: Go to the next step in the plan that was receive
d from Update Steps Planner.
```

How it works...

Essentially, SSL Certificate Automation Tool takes the certificate and private keys that were previously generated by the tool during the request process and automatically replaces the default self-signed certificate for the Single Sign-On service while starting and stopping the appropriate services during the process.

Registering the Inventory Service certificate

The Inventory Service certificate needs to be bound to the corresponding service in order for the neighboring services to trust the service and not prompt for verification. The default certificate is self-signed and not trusted by any remote machine.

Getting started

In order to proceed, we require access to the directory that holds the certificate and private key that were generated as a result of the certificate request completed earlier. In our example, the certificates are located in the C:\Certificates\SSLTool\ requests\<service name> folder.

Ensure that the command prompt account has administrative access to the vCenter and local servers.

How to do it...

Perform the following steps:

1. Open the command prompt on the local vCenter server with administrator rights.

2. Navigate to the location where VMware SSL Certificate Automation Tool has been installed (in our example, `C:\Certificates\SSLTool`).

3. Run `ssl-updater.bat`.

4. From the main menu, enter 4 to update Inventory Service.

5. Next, enter 3 to update the Inventory Service SSL certificate.

```
==================================================================
Main menu

Enter the action you want to run
    1. Plan your steps to update SSL certificates(Update Steps Planner)
    2. Generate Certificate Signing Requests
    3. Update Single Sign-On
    4. Update Inventory Service
    5. Update vCenter Server
    6. Update vCenter Orchestrator(vCO)
    7. Update vSphere Web Client and Log Browser
    8. Update vSphere Update Manager(VUM)
    9. End the update process and exit

The chosen action is: 4

==================================================================
4. Update the Inventory Service SSL Certificate

    1. Update the Inventory Service Trust to Single Sign-On
    2. Update the Inventory Service Trust to vCenter Server
    3. Update the Inventory Service SSL Certificate
    4. Rollback to the previous Inventory Service SSL Certificate
    5. Return to the main menu to update other services

The chosen service is: 3_
```

6. Ensure that the SSL chain is set to the location of the Single Sign-On certificate (in our example, `C:\Certificates\SSLTool\requests\vCenterInventoryService-VCENTER55\rui.crt`).

7. Ensure that the private key is set to the location of the Single Sign-On private key (in our example, `C:\Certificates\SSLTool\requests\vCenterInventoryService-VCENTER55\rui.key`).

8. Enter the username and password for the Single Sign-On administrative account.

9. The process will stop and restart the related services and indicate that the update was completed successfully.

```
Enter the location to the new Inventory Service SSL chain: C:\Certificates\SSLTo
ol\requests\vCenterInventoryService-VCENTER55\rui.crt
Enter the location to the new Inventory Service private key: C:\Certificates\SSL
Tool\requests\vCenterInventoryService-VCENTER55\rui.key
Enter the Single Sign-On Administrator user (default value is: administrator@vsp
here.local):
Enter the Single Sign-On Administrator password (will not be echoed):

[.] The supplied certificate chain is valid.

[Wed 08/06/2014 - 16:06:52.35]: Last operation update Inventory Service SSL cert
ificate completed successfully.
```

How it works...

SSL Certificate Automation Tool takes the certificate and private keys that were previously generated by the tool during the request process and automatically replaces the default self-signed certificate with the Inventory Service certificate while starting and stopping the appropriate services during the process.

There is also an option to update the trust between certificates; if a new certificate is generated for a particular service that is different from the existing service certificates, a trust might need to be updated.

Registering the vCenter certificate

The vCenter certificate needs to be bound to the corresponding service for the neighboring services to trust the service and not prompt for verification. The default certificate is self-signed and is not trusted by any remote machine.

Getting started

In order to proceed, we require access to the directory that holds the certificate and private key that were generated as a result of the certificate request completed earlier. In our example, the certificates are located in the `C:\Certificates\SSLTool\requests\<service name>` folder.

Ensure that the command prompt account has administrative access to the vCenter and local servers.

How to do it...

Perform the following steps:

1. Open a command prompt as an administrator on the local vCenter server.

2. Navigate to the location where VMware SSL Certificate Automation Tool has been installed (in our example, `C:\Certificates\SSLTool`).

3. Run `ssl-updater.bat`.

4. From the main menu, enter 5 to update the vCenter server.

5. Next, enter 2 to update the vCenter server SSL certificate.

6. Ensure that the SSL chain is set to the location of the vCenter server certificate (in our example, `C:\Certificates\SSLTool\requests\vCenterServer-VCENTER55\rui.crt`).

7. Ensure that the private key is set to the location of the Single Sign-On private key (in our example, `C:\Certificates\SSLTool\requests\vCenterServer-VCENTER55\rui.key`).

8. Enter the username and password for the vCenter server administrative account.

9. Enter the vCenter server original database password.

10. Enter the username and password for the Single Sign-On administrative account.

11. The process will stop and restart the related services and indicate that the update completed successfully.

How it works...

SSL Certificate Automation Tool takes the certificate and private keys that were previously generated by the tool during the request process and automatically replaces the default self-signed certificate with the vCenter server while starting and stopping the appropriate services during the process.

> The original database password can often be difficult for an administrator to remember. The password can be changed if required. It is always a best practice to take a snapshot of the vCenter server prior to applying any certificates if that server is virtual.

The vCenter server certificate is the most visible example that a self-signed certificate is be ng used, and this communication between the endpoint and the server might be vulnerable to man-in-the-middle attacks. The certificate warning, as seen in the following screenshot, is almost always ignored even during the production of vSphere deployments:

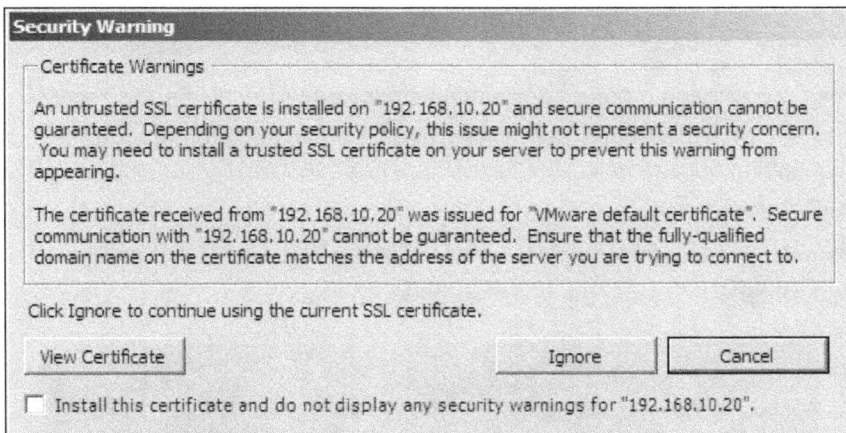

In 9 out of 10 VMware environments visited, this dialog is present or the administrator has selected **Ignore**; so, the warning is not displayed any longer.

Registering the Web Client certificate

The Web Client certificate needs to be bound to the corresponding service in order for the neighboring services to trust the service and not prompt for verification. The default certificate is self-signed and not trusted by any remote machine.

Getting started

In order to proceed, we require access to the directory that holds the certificate and private key that were generated as a result of the certificate request completed earlier. In our example, the certificates are located in the `C:\Certificates\SSLTool\requests\<service name>` folder.

Ensure that the command prompt account has administrative access to the vCenter and local servers.

How to do it...

Perform the following steps:

1. Open a command prompt as an administrator on the local vCenter server.
2. Navigate to the location where VMware SSL Certificate Automation Tool has been installed (in our example, `C:\Certificates\SSLTool`).
3. Run `ssl-updater.bat`.
4. From the main menu, enter 7 to update vSphere Web Client and Log Browser.
5. Next, enter 4 to update the Web Client SSL certificate.

6. Ensure that the SSL chain is set to the location of the vCenter server certificate (in our example, `C:\Certificates\SSLTool\requests\vCenterWebClient-VCENTER55\rui.crt`).

7. Ensure that the private key is set to the location of the Single Sign-On private key (in our example, `C:\Certificates\SSLTool\requests\vCenterWebClient-VCENTER55\rui.key`).

8. Enter the username and password for the Single Sign-On administrative account.

9. The process will stop and restart the related services and indicate that the update completed successfully.

```
[Wed 08/06/2014 - 16:39:42.49]: The services that are restarted as a part of thi
s operation are: vSphere Web Client
Enter location to the new Web Client SSL chain: C:\Certificates\SSLTool\requests
\vCenterWebClient-VCENTER55\rui.crt
Enter location to the new Web Client private key: C:\Certificates\SSLTool\reques
ts\vCenterWebClient-VCENTER55\rui.key
Enter Single Sign-On Administrator user (default value is: administrator@vsphere
.local):
Enter Single Sign-On Administrator password (will not be echoed):

[.] The supplied certificate chain is valid.
Stopping the vSphere Web Client...
vSphere Web Client stopped.
Starting vSphere Web Client... (this may take some time)
vSphere Web Client started.

[Wed 08/06/2014 - 16:48:20.15]: Last operation update vSphere Web Client SSL cer
tificate completed successfully.
```

How it works...

SSL Certificate Automation Tool takes the certificate and private keys that were previously generated by the tool during the request process and automatically replaces the default self-signed certificate with the vCenter Web Client certificate while starting and stopping the appropriate services during the process.

vCenter Web Client must be correctly configured with a trusted certificate to avoid attack by man-in-the-middle or endpoint spoofing.

Registering the Log Browser certificate

The Log Browser certificate allows for the viewing, searching, and exporting of vCenter Server and ESXi logfiles. The Log Browser certificate needs to be bound to the corresponding service in order for the neighboring services to trust the service and not prompt for verification. The default certificate is self-signed and not trusted by any remote machine.

Getting started

In order to proceed, we require access to the directory that holds the certificate and private key that were generated as a result of the certificate request completed earlier. In our example, the certificates are located in the `C:\Certificates\SSLTool\requests\<service name>` folder.

Ensure that the command prompt account has administrative access to the vCenter and local servers.

How to do it...

Perform the following steps:

1. Open a command prompt as an administrator on the local vCenter server.

2. Navigate to the location where VMware SSL Certificate Automation Tool has been installed (in our example, `C:\Certificates\SSLTool`).

3. Run `ssl-updater.bat`.

4. From the main menu, enter 7 to update vSphere Web Client and Log Browser.

5. Next, enter 6 to update the Log Browser SSL certificate.

```
========================================================================
7. Update the vSphere Web Client and Log Browser SSL Certificates
         1. Update the Web Client Trust to Single Sign-On
         2. Update the Web Client Trust to Inventory Service
         3. Update the Web Client Trust to vCenter Server
         4. Update the Web Client SSL Certificate
         5. Update the Log Browser Trust to Single Sign-On
         6. Update the Log Browser SSL Certificate
         7. Rollback to the previous Web Client SSL Certificate
         8. Rollback to the previous Log Browser SSL Certificate
         9. Return to the main menu to update other services

The chosen service is: 6
```

6. Ensure that the SSL chain is set to the location of the vCenter server certificate (in our example, `C:\Certificates\SSLTool\requests\vCenterLogBrowser-VCENTER55\rui.crt`).

7. Ensure that the private key is set to the location of the Single Sign-On private key (in our example, `C:\Certificates\SSLTool\requests\vCenterLogBrowser-VCENTER55\rui.key`).

8. Enter the username and password for the Single Sign-On administrative account.

9. The process will stop and restart the related services and indicate the update completed successfully.

```
[Wed 08/06/2014 - 16:56:00.81]: The services that are restarted as a part of thi
s operation are: VMware Log Browser
Enter location to the new Log Browser SSL chain: C:\Certificates\SSLTool\request
s\vCenterLogBrowser-VCENTER55\rui.crt
Enter location to the new Log Browser private key: C:\Certificates\SSLTool\reque
sts\vCenterLogBrowser-VCENTER55\rui.key
Enter Single Sign-On Administrator user (default value is: administrator@vsphere
.local):
Enter Single Sign-On Administrator password (will not be echoed):

[.] The supplied certificate chain is valid.

[Wed 08/06/2014 - 17:07:24.10]: Last operation update Log Browser SSL certificat
e completed successfully.
```

How it works...

SSL Certificate Automation Tool takes the certificate and private keys that were previously generated by the tool during the request process and automatically replaces the default self-signed certificate with the Log Browser certificate while starting and stopping the appropriate services during the process. When the Log Browser certificate is not trusted, viewing the **Tasks & Events** tab will produce a certificate trust dialog box.

Registering the Update Manager certificate

The Update Manager certificate needs to be bound to the corresponding service in order for the neighboring services to trust the service and not prompt for verification. The default certificate is self-signed and not trusted by any remote machine.

> Update Manager is an optional component and, although common, might not be present in all deployments.

Getting started

In order to proceed, we require access to the directory that holds the certificate and private key that were generated as a result of the certificate request completed earlier. In our example, the certificates are located in the C:\Certificates\SSLTool\ requests\<service name> folder.

Ensure that the command prompt account has administrative access to the vCenter and local servers.

How to do it...

Perform the following steps:

1. Open a command prompt as an administrator on the local vCenter server.

2. Navigate to the location where VMware SSL Certificate Automation Tool has been installed (in our example, `C:\Certificates\SSLTool`).

3. Run `ssl-updater.bat`.

4. From the main menu, enter `8` to update **vSphere Update Manager** (**VUM**).

5. Next, enter `1` to update the **vSphere Update Manager** (**VUM**) SSL certificate.

```
=======+===========================================================
Main menu

Enter the action you want to run
    1. Plan your steps to update SSL certificates(Update Steps Planner)
    2. Generate Certificate Signing Requests
    3. Update Single Sign-On
    4. Update Inventory Service
    5. Update vCenter Server
    6. Update vCenter Orchestrator(vCO)
    7. Update vSphere Web Client and Log Browser
    8. Update vSphere Update Manager(VUM)
    9. End the update process and exit

The chosen action is: 8

===================================================================
8. Update the vSphere Update Manager(VUM) SSL Certificate

    1. Update the vSphere Update Manager(VUM) SSL Certificate
    2. Update the vSphere Update Manager(VUM) Trust to vCenter Server
    3. Rollback to the previous vSphere Update Manager SSL Certificate
    4. Return to the main menu to update other services

The chosen service is: 1
```

6. Ensure that the SSL chain is set to the location of the vCenter server certificate (in our example, `C:\Certificates\SSLTool\requests\ VMwareUpdateManager-VCENTER55\rui.crt`).

7. Ensure that the private key is set to the location of the Single Sign-On private key (in our example, `C:\Certificates\SSLTool\requests\ VMwareUpdateManager-VCENTER55\rui.key`).

8. Enter the username and password for the Single Sign-On administrative account.

9. The process will typically complete successfully after stopping and starting the required services. In our example, the process failed due to Update Manager not being installed.

```
[Wed 08/06/2014 - 17:11:19.85]: The services that are restarted as a part of thi
s operation are: VMware vSphere Update Manager (VMware vSphere Update Manager UF
A service will also be stopped).
Enter location to the new vSphere Update Manager SSL chain: C:\Certificates\SSLT
ool\requests\VMwareUpdateManager-VCENTER55\rui.crt
Enter location to the new vSphere Update Manager private key: C:\Certificates\SS
LTool\requests\VMwareUpdateManager-VCENTER55\rui.key
Enter vCenter Server administrator user name (default value is: training\adminis
trator):
Enter vCenter Server administrator password (will not be echoed):

[.] The supplied certificate chain is valid.

[Wed 08/06/2014 - 17:13:44.28]: Last operation update vSphere Update Manager SSL
 certificate failed :
[Wed 08/06/2014 - 17:13:44.29]: The service is not installed on that machine.
```

How it works...

SSL Certificate Automation Tool takes the certificate and private keys that were previously generated by the tool during the request process and automatically replaces the default self-signed certificate with the vSphere Update Manager certificate while starting and stopping the appropriate services during the process.

Installing an ESXi host certificate

Updating the certificate on an ESXi host is not currently supported by SSL Certificate Automation Tool. The certificate and private key files must be manually copied to the corresponding ESXi host for deployment.

Getting started

In order to proceed, we require access to the directory that holds the certificate and private key that were generated as a result of the certificate request completed earlier. In our example, the certificates are located in the `C:\Certificates\SSLTool\requests\<service name>` folder.

Ensure that the command prompt account has administrative access to the vCenter and local servers.

Ensure that the root username and password for the host are available if needed.

How to do it...

Perform the following steps:

1. Enable SSH on the specified host (in our example, **esx5502.training.lab**).

2. Put the host in maintenance mode.

3. Navigate to the location where VMware SSL Certificate Automation Tool has saved the certificate and private key (in our example, `C:\Certificates\SSLTool\requests\esxi-esx5502`).

4. Copy both the `rui.cert` and `rui.key` files from the directory to the `/etc/vmware/ssl` ESXi host directory. In our example, we'll use WinSCP for the copy.

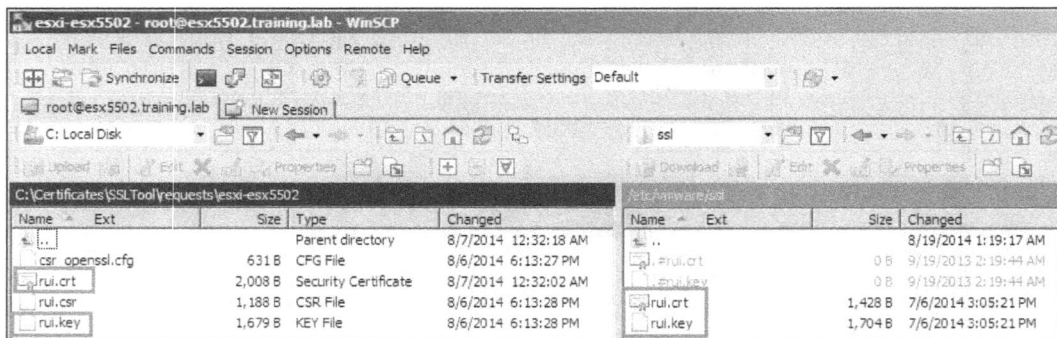

5. Restart the management agents on the host.

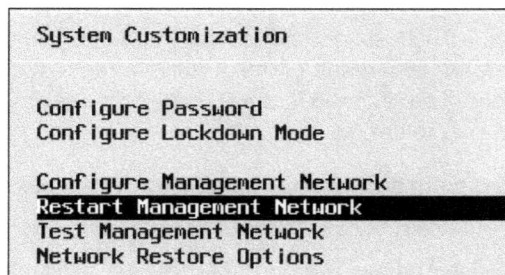

6. Remove the host from maintenance mode.

7. Disconnect and reconnect the host to the vCenter cluster.

8. Disable SSH on the specified host (in our example, **esx5502.training.lab**).

How it works...

When SSL Certificate Automation Tool automates the copying of the certificate and private keys as well as stopping and starting services, the host installation is not automated. The host certificate and key files must be copied manually to the host. Once the files are copied, the management agents must be restarted.

If the host is already part of an existing vCenter cluster, there are additional steps that need to be completed. The host should be disconnected and then reconnected to the cluster. Note that this will disable **High Availability** (**HA**) and other vCenter services. The virtual machines running on the host will not be affected directly. Once the host has been reconnected, it will function normally.

The certificate validity can be confirmed by pointing a web browser to the ESXi **Fully Qualified Domain Name** (**FQDN**). If the certificate is invalid in any way, including self-signed, a dialog similar to the one shown in the following screenshot will be shown:

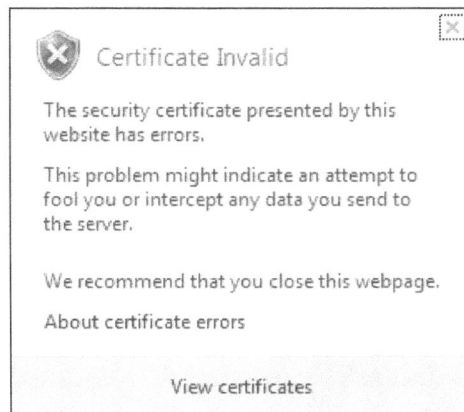

Once a proper certificate has been installed, the web browser will display a dialog similar to the one shown in the following screenshot, indicating that a trusted certificate is installed:

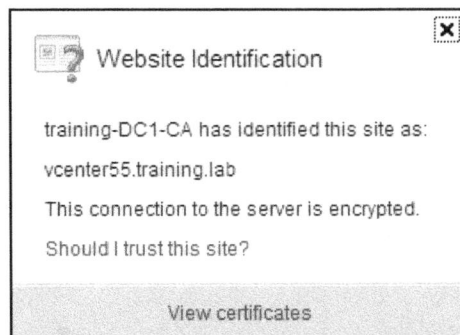

13
Configuring vShield VXLAN Virtual Wires

In this chapter, we will cover the following recipes:

- ▶ Prerequisites for configuring VXLAN virtual wires
- ▶ Configuring VXLAN virtual wires
- ▶ Testing VXLAN virtual wires
- ▶ Configuring firewall rules for VXLAN virtual wires

Introduction

The vShield VXLAN virtual wire is a layer 2 overlay network segment that enables a scalable network segment that is not tied to any physical network fabric. A VXLAN virtual wire can span multiple distributed switches to provide a virtual layer 2 network between multiple vSphere clusters.

The power of VXLAN virtual wires is the ability to implement a layer 2 segment on top of the existing layer 3 networks through encapsulation, which allows traffic to traverse geographically dispersed clusters. This is particularly useful in a cloud design where a physical layer 2 network does not exist between datacenters. A virtual wire allows a network shortcut between distributed virtual switches located on two completely separate physical and virtual infrastructures that are managed by the same vCenter. By allowing application traffic at layer 2 between clusters, VXLAN virtual wires provide the capability to vMotion virtual machines from one cluster to another. Placement on a underutilized cluster allows for better use of resources for higher virtual efficiency.

This chapter assumes that at least one vSphere distributed switch is set up and functional on a minimum of a single vSphere cluster. The basic setup and configuration of vSphere distributed switches is outside the scope of this book. For more information on the licensing required for distributed switch functionality and setup steps, please visit `http://www.vmware.com/in/support/support-resources/licensing/` and `http://www.vmware.com/products/vsphere/features/distributed-switch`.

Prerequisites for configuring VXLAN virtual wires

Configuring VXLAN virtual wires starts with verifying some prerequisites that are required prior to the actual configuration of the first virtual wire. Please confer with the network administrator for information regarding the settings on your physical network equipment if concepts are unfamiliar. Making changes to the physical network equipment can adversely affect machines and users outside of the virtual infrastructure. The settings should be first tested in an isolated network if at all possible.

Getting started

In order to proceed, we require access to vShield App through the vSphere Client plugin. The plugin can be enabled through the **Plug-ins** menu in vSphere Client. The client can be run on any modern Windows desktop operating system or server operating system.

> The vShield vSphere Client plugin requires Adobe Flash, which is not supported on Linux operating systems at this time.

vShield Manager must be installed and the vCenter account used for login should have Enterprise administrator rights to vShield Manager.

The network must be prepared prior to configuring VXLAN virtual wires. The prerequisites are as follows:

- The VMware vCenter Server, ESXi, and vSphere distributed switch versions must be Version 5.1 or greater
- The Managed IP address for any vCenter server that will manage a VXLAN virtual wire must be set to a valid value

▸ DHCP must be available on the underlying VLANs that support VXLAN virtual wires

▸ A multicast address range and segment ID pool must be configured

▸ **Internet Group Management Protocol** (**IGMP**) snooping must be enabled on layer 2 switches and the IGMP querier must be enabled on a router or layer 3 switches connecting the VXLAN participating hosts

▸ The physical network must support a **Maximum Transmission Unit** (**MTU**) of at least 1550 (1600 is recommended)

For a complete list of physical switch prerequisites, visit http://kb.vmware.com/ selfservice/microsites/search.do?language=en_US&cmd=displayKC&externa lId=2050697.

How to do it...

In order to set up the prerequisite configurations to be completed, this *How to do it...* section is broken down into milestones.

Ensuring the Managed IP address of vCenter is set

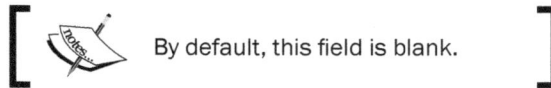

By default, this field is blank.

To ensure that the Managed IP address of vCenter is set, perform the following steps:

1. Launch vSphere Client using an account with administrative rights, if it is not already open.

2. Navigate to **Home** from the menu bar.

3. Select **vCenter Server Settings**.

4. Select **Runtime Settings** from the option list on the left-hand side.

5.   Enter the IP address for **vCenter Server Managed IP** (in our example,
      192.168.10.20).

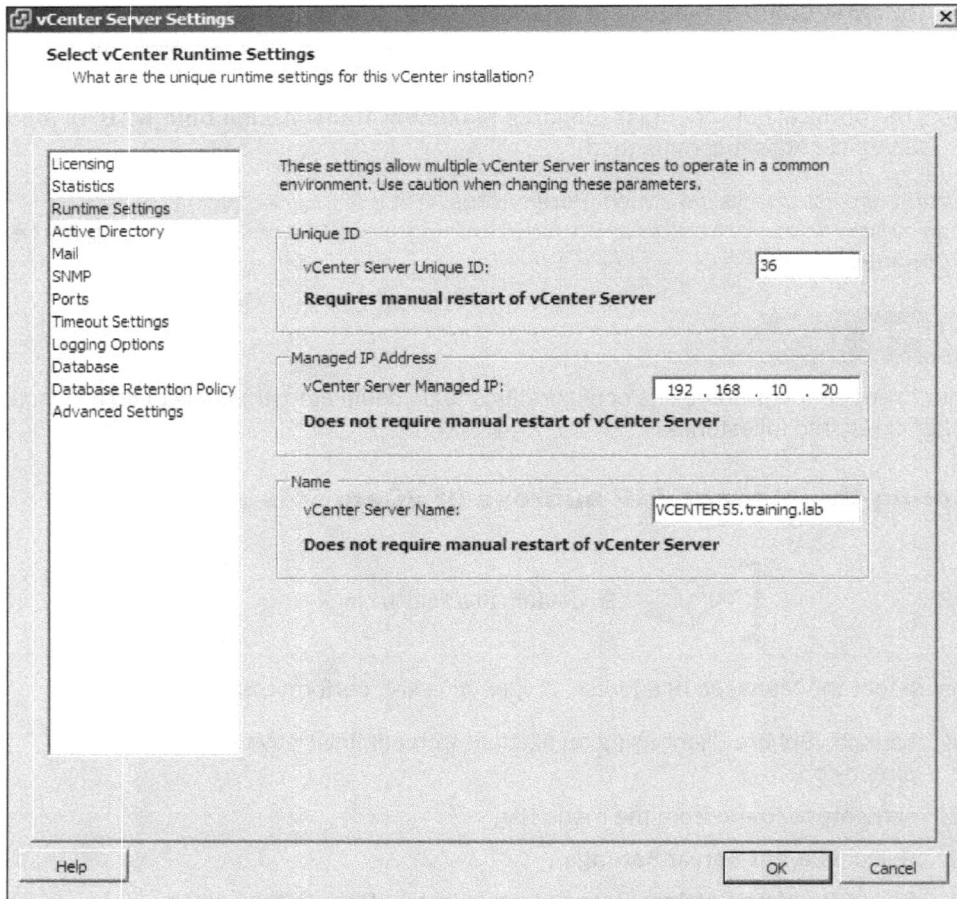

6.   Click on **OK** to save the settings.

Ensuring DHCP availability

To ensure DHCP availability, perform the following steps:

1.   Navigate to **Home** | **Inventory** | **Networking** from the menu bar.

2.   Select a valid datacenter (in our example, **Datacenter**).

3.   Select the **IP Pools** tab and click on **Add...**.

4.   Enter a valid **IP Pool Name** (in our example, **VXLAN Pool**).

5.   Enter a valid **Subnet** (in our example, **172.21.10.0/24**).

6. Enter a valid **Gateway** (in our example, **172.21.10.1**).

7. Enter a valid scope in **Ranges** (in our example, **172.21.10.10#101**).

8. Click on **view** to confirm the address range.

9. Select the **Associations** tab from the **VXLAN Pool Properties** window.

10. Check the networks that should use this IP pool (in our example, **VX_transport_dvPortGroup**).

11. Click on **OK** to save the changes.

Setting a multicast address range and segment ID pool

1. Navigate to **Home | Inventory | Hosts and Clusters** from the menu bar.

2. Select a valid datacenter (in our example, **Datacenter**).

3. Select the **Preparation** option under the **Network Virtualization** tab.

4. Click on **Segment ID,** and then click on **Edit...**.

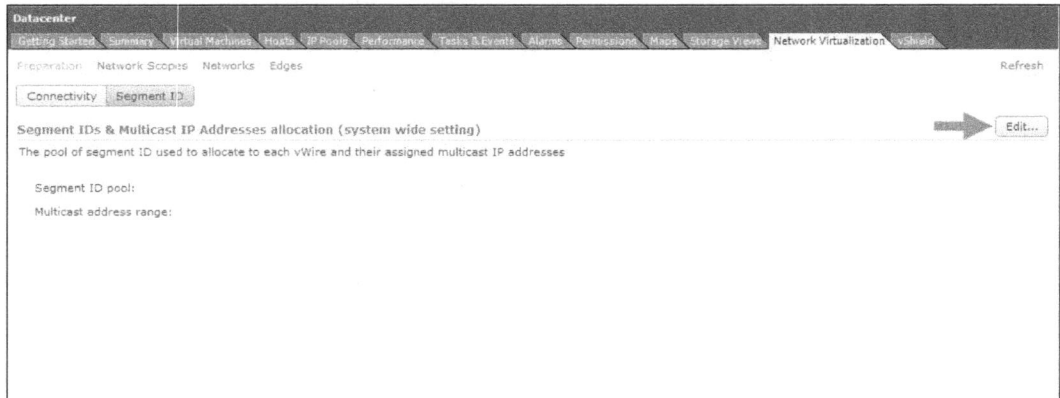

5. Set the range for **Segment ID pool** (in our example, **5000-5200)**. The **Segment ID pool** field specifies the number of logical L2 networks that can possibly be created.

6. Set the **Multicast addresses** (in our example, **224.1.1.100-244.1.1.200**).

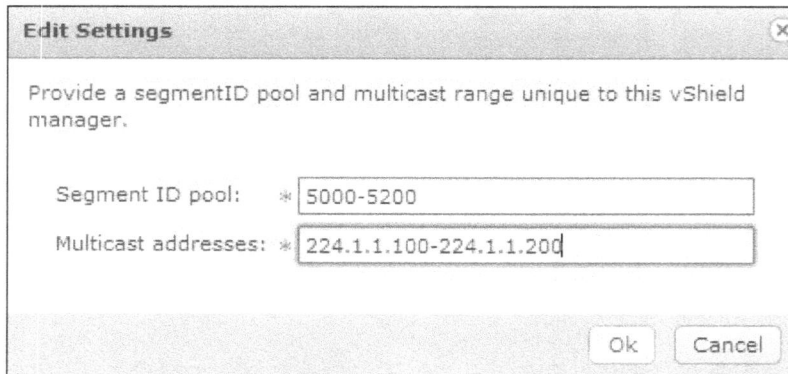

7. Click on **Ok** to save the settings.

Setting up network connectivity for VXLAN traffic

Perform the following steps:

1. Navigate to **Home | Inventory | Hosts and Clusters** from the menu bar.
2. Select a valid datacenter (in our example, **Datacenter**).
3. Select the **Network Virtualization** tab and select the **Preparation** option.
4. Click on **Connectivity,** and then click on **Edit...**.

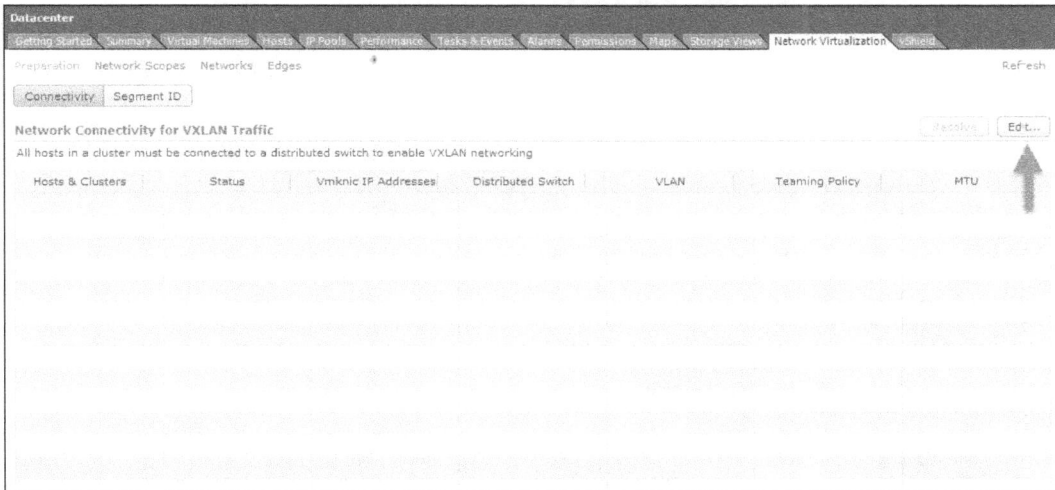

5. Select a valid **Cluster**, **Distributed Switch**, and **VLAN** (in our example, **Lab Cluster**, **dvSwitch1**, and **20** respectively).

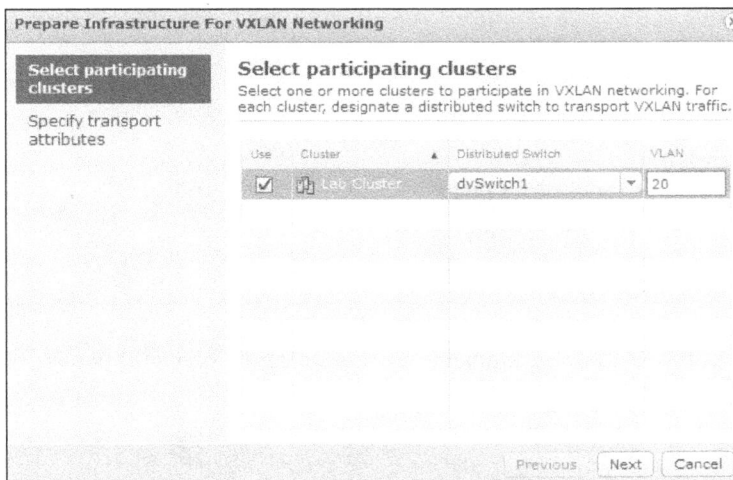

6. Click on **Next**.

7. Accept the default values for **Teaming Policy (Static EtherChannel)** and **MTU (1600)**.

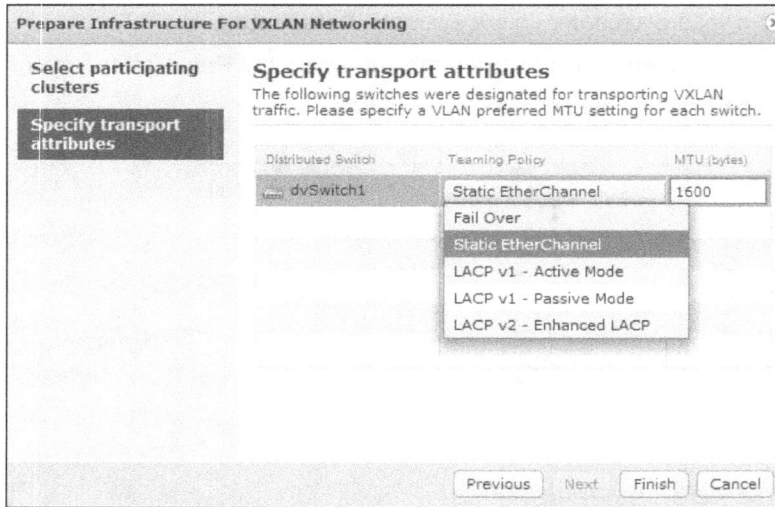

8. Click on **Finish**.

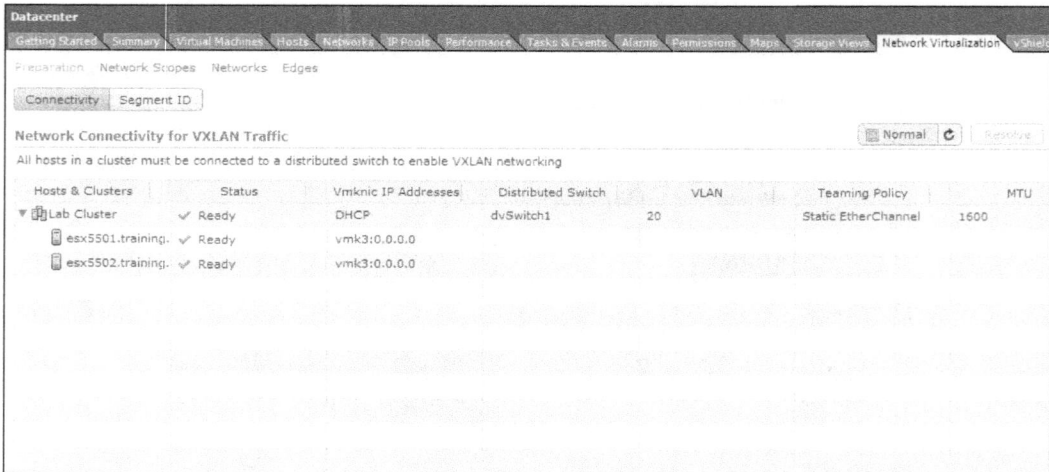

9. Note that the **Status** will change to **Normal** after the configuration is complete.

Verifying the distributed switch MTU setting

To verify the distributed switch MTU setting, perform the following steps:

1. Navigate to **Home** | **Inventory** | **Networking** from the menu bar.

2. Select a valid distributed switch (in our example, **dvSwitch1**).

3. Right-click on **dvSwitch1** and select **Edit Settings**.

4. Select **Advanced** from the **Properties** tab.

> Ensure that the value of **Maximum MTU** is greater than 1550 (in our example, **1600**). This will prevent packet fragmentation due to the increased size of the VXLAN frames.

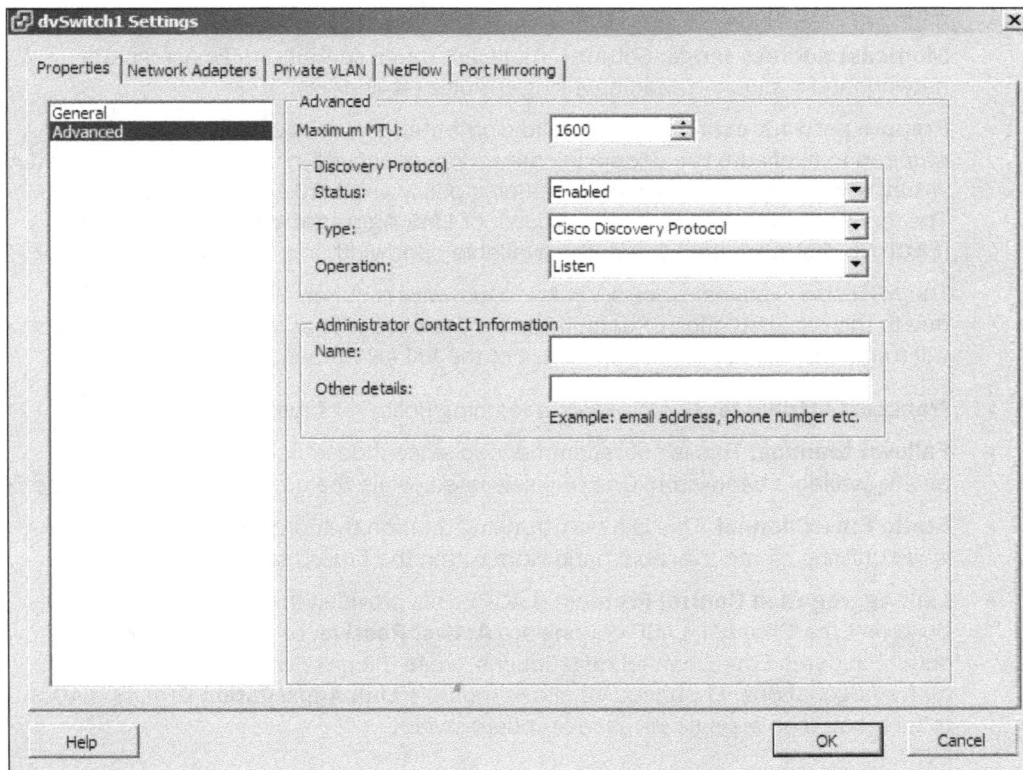

5. Click on **OK** to close the window.

How it works...

Configuring the prerequisites correctly will often involve the skill of the network administrator to ensure that the physical and virtual settings do not conflict with one another. Each of the prerequisites is configured within the vSphere environment with the exception of DHCP, which will likely already have a configured scope in place:

- **Managed IP address of vCenter server**: This setting is required to ensure that the services and servers are able to identify the vCenter server based on both its fully qualified domain name in addition to its IP address.

- **Ensure DHCP is available by IP Pool**: When creating a VXLAN virtual wire, DHCP is used for IP address provisioning by default. If a VXLAN network is set up with an address range or segment that does not have access to a valid DHCP scope or pool, a manual IP address can be used.

- **Multicast address range**: Setting a multicast range spreads traffic across the network and avoids overloading a single multicast address.

- **Prepare network connectivity**: A valid distributed switch, cluster, and VLAN are required to configure the underlying network connectivity in preparation for the VXLAN virtual wire creation. In addition, a teaming policy and MTU size must be specified. The teaming policy will usually be a flavor of **Link Aggregation Control Protocol** (**LACP**) to make the best use of the available bandwidth in a fault tolerant manner.

  The MTU size is critical since a VXLAN virtual wire requires additional information due to the encapsulation of data. If the MTU is not set to at least `1550`, the packet will fragment due to the increased size of the VXLAN frames.

- **Transport Attributes**: This provides a teaming policy for fault tolerance.

- **Failover teaming**: This is not recommended since it does not take advantage of all the available bandwidth. One uplink is used, while the other is in standby mode.

- **Static EtherChannel**: This is a port trunking method that provides fault tolerance while utilizing all the available bandwidth within the EtherChannel configuration.

- **Link Aggregation Control Protocol** (**LACP**): This provides the ability to dynamically build an EtherChannel. LACP options are **Active**, **Passive**, or **Enhanced v2**. The active setting initiates EtherChannel negotiations, while the passive setting responds to active negotiations. Enhanced v2 allows multiple **Link Aggregation Groups** (**LAG**s) to be created on a single virtual distributed switch.

There's more

- For more information on Enhanced LACP support in vSphere 5.5, visit `http://kb.vmware.com/selfservice/microsites/search.do?language=en_US&cmd=displayKC&externalId=2051826`

Configuring VXLAN virtual wires

Once the network is ready for the VXLAN virtual wires configuration, the network scopes, networks, and edge configurations can be completed. Prior to proceeding, ensure that the list of applications to be included is available.

Getting started

In order to proceed, we require access to vShield App through the vSphere Client plugin. The plugin can be enabled through the **Plug-ins** menu in vSphere Client. The client can be run on any modern Windows desktop operating system or server operating system.

> The vShield vSphere Client plugin requires Adobe Flash, which is not supported on Linux operating systems at this time.

vShield Manager must be installed and the vCenter account used for login should have Enterprise administrator rights to vShield Manager.

The network must be prepared according to the prerequisites configured in the previous section prior to configuring VXLAN virtual wires.

How to do it...

In this section, we'll be configuring our VXLAN virtual wire to support a SQL server that runs our data warehouse. We want to place this on an isolated network with the ability to vMotion to an alternate datacenter if required. This *How to do it...* section is broken down into milestones.

Adding a VXLAN network scope

Perform the following steps:

1. Navigate to **Home | Inventory | Hosts and Clusters** from the menu bar.
2. Select a valid datacenter (in our example, **Datacenter**).
3. Select the **Network Scopes** option under the **Network Virtualization** tab.
4. Click on **+** to add a scope.
5. Enter a name in the **Name** field (in our example, **Database Virtual Wire**).
6. Enter a **Description** (in our example, **SQL Server connectivity**). This scope will support our SQL database communications.

7. Select a valid cluster (in our example, **Lab Cluster**).

Add Network Scope			⊗
Name	* Database Virtual Wire		
Description	SQL Server connectivity		

Select One or More Clusters to Add to this Network Scope

Clusters	Distributed Switch	Readiness
☑ 🗂 Lab Cluster	dvSwitch1	✓ Ready

Ok | Cancel

8. Click on **Ok** to save the changes.

Adding a VXLAN virtual wire

Perform the following steps:

1. Choose **Home | Inventory | Hosts and Clusters** from the menu bar.
2. Select a valid datacenter (in our example, **Datacenter**).
3. Select the **Networks** option under the **Network Virtualization** tab.
4. Click on **+** to add a scope.
5. Enter a name in the **Name** field (in our example, **SQL_DB_DW**).
6. Enter a description in the **Description** field.
7. Select a valid entry for the **Network Scope** field (in our example, **Database Virtual Wire** is the only option). To this point, only one virtual wire has been created and is the only choice.
8. Note the **Scope Details**.

Create VXLAN Network

Name   * SQL_DB_DW

Description   SQL Data Warehouse Network

Network Scope   Database Virtual Wire   ▼
                  Database Virtual Wire

Scope Details

Name   Database Virtual Wire

Description   SQL Server connectivity

▾ Clusters

Lab Cluster   Ready

▾ Available Services

                                              Ok   Cancel

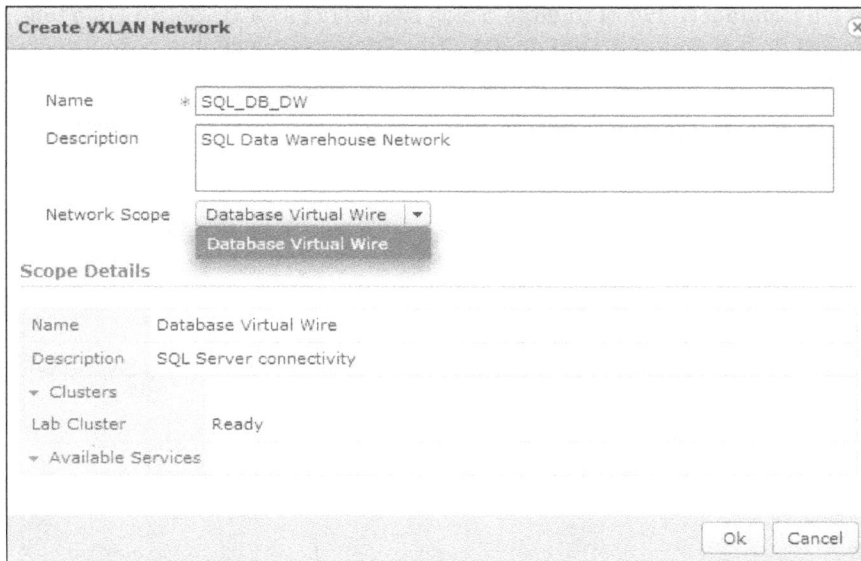

9. Click on **Ok** to create the virtual wire.

Connecting a VXLAN virtual wire to vShield Edge

Perform the following steps:

1. Navigate to **Home | Inventory | Hosts and Clusters** from the menu bar.
2. Select a valid datacenter (in our example, **Datacenter**).
3. Select the **Networks** option under the **Network Virtualization** tab.
4. Highlight the virtual wire (in our example, **SQL_DB_DW**).
5. Click on the gear, and then click on **Connect to Edge...**.

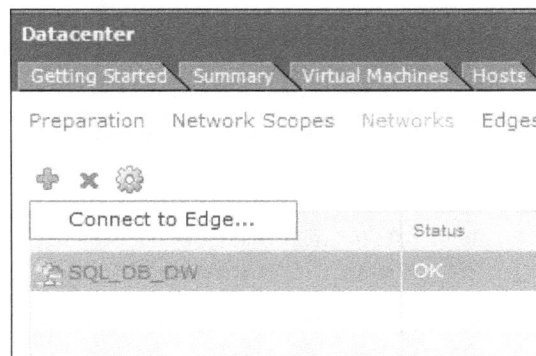

Datacenter

Getting Started Summary Virtual Machines Hosts

Preparation Network Scopes Networks Edges

➕ ✖ ⚙

Connect to Edge...   Status

SQL_DB_DW   OK

6. In the **Connect Network to Edge** dialog box, select a valid vShield Edge from the list (in our example, **LabEdge01**). This Edge was configured previously in *Chapter 9, Configuring vShield Edge.*

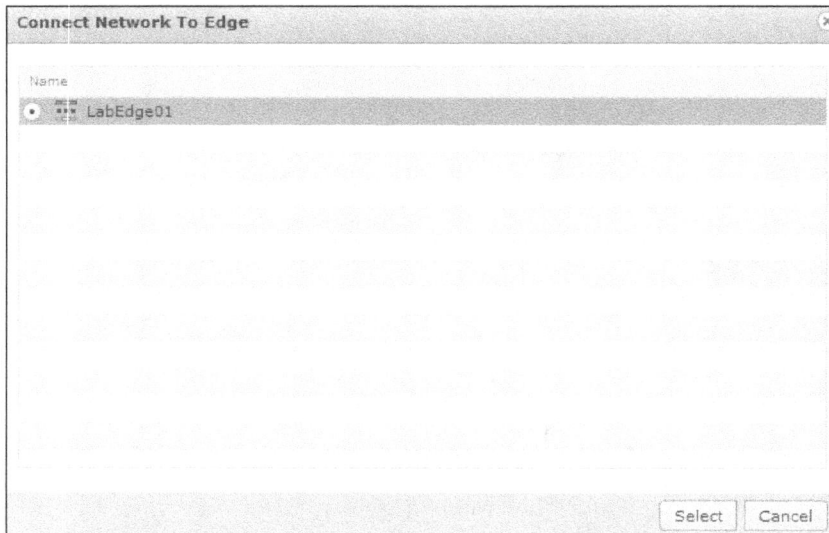

7. Click on **Select**.
8. Click on **Continue** in the prompted window.
9. Within the **Edit Edge Interface** dialog box, create a valid **Name** (in our example, **LabEdge01_VXLAN_SQL**). This name identifies the interface as a VXLAN conduit connected to the vShield Edge for SQL traffic.
10. Set the **Type** option to **Internal**.
11. Verify that **Connected To** is set to **SQL_DB_DW**.
12. Set the **Connectivity Status** option to **Connected**.

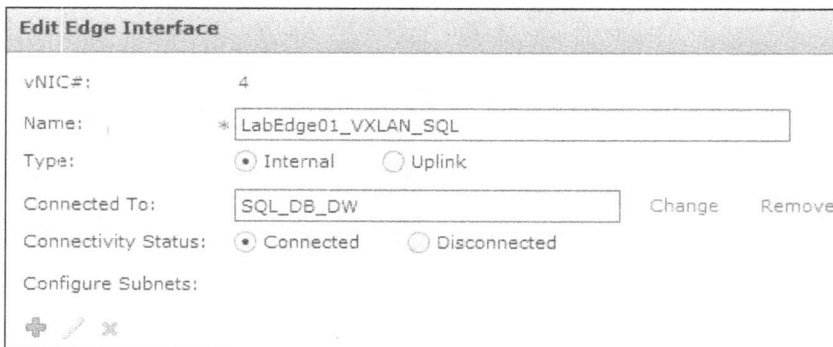

13. Click on **+** to configure a subnet.

14. Within the **Add Subnet** dialog box, add a valid **IP Address** (in our example, **172.21.10.1**).

15. Add a valid **Subnet Mask** (in our example, **255.255.255.0**).

Add Subnet

Specify the IP addresses in the subnet: *

Primary IP	IP Address
●	172.21.10.1

Subnet Mask: * 255.255.255.0

Save   Cancel

16. Click on **Save** to close.

17. Within the **Edit Edge Interface** window, set the value of **MTU** to **1600**. This setting prevents fragmentation caused by the VXLAN frame being added to the packet.

Edit Edge Interface

172.21.10.1*   255.255.255.0

MAC Addresses:

You can specify a MAC address or leave it blank for auto generation. In case of HA, two different MAC addresses are required.

MTU: 1600

Options: ☐ Enable Proxy ARP   ☑ Send ICMP Redirect

Fence Parameters:

Example: ethernet0.filter1.param1=1

Save   Cancel

18. Click on **Save**.

19. Note the new vShield Edge interface.

vNIC	Name	Type	IP Address	Subnet Mask	Connected To	Status
0	LabEdge01_Uplink01	Uplink	10.10.10.1*	255.255.255.0	DMZ Network	✓
1	LabEdge01_Mgmt01	Internal	192.168.10.2*	255.255.255.0	Internal Network	✓
2	LabEdge01_PII_Net01	Internal	10.10.30.1*	255.255.255.0	PII_dvPortGroup	✓
3	LabEdge01_Public	Uplink	67.154.180.244*	255.255.255.224	Virtual Switch Tagged VST	✓
4	LabEdge01_vXLAN_SQL	Internal	172.21.10.1*	255.255.255.0	SQL_DB_DW	
5	vnic5	Internal				⊘
6	vnic6	Internal				⊘
7	vnic7	Internal				⊘
8	vnic8	Internal				⊘
9	vnic9	Internal				⊘

Enabling services for the VXLAN virtual wire

Perform the following steps:

1. Navigate to **Home | Inventory | Hosts and Clusters** from the menu bar.

2. Select a valid datacenter (in our example, **Datacenter**).

3. Select the **Networks** option from the **Network Virtualization** tab.

4. Click on the hyperlink name of the virtual wire (in our example, **SQL_DB_DW**).

5. Select the **Summary** view.

6. Click on **Enable Services...**.

7. Select a valid **Service** (in our example, **Port Profile**).

8. Select a valid **Service Profile** (in our example, **vxlan test service**).

9. Click on **Apply** to save the service profile information. This successfully enables the port profile service for our virtual wire.

Connecting a virtual machine to a VXLAN virtual wire

Perform the following steps:

1. Choose **Home | Inventory | Hosts and Clusters** from the menu bar.

2. Select a valid datacenter (in our example, **Datacenter**).

3. Select the **Networks** option under the **Network Virtualization** tab.

4. Click on the hyperlink name of the virtual wire (in our example, **SQL_DB_DW**).

5. Select the **Virtual Machines** view.

6. Click on **+** to add a virtual machine to the VXLAN.

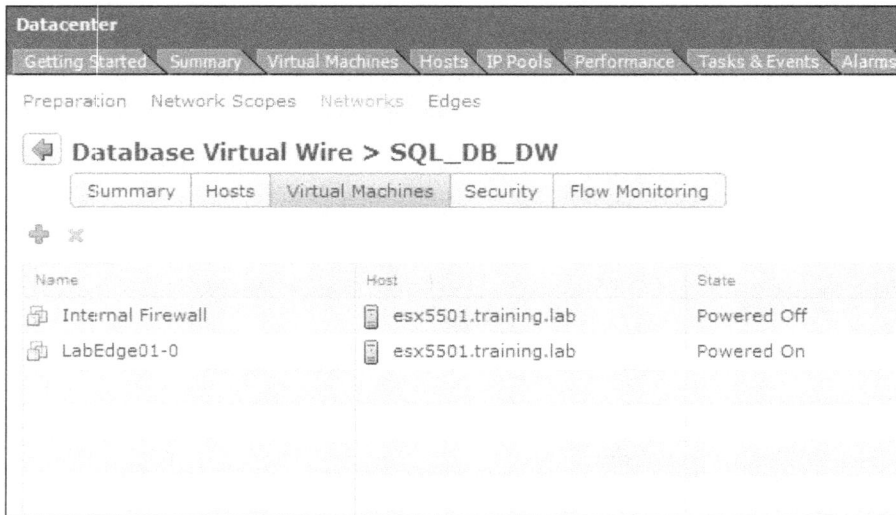

7. Within the **Connect VNics to this Network** dialog box, click on the search icon.

8. Select the virtual NIC of the virtual machine to join the VXLAN (in our example, **SQL DataWarehouse 1**).

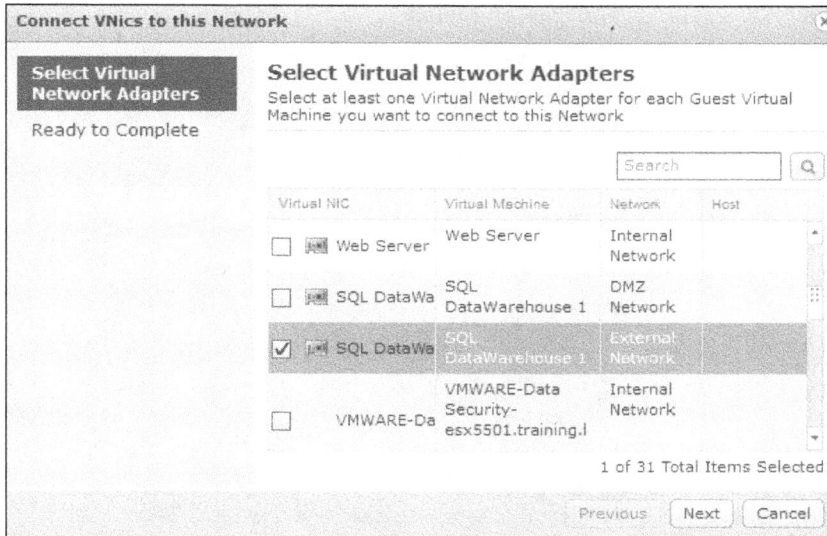

9. Click on **Next**.

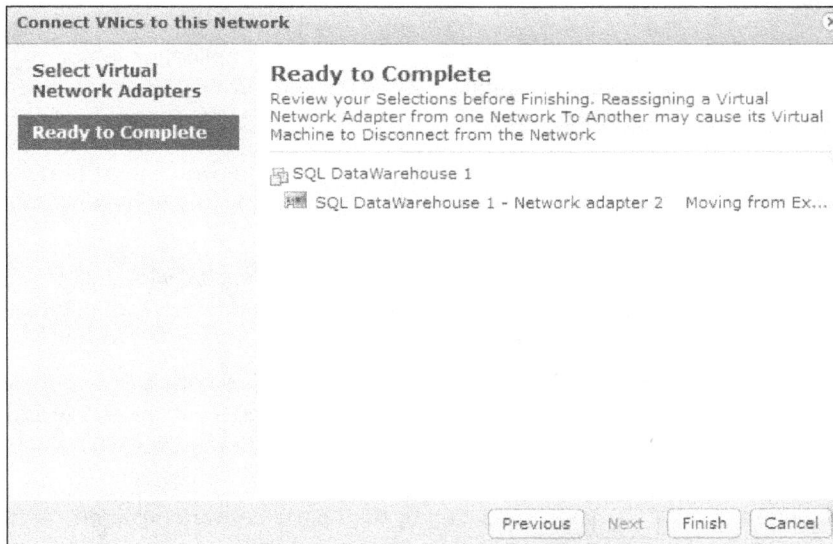

10. Confirm the settings and click on **Finish**.

Note the virtual machine has been added.

Datacenter

Getting Started | Summary | Virtual Machines | Hosts | IP Pools | Perfo

Preparation   Network Scopes   Networks   Edges

Database Virtual Wire > SQL_DB_DW

Summary | Hosts | Virtual Machines | Security | Flow

Name	Host
Internal Firewall	esx5501.training.lab
SQL DataWarehouse 1	esx5501.training.lab
LabEdge01-0	esx5501.training.lab

How it works...

A VXLAN virtual wire is usually configured to support a specific application or set of applications. In our example, we are creating a VXLAN to support SQL Server data warehouse traffic for an isolated set of data warehouse servers:

▶ **Add a VXLAN network scope**: This adds an identified network space that can contain multiple VXLAN virtual wires, organizing similarly functioning VXLANs into a single container.

▶ **Add a VXLAN virtual wire**: This adds an actual VXLAN virtual wire that provides the layer 2 network abstraction to allow any virtual machine vNIC to connect as they will in a standard port group.

▶ **Connect VXLAN Virtual Wire to vShield Edge**: This follows the same process as connecting a non-VXLAN network to a vShield Edge. The link type and IP address are required. In the case of a VXLAN virtual wire, ensure that the MTU is set to 1600. vShield Edge provides isolation for the VXLAN as well as security.

▶ **Enable Services**: This can be provided by third-party network providers, and in our example, we have the mock service known as vxlan test service as no third-party providers were available.

▶ **Connect Virtual Machine to VXLAN**: This can be accomplished by either altering the properties of the virtual machine itself, or by accessing the properties of the virtual wire itself. To add a virtual machine, simply search for a valid vNIC for the virtual machine and add it to the VXLAN. The vNIC will be reassigned to the VXLAN virtual wire from its original network.

Testing VXLAN virtual wires

Once the setup of the VXLAN virtual wire has been completed, the network should be tested to confirm proper connectivity. **Internet Control Message Protocol** (**ICMP**) and broadcast tests are available. The connectivity should be verified between each endpoint host of the virtual wire.

Getting started

To proceed, we'll require access to vShield App through the vSphere Client plugin. The plugin can be enabled through the **Plug-ins** menu in vSphere Client. The client can be run on any modern Windows desktop operating system or server operating system.

> The vShield vSphere Client plugin requires Adobe Flash, which is not supported on Linux operating systems at this time.

vShield Manager must be installed and the vCenter account used for login should have Enterprise administrator rights to vShield Manager.

How to do it...

Perform the following steps:

1. Navigate to **Home | Inventory | Hosts and Clusters** from the menu bar.
2. Select a valid datacenter (in our example, **Datacenter**).
3. Select the **Networks** option under the **Network Virtualization** tab.
4. Click on the hyperlink name of the virtual wire (in our example, **SQL_DB_DW**).
5. Select the **Hosts** view.
6. Highlight a host, click on the gear icon, and then select **Test Connectivity...**.

7. Select a valid **Source host** (in our example, **esx5501.training.lab**).

8. Select a valid **Destination host** (in our example, **esx5502.training.lab**).

9. Pick a valid value for **Size of test packet** from the drop-down options (in our example, **VXLAN standard**). The alternate size is the standard TCP/IP packet size.

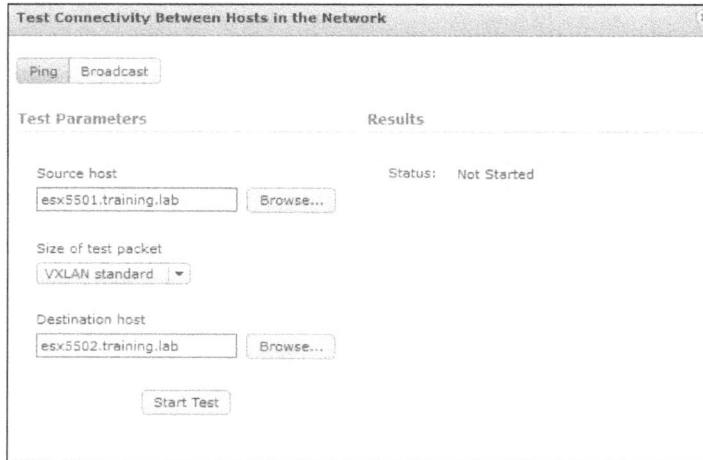

10. Click on **Start Test**.

> A bug exists in vShield 5.5.0 build 1447281 used in this book, which causes the test to fail with an *unknown interface* error.

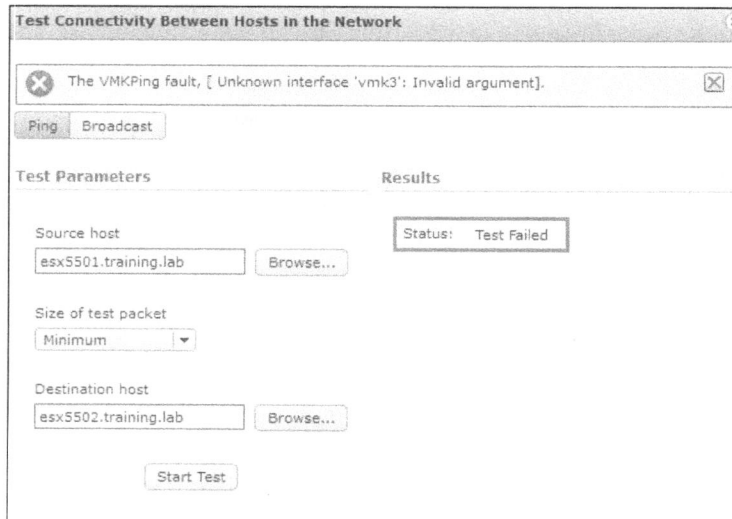

11. There is a workaround to test connectivity with `vmkping` through an SSH connection. Open an SSH connect to a valid ESXi host (in our example, we'll use `Putty.exe` to make a connection).

12. After connecting with an administrative account, run `esxcfg-vmknic -l` to list the virtual network adapters; **vmk3** is the vNIC that failed the connection test.

```
~ # esxcfg-vmknic -l
Interface  Port Group/DVPort   IP Family IP Address
 Netmask            Broadcast       MAC Address       MTU     TSO MSS   Enabled Typ
e
vmk0        Management Network   IPv4        192.168.10.10
 255.255.255.0   192.168.10.255  00:50:56:9f:7f:3d 1500    65535     true    STA
TIC
vmk1        vmservice-vmknic-pg IPv4        169.254.1.1
 255.255.255.0   169.254.1.255   00:50:56:6e:bf:05 1500    65535     true    STA
TIC
vmk2        iSCSI                IPv4        10.10.10.10
 255.255.255.0   10.10.10.255    00:50:56:67:80:98 1500    65535     true    STA
TIC
vmk3        541                  IPv4        172.21.10.2
 255.255.255.0   172.21.10.255   00:50:56:64:90:1e 1600    65535     true    STA
TIC
```

13. Running `vmkping 192.168.10.11 -I vmk0` confirms that the vmk0 vNIC is connected as expected.

```
~ # vmkping 192.168.10.11 -I vmk0
PING 192.168.10.11 (192.168.10.11): 56 data bytes
64 bytes from 192.168.10.11: icmp_seq=0 ttl=64 time=1.567 ms
64 bytes from 192.168.10.11: icmp_seq=1 ttl=64 time=0.600 ms
64 bytes from 192.168.10.11: icmp_seq=2 ttl=64 time=0.518 ms

--- 192.168.10.11 ping statistics ---
3 packets transmitted, 3 packets received, 0% packet loss
round-trip min/avg/max = 0.518/0.895/1.567 ms
```

14. Running `vmkping 172.21.10.3 -I vmk3` returns the same error as vSphere Client. This command executes the same test that failed in the GUI.

15. Running `vmkping ++netstack=vlan 172.21.10.3 -I vmk3` directs the ping to use the specific network stack of VXLAN. This command succeeds because the extra parameter that identifies the network stack is defined.

```
~ # vmkping 172.21.10.3 -I vmk3
Unknown interface 'vmk3': Invalid argument
~ # vmkping ++netstack=vxlan 172.21.10.3 -I vmk3
PING 172.21.10.3 (172.21.10.3): 56 data bytes
64 bytes from 172.21.10.3: icmp_seq=0 ttl=64 time=0.089 ms
64 bytes from 172.21.10.3: icmp_seq=1 ttl=64 time=0.060 ms
64 bytes from 172.21.10.3: icmp_seq=2 ttl=64 time=0.068 ms

--- 172.21.10.3 ping statistics ---
3 packets transmitted, 3 packets received, 0% packet loss
round-trip min/avg/max = 0.060/0.072/0.089 ms
~ #
```

16. The connectivity test now succeeds with the correct network stack.

How it works...

Before utilizing the new VXLAN, the virtual wire connectivity should be tested between the hosts that will serve as endpoints to the virtual wire. These hosts will likely be located on several different clusters in a larger virtualization infrastructure. When there is a bug in the vShield connectivity test, the test can be accomplished as shown, using the `vmkping` command. The `vmkping` command is a common ESXi command used to test the connectivity of a VMkernel port.

There's more

▶ Information specific to this bug and the specified workaround can be found at `https://communities.vmware.com/thread/459736?start=0&tstart=0`

▶ For more information on `vmkping` and its command options, refer to `http://kb.vmware.com/selfservice/microsites/search.do?language=en_US&cmd=displayKC&externalId=1003728`

Configuring firewall rules for VXLAN virtual wires

VXLAN virtual wires rely on vShield Edge to provide port-level firewall functionality to isolate and allow specific traffic between networks configured on a given vShield Edge gateway. The firewall rule management consists of source, destination, and traffic types as categorized by predefined services. Since vShield Edge integrates with VXLAN, it is more efficient to configure firewall rules through vShield Edge to ensure traffic flow to VMs on the virtual wires.

Getting started

To proceed, we'll require access to vShield App through the vSphere Client plugin. The plugin can be enabled through the **Plug-ins** menu in vSphere Client. The client can be run on any modern Windows desktop operating system or server operating system.

> The vShield vSphere Client plugin requires Adobe Flash, which is not supported on Linux operating systems at this time.

vShield Manager must be installed and the vCenter account used for login should have Enterprise administrator rights to vShield Manager.

How to do it...

Perform the following steps:

1. Launch vSphere Client using an account with administrative rights, if it is not already open.

2. Navigate to **Home | Inventory | Hosts and Clusters** from the menu bar.

3. Navigate to **Datacenter** and select the **Network Virtualization** tab.

4. Select **Networks**.

5. Click on a valid network hyperlink (in our example, **SQL_DB_DW**).

6. Select **Security** from the menu bar and note that the **Default Rule** option is set to allow all.

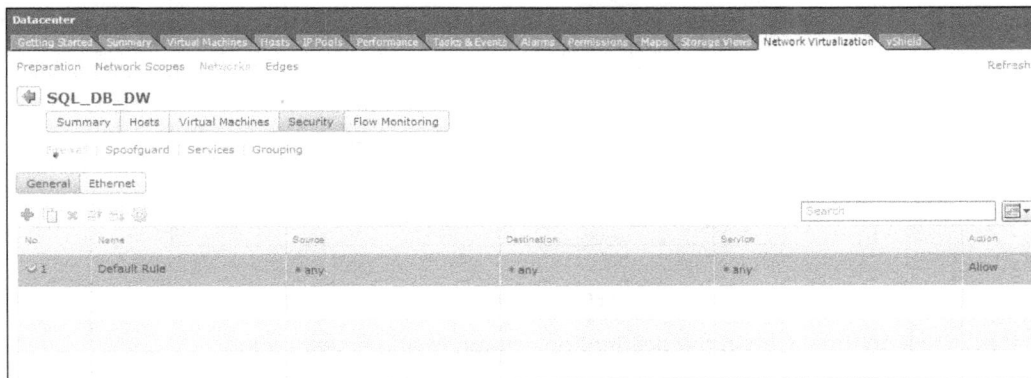

7. Click on the **+** icon to add a rule.

8. Type in a name for the **Rule Name** field (in our example, **SQL Browser**).

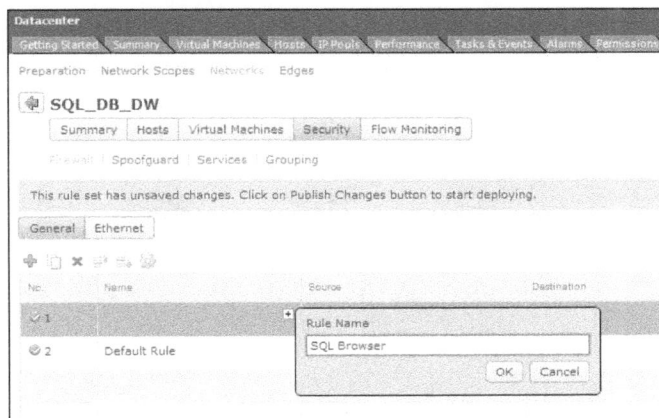

9. Click on **OK** to accept the name.

10. Click on the **+** icon in the source column to add a source.

11. Select a valid entry for **Virtual Wire** (in our case, **SQL_DB_DW**).

12. Add the virtual wire to the selected column from the available column by using the arrow.

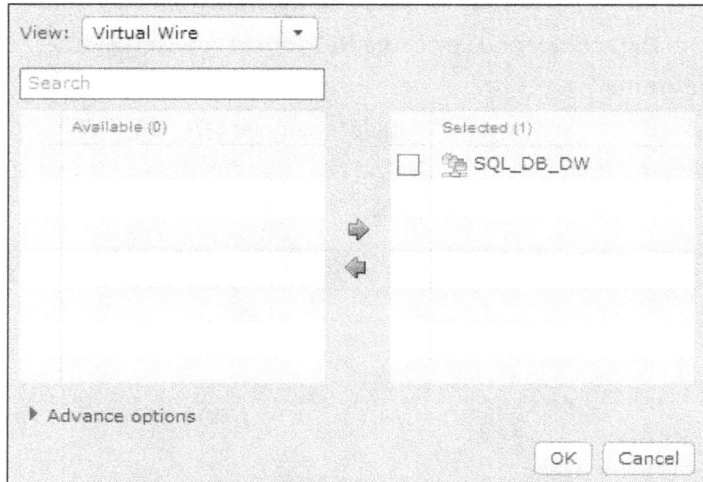

13. Click on **OK** to accept all the performed actions.

14. Click on the **+** icon in the destination column to add a destination.

15. Select a valid **vNIC** from the list (in our example, **SQL DataWarehouse 1**).

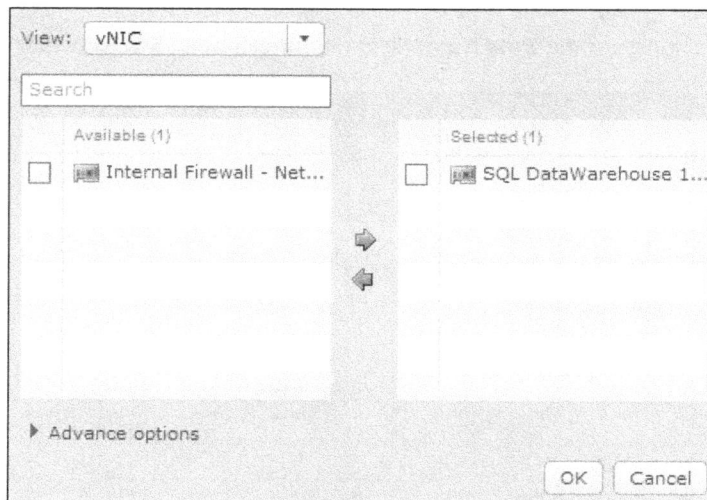

16. Click on **OK** to accept the changes.
17. Click on the **+** icon in the service column to add **SQL Server Browser service**.
18. Select **SQL Browser service** from the **Available** list and add it to the **Selected** column.

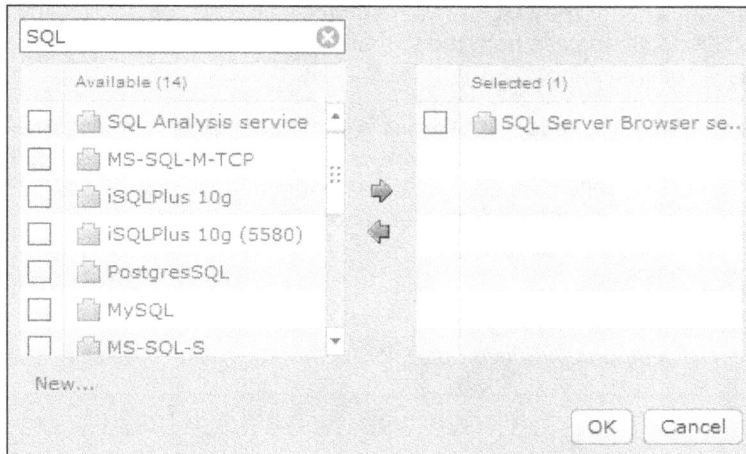

19. Click on **OK** to accept the changes.
20. Click on **Publish Changes** to activate the rule.

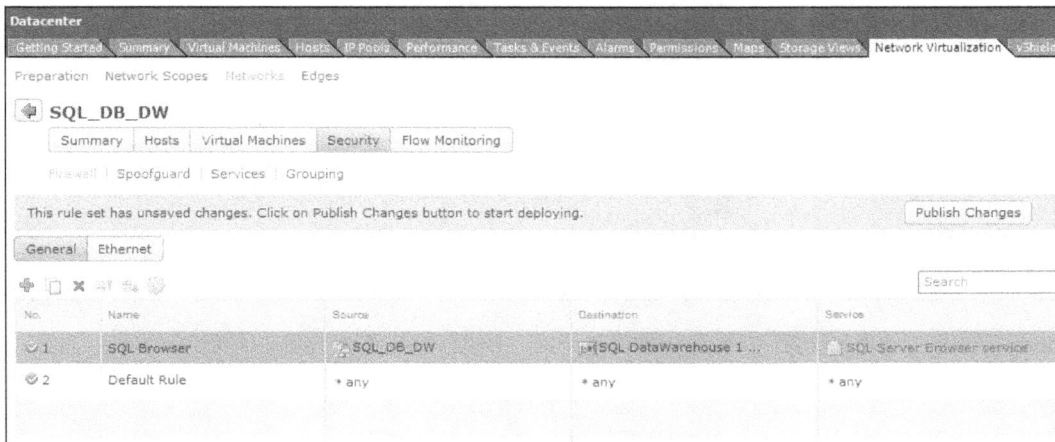

The rule is now active.

How it works...

The vShield Edge firewall allows both the source and destination rule definitions to be defined by virtual wire, security group, virtual machine, vNIC, or IP address. In our example, we selected a virtual wire for the **SQL Browser service** rule. This rule allows any SQL browser traffic, TCP 1434, to pass from the virtual wire to the vNIC of the SQL DataWarehouse virtual machine.

Once the configuration of the required services is complete, the default **any** rule will be changed to the default **deny** rule to ensure that only specified traffic is passing through the virtual wire to the specific vNIC connections. Care should be taken when assigning rules within vShield Edge to ensure proper security and functionality.

See also

▶ *Chapter 9, Configuring vShield Edge*, for further details on firewall configuration

Index

[PACKT] enterprise
PUBLISHING
professional expertise distilled

Thank you for buying
VMware vSphere Security Cookbook

About Packt Publishing

Packt, pronounced 'packed', published its first book "*Mastering phpMyAdmin for Effective MySQL Management*" in April 2004 and subsequently continued to specialize in publishing highly focused books on specific technologies and solutions.

Our books and publications share the experiences of your fellow IT professionals in adapting and customizing today's systems, applications, and frameworks. Our solution-based books give you the knowledge and power to customize the software and technologies you're using to get the job done. Packt books are more specific and less general than the IT books you have seen in the past. Our unique business model allows us to bring you more focused information, giving you more of what you need to know, and less of what you don't.

Packt is a modern, yet unique publishing company, which focuses on producing quality, cutting-edge books for communities of developers, administrators, and newbies alike. For more information, please visit our website: www.PacktPub.com.

About Packt Enterprise

In 2010, Packt launched two new brands, Packt Enterprise and Packt Open Source, in order to continue its focus on specialization. This book is part of the Packt Enterprise brand, home to books published on enterprise software – software created by major vendors, including (but not limited to) IBM, Microsoft and Oracle, often for use in other corporations. Its titles will offer information relevant to a range of users of this software, including administrators, developers, architects, and end users.

Writing for Packt

We welcome all inquiries from people who are interested in authoring. Book proposals should be sent to author@packtpub.com. If your book idea is still at an early stage and you would like to discuss it first before writing a formal book proposal, contact us; one of our commissioning editors will get in touch with you.

We're not just looking for published authors; if you have strong technical skills but no writing experience, our experienced editors can help you develop a writing career, or simply get some additional reward for your expertise.

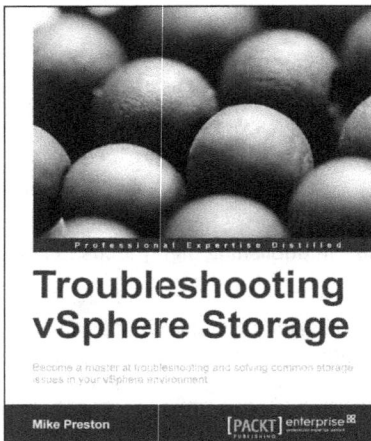

Troubleshooting vSphere Storage

ISBN: 978-1-78217-206-2   Paperback: 150 pages

Become a master at troubleshooting and solving common storage issues in your vSphere environment

1.   Identify key issues that affect vSphere storage visibility, performance, and capacity.

2.   Comprehend the storage metrics and statistics that are collected in vSphere.

3.   Get acquainted with the many vSphere features that can proactively protect your environment.

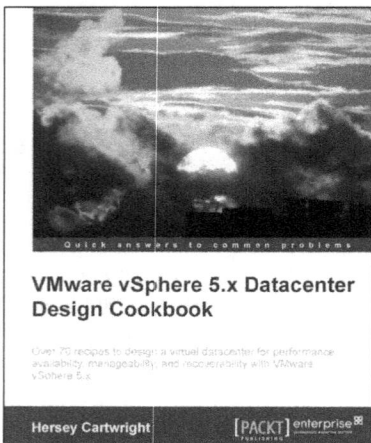

VMware vSphere 5.x Datacenter Design Cookbook

ISBN: 978-1-78217-700-5   Paperback: 260 pages

Over 70 recipes to design a virtual datacenter for performance, availability, manageability, and recoverability with VMware vSphere 5.x

1.   Innovative recipes, offering numerous practical solutions when designing virtualized datacenters.

2.   Identify the design factors—requirements, assumptions, constraints, and risks—by conducting stakeholder interviews and performing technical assessments.

3.   Increase and guarantee performance, availability, and workload efficiency with practical steps and design considerations.

Please check **www.PacktPub.com** for information on our titles

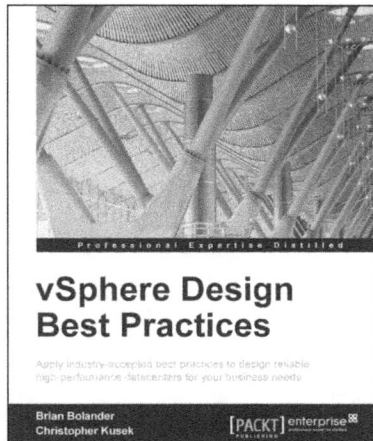

vSphere Design Best Practices

ISBN: 978-1-78217-626-8   Paperback: 126 pages

Apply industry-accepted best practices to design reliable high-performance datacenters for your business needs

1. Learn how to utilize the robust features of VMware to design, architect, and operate a virtual infrastructure using the VMware vSphere platform.

2. Customize your vSphere Infrastructure to fit your business needs with specific use-cases for live production environments.

3. Explore the vast opportunities available to fully leverage your virtualization infrastructure.

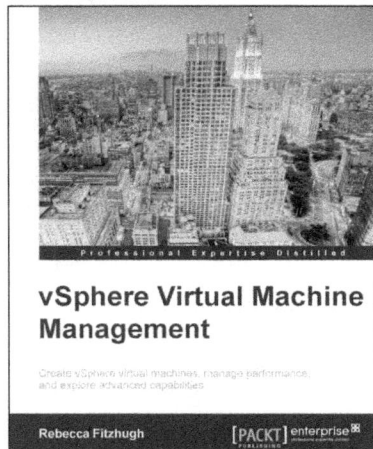

vSphere Virtual Machine Management

ISBN: 978-1-78217-218-5   Paperback: 326 pages

Create vSphere virtual machines, manage performance, and explore advanced capabilities

1. Create virtual machines using the wizard, cloning, deploying from a template, and using OVF templates.

2. Manage multi-tiered applications using vApps.

3. Learn how to optimize virtual machine performance and resource allocation.

Please check **www.PacktPub.com** for information on our titles

www.ingramcontent.com/pod-product-compliance
Lightning Source LLC
Chambersburg PA
CBHW082107220326
41598CB00066BA/5645